# How the West Really Lost God

# How the West Really Lost God

*A New Theory of Secularization*

Mary Eberstadt

TEMPLETON PRESS

Templeton Press
300 Conshohocken State Road, Suite 500
West Conshohocken, PA 19428
www.templetonpress.org

Typeset and designed by Gopa & Ted2, Inc.

Library of Congress Cataloging-in-Publication Data

Eberstadt, Mary.
 How the West really lost God : a new theory
of secularization / Mary Eberstadt.
   pages cm
 Includes bibliographical references and index.
 ISBN 978-1-59947-379-6 (hardbound : alk. paper)
 ISBN 978-1-59947-466-3 (paperback : alk. paper)
 1. Secularization (Theology) 2. Secularism. I. Title.
 BT83.7.E24 2013
 270.8—dc23

                                        2012043415

Printed in the United States of America

14 15 16 17 18 19    10 9 8 7 6 5 4 3 2 1

"How could we drink up the sea? Who gave us the sponge to wipe away the entire horizon?"
—FRIEDRICH NIETZSCHE, "The Parable of the Madman," *The Gay Science*, 1882

"It is in my lifetime that the people have forsaken formal Christian religion, and the churches have entered seemingly terminal decline. It matters that we understand why."
—CALLUM G. BROWN, *The Death of Christian Britain*, 2001

For Frederick, Catherine, Isabel, and Alexandra

# Table of Contents

How the West Really Lost God

# Introduction

MOST BOOKS have their origin in some kind of enduring mental distraction that has grown so large and ungainly in the author's mind that only hammering it out at book length will fully exorcise the thing. The volume you are reading on your screen right now or holding in your hands is no exception. The particular puzzle that started this effort happens to be—at least to some people—one of the most interesting questions in all the modern world. It is this: *How and why has Christianity really come to decline in important parts of the West?*[1]

Note that use of the word "really," which is also in the book's title. In some contexts, it is a freighted term suggesting that a nefarious plot is afoot to conceal the truth about something or another. But such is not its meaning here. In choosing that qualifier "really," I do not mean to question the good intentions of other curious armchair theorists pushing around the pieces of this same puzzle during the past hundred and twenty-five years or so. Quite the contrary. The list of scholars and other thinkers who have prophesied, studied, decried, celebrated, and otherwise sought to explain what they saw as the decline of Western Christianity is a monumentally long and impressive one—in part a roll call of the greatest minds of modernity, including Karl Marx and Charles Darwin, Auguste Comte and Sigmund Freud, Émile Durkheim and Max Weber, and many more. Also running in that distinguished pack, of course, is the German philosopher Friedrich Nietzsche, whose parable of the madman in the marketplace foretelling the death of God remains the paradigm through which many sophisticated people understand secularization right down to this day.

Far from ignoring them, I hope in this book to do some brief justice to preceding attempts to explain what really happened to the "Sea of Faith," as the Victorian poet Matthew Arnold immortally dubbed the Christianity of yesteryear. Once, he wrote, that sea was swollen and full; but today it has retreated far and seemingly permanently from the high-water mark.[2] Some time back, the great majority of people living in what can still broadly be called Western civilization believed in certain things: *God created the world; He has a plan for humanity; He promises everlasting life to those who live by His Word*; and other items of faith that Judeo-Christianity bequeathed to the world. Today—especially, though not only, in Western Europe—no great majority continues to believe in all such particulars. To judge by the evidence of one's senses, including extensive survey data, both belief and practice are diminishing among Christian populations in almost every European country—and not only in Europe; the percentage of people who claim no faith at all has also risen steadily in the United States.[3] Religious stories and music and rituals honed for millennia, studied generation after generation by believers both literate and illiterate, have become for many modern people of the West artifacts as remote as the cave paintings of Lascaux—of some enduring aesthetic and historical interest, to be sure, but having no more bearing on the present day than Paleolithic art.

What happened? Why was belief in the Christian God and his churchly doings apparently taken for granted by most Europeans, say, six hundred years ago—whereas today merely alluding to the *possibility* of the existence of that same God is now guaranteed to provoke uneasy dissent in some sophisticated quarters and savage ridicule in others? How much did the Enlightenment and rationalism and scientific thinking have to do with this enormous transformation—this sea change from a civilization that widely fears God, to one that now often jeers him? How much did various historical influences figure into this reshaping of our shared civilization—factors like technology, the world wars, politics, church scandals, the changing social status of women, and more?

These and other large questions will be considered in the pages ahead—including, at the outset, the radical question raised by some scholars, which is whether Western Christianity has even declined in the first place.

It is the contention of this book that just about everyone working on this great puzzle has come up with some piece of the truth—and yet that one particular piece needed to hold the others together still has gone missing. Urbanization, industrialization, belief and disbelief, technology, shrinking population: yes, yes, and yes to all those factors statistically and otherwise correlated with secularization. Yet, even taking them all into account, the picture remains incomplete, as chapter 2 goes to show. It is as if the modern mind has lined up all the different pieces on the collective table, only to press them together in a way that looks whole from a distance but still leaves something critical out.

This book is an attempt to supply that missing piece. It moves the human family from the periphery to the center of this debate over how and why Christianity exercises less influence over Western minds and hearts today than it did in the past. Its purpose is to offer an alternative account of what Nietzsche's madman really saw in what he called the "tombs" (read, the churches and cathedrals) of Europe.

Its argument, in brief, is that the Western record suggests that family decline is not merely a *consequence* of religious decline, as conventional thinking has understood that relationship. It also is plausible—and, I will argue, appears to be true—that *family decline in turn helps to power religious decline*. And if this way of augmenting the conventional explanation for the collapse of Christian faith in Europe is correct, then certain things, including some radical things, follow from it, as we shall see.

The pages ahead amount to an argument in three parts. The first section gives an overview of the present intellectual scene, including the conventional explanations for secularization and the various problems with those explanations as they stand (chapters 1 and 2). In other words, those chapters amount to a brief about why our current understanding of secularization is insufficient. The second part of the book puts forth evidence for an alternative theory of what has happened (chapters 3 through 7). It argues that (a) the alternative theory is consistent with the historical fact that family decline and Christian decline have gone hand in hand; and (b) that the alternative theory has the added attraction of "solving" certain problems that the existing theories cannot solve. Chapter 7 concerns broad matters of religious anthropology. It asks—and attempts to answer—why this theory works: i.e., just what the mechanisms might be that make family and faith so intricately bound together.

The concluding chapters change gears once more and take on the practical question of why anyone should care about the exact mechanism of secularization in the first place—including speculation about what this new theory might suggest about the future of both Western Christianity and the Western family. The conclusion makes the case that contrary to what many seem to think, everyone has a dog of one kind or another in the fight over secularization—ardent secularists and pious churchgoers alike.

Let us begin by stepping back for a moment and putting these two essential pieces of the puzzle side by side, in part simply to introduce them and to contemplate their enormity: the decline of Christianity in parts of the advanced West on the one side, and the decline of the natural family—meaning the family built on irreducible biological ties—on the other.[4]

The dramatic decay of Christian belief and practice, notably though not only in Western Europe, is by now both familiar and much remarked upon—so much so that it has even become common intellectual practice to refer to parts of the Continent as "post-Christian." As the data from the European Values Survey (cited in endnote 3) go to show, people across Europe go to church less, believe in the Christian creed less, and believe in God himself less than they did even eighteen years ago.

In addition to being "post"-Christian, some parts of this landscape are also notably *anti*-Christian—as a lengthening list of public events disfigured by aggressive atheist or secular protests goes to show. Some observers have even used the term "Christophobic" to capture the vehemence with which some Europeans, including high-ranking public figures, have come to renounce the influence of Christianity on the Western present and past.[5]

This religious turnaround in the former heart of Christendom itself in turn has had massive consequences for the way most people in those countries now lead their lives. For Western Europeans, the waning of religious belief has transformed practically every aspect of life from birth to death: their politics, laws, marriages (or lack thereof), arts, education, music, popular culture, and other activities from the sublime to the prosaic that were once influenced and even dominated by the church—and are no more. In some countries, laws that once discriminated in favor of Christians now actively discriminate against them.[6] A growing number of Western individuals greet the milestones of life with no religious framework at all. They are born without being baptized; they have children without being married; they contract civil marriages instead of religious ones.

They darken church doors infrequently, if ever, and upon dying their bodies are incinerated and scattered to the winds, rather than prayed over whole in the ground as Christian ritual and dogma had hitherto commanded.

It is true, as is sometimes noted, that there are exceptions to this general rule of Western religious decline.[7] As is often pointed out, for example, certain evangelical Protestant denominations are apparently thriving despite the secular trend. Not only that, but some strikingly powerful renewal movements have meanwhile sprung up within both Catholic and Protestant ranks. Other signs of Christian life also abound for those who look for them—including in societies where atheism and aggressive secularism are flourishing too, and have inadvertently generated movements of religious counterculture.

Evangelical renewal within the Anglican community in Britain, to take one example of such itinerant vitality, has led to a newly popular program in Christian education called the "Alpha course."[8] It has been taken by over seventeen million people, according to the group, and is now being used by a range of other Christians outside of Great Britain as well as in it, including Presbyterians, Pentecostals, Lutherans, Baptists, and Methodists. In another measure of ongoing religious devotion, Catholic pilgrimages continue to attract millions each year across Europe, and some, such as Santiago de Compostela in northern Spain, have lately grown extraordinarily.[9] Within or around the Catholic church, for its part, some potent renewal movements have sprung up precisely as a response to modernity, including Opus Dei and Comunione e Liberazione (Communion and Liberation), both of which have spread from Europe to other parts of the world. And to repeat—as the latter two examples suggest, and as hopeful clerics and believers who are also scholars in these matters like to point out—in many places outside the advanced nations, Christianity both Protestant and Catholic remains vigorously on the march.

Nevertheless, to keep our eyes fixed on Europe and important swaths of the rest of the West—particularly elite swaths, like secular higher education—is to understand that many people in these places now judge the churches to be mere artifacts, including embarrassing and sometimes despised artifacts of what is thought to be a regrettable past riddled with corruption, oppression, religious wars, and the rest of the dark side of the historical record. From once-devout Ireland over to Germany, former seat of the Holy Roman Empire; from thoroughly secular Scandinavia on down to the former Christian strongholds of Spain and France and even Italy; in sum, across Western Europe today, the religion symbolized by the cross appears to many informed people to be an endangered historical species— where indeed it is not already extinct.

Then there are the human faces of this massive change, just a handful of which we might briefly contemplate here. Across the Continent, elderly altar servers shuffle in childless churches attended by mere handfuls of pensioners. Tourist throngs in Notre Dame and other cathedrals circle ever-emptier pews roped off for worshippers. Former abbeys and convents and monasteries find themselves remade into luxury hotels and sybaritic spas. Churches shuttered for decades become apartments or discos—sometimes even mosques. The Church of England, to take one significant example of the collision between religion and real estate, closed some 1,700 structures between 1970 and 2005—10 percent of the total across the land; and in London, some five hundred churches of varying denominations have been transformed since 2001.[10] The emptiness of the churches makes the bustling of the mosques more noticeable; not surprisingly, a number of books pondering the decline of Christianity and the rise of Islam have lately been added to the shelves.[11]

In one more measure of its seismic effects, the waning of Christian influence in Europe has also led to a markedly different public atmosphere across the Continent than the starchiness of the phrase "Old Country" would seem to suggest. Famously liberal and libertine capitals like Amsterdam and Berlin sport some of the leading sex districts of the world. The transformation in public mores filters down to the most mundane venues. Pornography is openly displayed on newsstands far more commonly than in the United States, nudity is a commonplace of fashionable beaches, and among sophisticated politicians and intellectuals and celebrities, denigration of relative American "puritanism" is a parlor sport of choice—as any Yankee traipsing around the Continent soon discovers.

Also as part of this same sea change, open hostility to religion—especially Christianity—appears to be at an all-time postwar high. A few years ago, best-selling books by leading atheists rode the antireligious wave to remarkable commercial success, in the process seeming to compete with one another for worst-case accounts of Christian beliefs and Christian history.[12] Even so, these bracing manifestos seem positively genteel compared to some other developments.

As events of the past few years have also gone to show, for example, ceremonial visits to other nations by the pope or other high-ranking Catholic officials have become reliable lightning rods of anti-Christianism. Once upon a time occasions of intense public veneration, such trips are now guaranteed to produce public demonstrations from Madrid to London to Berlin, to take a few examples from the recent past—and for that matter even at Sapienza University, in the Vatican's very own backyard of Rome.[13] Not only the fact of these demonstrations, but also their characteristically vituperative tone, speak to a deep festering within secularism itself—a seeming inability to desist from opening and reopening what are perceived to be the wounds inflicted by religious history and religious belief. In fact, so hostile and obscene are some of these protests that tolerant people might be expected to criticize them—if the object of their hatred were anything *but* Christianity, that is.[14]

Such are just a few of the visible faces of the Continent's dramatically changed human landscape, sketched here to give the merest sense of the scope and speed of religious change there.

Now let us set aside those faces to look briefly but intensely at the shape of the second great decline of our times: that of the natural family, which has also occurred across the advanced West.[15]

Like the collapse of Christianity in many of the same places, the collapse of the natural family has reshaped the known world of just about every man, woman, and child alive in the Western world today. For years now, secular sociologists have debated the meaning of the changes that have diminished the hold that the natural family once had over an individual's life. Divorce, single parenthood, widespread use of contraception, legal abortion, the sharp drop in the Western birthrate: these are just some of the prodigious transformations in family structure on which experts train their sights. And while scholars as well as nonscholars take sides on the question of whether these are good things or bad things for society, no one seriously suggests that radical family change hasn't *happened* across the Western world. Obviously, it has.

Consider for starters the most obvious of these changes: the ongoing decline in the birthrate. According to Eurostat, the most authoritative source for European statistics, between 1960 and 2010 the birthrate dropped in every single country and plunged in most.[16] One does not need to be a statistician (I certainly am not) to grasp the overall direction of this social change concerning babies. Blips aside, births have obviously dropped dramatically. As Eurostat notes, despite the fact that the numbers have trended slightly upward of late, "The total fertility rate declined steeply between 1980 and 2000–2003 in many Member States, falling far below replacement level."

Much has been written lately about the implications of this demographic revolution, and some of the relevant experts will appear later on. For now, however, let us limit ourselves to a single uncontroversial point: *the drop in the Western birthrate is one demographic fact that has radically remade the families of today and tomorrow.*[17]

Add to that some other changes: historically high rates of both divorce and out-of-wedlock births. These family phenomena too have increased sharply in the West during the same years that the birthrate has been falling. Let us confine ourselves to the out-of-wedlock measure, again for the years 1960–2010 and again using Eurostat's numbers. During that time, the proportion of births outside marriage—what was once called bastardy, then illegitimacy—rose steadily in every European country (as well as in the United States).[18] It does not take an expert here, either, to grasp the overall direction of this change in the world to which many Western children are now born.

Once again, our purpose here is not to militate for or against any of these changes. Neither is it to split academic hairs over any particular chart or graph or timeline. What we want instead is merely to observe that these large shocks ripple out into society in a great number of ways. How could they not?[19] For decades scholars have struggled to understand the larger fallout of this new familial world, and their thoughts too will make appearances in the chapters ahead.[20]

For now, though, it's enough to establish that these large trends—fewer babies, more divorce, more homes with unmarried parents—are in themselves uncontroversial even among scholars, because they are so empirically clear. To say that the family has "declined," to repeat, is not to say that relatives love one another any less than they used to, or that children will ever stop wanting bedtime stories, or that an "end to men" or "end to women" is upon us, or any other reductionist formulation. It is rather to observe that—exactly as in the case of Christianity, and its simultaneously diminished role in the West—the family *as an institution* obviously has less power over its individual members than it used to have.

Underlying that loss of familial power is not only demographic reality but also the fundamental issue of identity—i.e., the fact that what were once considered by most people to be fixed and immutable ties are now frequently in flux.

Once upon a time, for example, whoever married your sister became your brother-in-law for life. Today, he remains your brother-in-law only so long as he and/or your sister decide to stay together—and if they divorce, many other brothers-in-law or significant-other brother-in-law-like people might theoretically take his place. At some point in the not-so-distant Western past—to put the matter conversely, from his point of view—whoever that person was had no option *but* to remain your brother-in-law once he married your sister (just as he would simultaneously remain your sister's husband, and your father's son-in-law, and your daughter's uncle, and so on, for life). Today, of course, every one of those identities that were once considered permanent can change according to his intentions or his wife's.

This is just one example of how the collision between the family and the modern world has resulted in a radical redefinition of the family. One can easily think of others. In the movie *The Godfather II*, protagonist Michael Corleone's mother consoles him in a moment of marital trouble, telling him firmly that it is impossible to lose your family. Such was true in her native, traditional-minded Sicily, perhaps; but as Michael knows, and Mamma does not, such is not the case in the modern West. Precisely because the family can now be redefined according to what its members decide to do—particularly its most powerful members—it is possible indeed to "lose" one's family as it never was before. Biological ties, and only biological ties, remain immutable.

Hence kinship, to repeat, does not define modern men and women as it once did our ancestors; for many people, "family" is instead, at least in part, a series of optional associations that can be and sometimes are discarded voluntarily depending on preference. To put it lightly, when measured against the sweep of human history, this is rather a new and potent sociological fact.

As with the decline of Christianity, however, who really needs sociology to convince us that the family is weaker than it once was? For most of us, personal or vicarious experience alone will suffice. It is family decline that powers, say, the steady parade of dysfunction on Western airwaves; think of televised divorce courts, televised paternity tests, televised breakups, and the rest of the inadvertently illuminating shows that exploit the weakened hearth to the hilt. If family decline didn't exist, reality TV would have to invent it.

Or, to offer a more consequential example of how the family has imploded, witness the economic crisis now threatening welfare states across the advanced world—the demonstrations that have made headline news on and off since 2008 from Athens to Madrid, London to Barcelona, and back again. For years now, financial markets have been racked by fears that Greece/Italy/Spain might collapse/default and bring the rest of the European Union down with them. Nor is this anxiety about what is called "contagion" a matter of financial accounting only. Picture-postcard Europe now sports bonfires, mobs, and gas masks—and rates of unemployment topping 25 percent in some countries. Why?

As does not seem to be well understood, at least as yet, this smoldering European economic crisis would not even exist without an underlying, multifaceted crisis brought on by the decline of the family. That is because the shrinkage of the family across the West in simple numerical terms has come to mean that in Western economies too few younger workers support the older ones—certainly fewer than the visionaries and politicians who authored the modern welfare states imagined. The fact that sustaining these welfare states has in effect become a Ponzi scheme is by now perhaps indeed the single most pressing fact of politics—and it is a fact grounded in turn on the changing Western family.

Just how tight *is* the connection between the Continent's economic woes on the one hand and its embrace of low fertility and related changes on the other? Demographer Nicholas Eberstadt, for one, has argued that the "costs associated with population aging are estimated to account *for about half* the public-debt run-up of the O.E.C.D. economies over the past 20 years [emphasis added]."[21] He and coauthor Hans Groth, chairman of the World Demographic Association, also calculate that every percentage point increase in an OECD (Organization for Economic Development) country's proportion of seniors sixty-five years and older is associated with a 7 percent point increase in the ratio of public debt to GDP.[22]

Demographic decline has also altered the "macro" picture in another pertinent way. Ali Alichi, an economist with the International Monetary Fund, has pointed out that older citizens, for example, have less incentive to repay debt—another prosaic fact now having global reverberations. "As the number of older voters relative to younger ones increases around the globe," he observes, "the creditworthiness of borrowing countries could decline—resulting in less external lending and more sovereign debt defaults."[23] It is hard to think of a single more succinct statement of demography's profound implications for politics today, or for that matter of a more accurate summation of what might be called modern demographic brinksmanship.

Third, the decline of the family has also put more pressure on those same welfare states that are already stretched beyond their fiscal limits—because more people now expect their governments to perform tasks once assumed by sons, daughters, maiden aunts, and the like. As families have shrunk, disbanded, re-formed, and otherwise come to reflect the reality that what were once permanent ties are now increasingly optional and fungible, Western men and women have ratcheted up the pressure on the state to operate as a family substitute—in particular, as a father substitute. This point was demonstrated perfectly if once more unwittingly in the United States in 2012, when a video made by President Barack Obama's reelection team chronicled a fictitious young woman named "Julia" benefiting from government assistance at each major stage of her life—every one of which forms of assistance, from day care to retirement, are government substitutes for what the extended family was once competent to do and often is no more.[24]

Alternatively, as the state has expanded to take on duties once shouldered instead by those nearest and dearest, the incentives to do the hard work of keeping a family together have increasingly elicited the tacit response, *why bother*? After all—or so it seemed for a while, at least, though we now know otherwise—the pension remains the same. In this way, one can argue, the expanded welfare state competes with the family as the dominant protector of the individual—in the process undercutting the power of the family itself.

In other words, family change has been an engine fueling statism —and statism in turn has been an engine fueling family decline. This too is a part of the larger social and political picture that we need to understand for purposes of what follows.

To repeat: this use of this term "decline" to describe what has happened to the Western family in the past century or so is not intended as a pejorative—any more than talk of "decline" of faith, say, is disrespectful of Christians *per se*. It is simply a fact, disputed by no one serious and easily observable everywhere, that the modern Western family does not exert the same force on individuals today that it has in most other places throughout human history—just as it is a fact that the Christian churches have less influence today over the lives of many who identify themselves as "Christians" than those same churches did in the distant and even recent past.

To summarize our brief tour so far: families in the advanced nations today are smaller than before; they are more scattered; they are less likely to be bound by marriage; they are more likely to be "blended" in one way or another; and they are more likely to include parents and children who are regularly out of the home for substantial periods of time.[25] Few families today are extended under the same roof; from day care to rehab centers to hospitals to nursing homes, invented institutions supply needs that were formerly met by the home. And in the petri dishes now home to tomorrow's family hybrids, the biological basis of the natural family is being further subverted or weakened by a number of practices that did not even exist until the past few decades—in vitro fertilization, surrogate motherhood, anonymous sperm donors, indefinite egg freezing, and other experiments offering radically new answers to the question of what makes a family today or tomorrow.

Once again, for our purposes here, it does not matter how you or I or anyone else *feels* about any of these changes. Of course some people—mainly traditionalists and conservatives—deplore the weakening of traditional family bonds, and believe that family decline has left individual men and women and children worse off in various ways than they were before. Of course some other people—mainly liberals and progressives—embrace these same changes and argue that contemporary innovations to the family help to humanize what had become an oppressive, sometimes authoritarian institution. Of course, too, other people who are not particularly ideological or religious have their own individual views of what makes families good or bad, desirable or undesirable, and worth defending or not.

Our business here is to transcend these familiar grooves of the culture wars and to move somewhere new once we have finished inspecting the big picture. As even this relatively brief tour goes to show, we modern people lead very different domestic lives than those typical of our ancestors and even our recent relatives—and one of the main reasons is that we have fewer biological relations, and more attenuated bonds to those we do have, than those people who came before us. As historian Peter Laslett put it memorably in his classic and still fascinating 1965 study, *The World We Have Lost: England before the Industrial Age*, "Time was when the whole of life went forward in the family, in a circle of loved, familiar faces. . . . That time has gone forever. It makes us very different from our ancestors."[26] The argument in the pages ahead depends in part upon grasping Laslett's point in full.

Also like the decline of religion, this decline of the family is not just a series of social trends debated by academics, but a profound change reflected in human faces. Some of them look contented indeed, or at least markedly less miserable than they would have been in earlier times: the adults who, under no-fault divorce, can choose without legal penalty to leave unhappy marriages for the prospect of fulfillment elsewhere; the single mothers and their children who would once have suffered stigma for hailing from a fatherless home, and who are now accepted instead as one possible social norm; the individual men and women whose personal erotic choices might have been stigmatized and prosecuted elsewhere in time; and so on.

Some other faces in this new world, for their part, reveal the darker side of these same changes: the aging, childless people who must now rely on friends or institutions for company, rather than on family members, when they get sick; the children of older and smaller families who will spend most of their adulthood with no immediate biological relatives and who will never know a robust extended family, for better or worse; and perhaps above all, the many children who will never know what most people previous to us could take for granted, namely, the presence in the home of two biologically related parents, and the persistence of those same two individuals through the generations—i.e., into the lives of their biological grandchildren.

At the extreme end of this spectrum of change there are some positively sepulchral images to ponder. What is the world to make of the fact that "donor children," those purposely created by anonymous fathers, are now so plentiful that roughly half of them worry about unintentional incest with a romantic partner in the future?[27] Or of the elderly Japanese who use electronic toys as substitutes for grandchildren?[28] Or of the unforeseen forms of heartbreak being ushered in by biotechnology—as in the recent story of an Indian woman whose own two children were orphaned when she died in childbirth serving as a paid surrogate mother to wealthy Westerners?[29] Once again, the point here is not to argue for these changes or against them, but merely to do some brief justice to their massive sweep and scope.

The decline of the Western family, in sum, has altered the rhythms of daily life from the moment of birth to that of death—from the ways that babies are cared for, to when school starts and how long it goes, to how the sick are tended, to what a deathbed looks like, and just about everything else in between.

Like the waning of Christianity, the waning of the traditional family means that all of us in the modern West lead lives our ancestors could not have imagined. We are less fettered than they in innumerable ways; we are perhaps the freest people in the history of all humanity. At the same time, we are also more deprived of the consolations of tight bonds of family and faith known to most of the men and women coming before us—and this fact, it will be argued, has had wider repercussions than have yet been understood.

In all, both these seismic shifts are only beginning to be mapped and explored. Our purpose here is to contribute to that effort in however modest a way, so that we might understand something new about this vastly altered social, economic, moral, and religious landscape.

With those two sketches of faith and family in the modern West in place before us, let us now ask the question to which this effort is dedicated. What is the actual relationship between these two momentous trends of modernity—religious decline on the one hand, and family decline on the other?

That is the chicken-or-egg question at the heart of this book. To my knowledge, it has not been explored at this length before, so both the question and the way it is answered in the pages ahead offer something new. The proposition of this book is that there was—and still is—a critical defect in the conventional secular story line about how and why Christianity has collapsed in parts of the West. The missing piece is what I will dub "the Family Factor."

Simply stated, what the "Family Factor" means to signal is a new idea. It is that the causal relationship between family and religion—

specifically, the religion of Christianity—is not just a one-way, but actually a two-way street. In other words, I will argue that family formation is not merely an *outcome* of religious belief, as secular sociology has regarded it. Rather, family formation can also be, and has been, a causal agent in its own right—one that also potentially affects any given human being's religious belief and practice. The process of secularization, I will argue, has not been properly understood because it has neglected to take into account this "Family Factor"—meaning *the active effect that participation in the family itself appears to have on religious belief and practice.*

In brief, this book means to turn the standard account of Western religious decline upside down. It does not argue that the conventional story line is all wrong—quite the opposite. But it does argue that this story line is radically incomplete—and that the *way* in which it is incomplete forces us to rethink the supposed inevitability of Christianity's fall from Western grace. That is one radical implication of the pages ahead, and one we will revisit in the book's conclusion.

What has been missed is a fact so prosaic that it has seemed to go without saying—namely, that the family has been an important, indeed irreplaceable, transmission belt for religious belief in a number of different ways that will be spelled out further in chapter 7, "Putting All the Pieces Together: Toward an Alternative Anthropology of Christian Belief."

To put the point yet one more way: the collapse of Christianity in Europe, and the collapse of the natural family there—via rising rates of divorce, illegitimacy, and the rest of the familiar trends of modernity—have obviously gone historically hand in hand (look again at that data mentioned earlier from the European Values Study and Eurostat).

Until now, however, people observing that constant conjunction have simply assumed that the former phenomenon was driving the latter—i.e., that the decline in the natural family was a mere *conse-quence* of the shrinking of belief. This book makes the case that the reverse is also true—in other words, that the ongoing deterioration of the natural family itself has both accompanied and accelerated the deterioration in the West of Christian belief.

To grasp the real nature of the relationship between these trends, we must move away from two-dimensional timelines trying to pin-point cause and effect toward a more nuanced three-dimensional model of how these two forces operate together. Amid the models considered and rejected as ultimate metaphors in this argument, perhaps the best literary option is to borrow from scientists James D. Watson and Francis Crick, discoverers of the structure of DNA.[30] What this book means to impress is that *family and faith are the invis-ible double helix of society—two spirals that when linked to one another can effectively reproduce, but whose strength and momentum depend on one another.* That is one way of stating the thesis here.

To summarize the argument in other, more familiar metaphorical terms, Nietzsche was right to declare that the great Christian cathe-drals of Europe had become tombs. But he and his many modern heirs have been wrong about what exactly had been buried in them. In outlining a new and complementary way of how Christian faith really appears to come and go in the world, we will, I hope, learn something new—something perhaps hitherto unseen—about faith, family, and what the pages ahead will argue is an intricate and nec-essary dynamic between the two.

Herewith a few words in closing about what this book is not. It is not an attempt to gauge the health of religion worldwide, as some dis-tinguished scholars and other thinkers have admirably attempted.[31] It is not a book about the state of other religions, including Judaism and Islam—or, for that matter, about any other non-Christian religion in Western Europe or anywhere else. To be sure, some of what is said would seem to apply beyond the case of Christianity alone; and more than once, the reader may find himself wondering where the Chinese or the Hindus or the Muslims or other people might fit into this picture. But this attempt to say something new about how Christianity *per se* might rise and fall has been more than enough ambition for one book. The implications of this extended speculation for other faiths remains a story, perhaps, for another time.

And this is not, finally, a work of advocacy, ideological or religious or otherwise.[32] Whatever my existential particulars or yours, the pages ahead are as objective and free of prejudice as I could make them. More to the point, someone with alternative preconceptions—an agnostic or an atheist, a Wiccan or a Buddhist—could have developed the same theory in possession of the same empirical and other evidence. In much modern writing on secularization, one senses that an ideological or religious tail is wagging the dog of theory. That is not the case here.[33]

I have also tried in these pages to translate what is often a frustratingly esoteric discussion into regular old English. This is not a book of "narratives" (let alone "metanarratives"), "scripts," or related sociological jargon. It is instead an attempt to engage the general reader in an effort to figure out something new about Christianity's decline—namely, the idea that the family played, and continues to play, a critical and hitherto silent role in that religion's current standing in the Western world. Some readers might find the scholarly details here and there to be more involved than they prefer; more likely, some scholars will think that a neophyte has gone where a neophyte ought not to go. I can only hope that this intellectual platypus of a book offers something for everyone, including critics.

At the outset of his widely acclaimed 2010 work, *A Secular Age*, renowned scholar Charles Taylor asks a question that is one way of opening the window to the past and present landscape. "Why," he asks, "was it virtually impossible not to believe in God in say, 1500 in our Western society, while in 2000 many of us find this not only easy, but even inescapable?"[34] Here as a friendly amendment is a different way of opening that same figurative window. For over 125 years, the Western discussion of the loss of Christian faith has revolved around Friedrich Nietzsche's metaphorical question: *Who or what killed the Christian God?* Maybe that is not quite the right question. If we ask instead, metaphorically, *Who or what **kills** the Christian God?* then I believe we will see things about the decline of Christianity in the West—and by implication, the possibilities for its future—that have not been seen this way before.

## Does Secularization Even Exist?

Now forget for a moment the impressionistic evidence just presented in the introduction about Christianity's decline in parts of the West. In this chapter, we will consider a radical response to all that: according to some theorists, the notion of decline is *itself* an illusion—one brought on by a failure to read the evidence in a sufficiently deep or nuanced way. The idea that the West is less Christian today than it once was, they argue, may indeed be widespread and widely accepted; but it is nevertheless based on a misreading of the facts.

This is a minority, contrarian view, to be sure; but the reason that we need to pay attention to it is simple: if it is correct—if Christianity, *pace* Matthew Arnold and *Time* magazine and other authorities, is *not* in fact in a downward spiral across the West—then rather obviously, the world does not need a new theory explaining its decline.[1] In fact, the world doesn't need any theory about secularization at all—because if these contrarian thinkers are correct, there is no decline to account *for*.

The second reason we need to examine this line of argument is that it sheds light on the same mystery at the heart of this book: namely, the fact that upon inspection, there is something seriously amiss—maybe even more than one thing—with the conventional sociological account of what has really happened to Christianity in the Western world. In the course of criticizing secularization theory *per se*, the scholars opposed to it have generated useful clarifications about the theory's limits. In fact, as two other noted scholars, Pippa Norris and Ronald Inglehart recently put it, "Secularization theory is currently experiencing the most sustained challenge in its long history"—an observation issuing not from critics of the theory, but from two of its leading representatives.[2]

In sum, there is figurative blood in the water surrounding this matter of secularization theory, and watchful parties on both sides know it. Let us see where the trail leads.

Contrarians in this debate believe that other scholars and especially secular scholars have misread the empirical evidence—in effect, that they have minimized the signs of the times that point to Christian vitality and/or revival, and maximized those signs that point to decline. Let us dub this contrarian mode of thought the "so-what" school of secularization theory—because the arguments amount to saying "So what?" when faced with evidence of what appears to be Christian religious decline.

The "so-what" school is not an actual school, of course. As sometimes happens in scholarship, it is instead the unintentional collective outcome of like minds thinking alike. But taken together, their arguments do bear a family resemblance to each other, so it seems fair to regard them as variations on the same wider theme—the theme being that Christianity is not in fact declining as many say it is.

*"The West hasn't really lost God, because recent events go to show that religion is thriving around the world."*

Since the jihadist attacks of 9/11 especially, many have remarked upon religion's unexpected resiliency in the world. Believers and nonbelievers alike have made the point that contrary to claims of God's obsolescence, the most monumental global events of recent years have been inspired or otherwise decisively affected by religious belief. In a sense, these observations are all footnotes to sociologist Peter Berger's famous observation of 1990 that "the assumption we live in a secularized world is false" because "the world is as furiously religious as ever."[3]

Consider just a smattering of the historical evidence bolstering the claim to religion's staying power. There was, first and perhaps foremost, the near-global routing over two decades ago of that most aggressively secularist ideology of them all: Marxist/Communism. To many observers, the demise of the Communist governments served as a proxy of sorts for the endurance of God. Not only did religion fail to wither away as the modern age with all its machinations wore on, as Marx had so hopefully predicted; rather—thanks to the Velvet Revolutions of 1989—it was instead Communism that was unceremoniously jettisoned from history, alongside Nazism and certain other professional enemies of Christianity, too.

Even so, the unforeseen speed and depth of the Communist collapse was especially striking—particularly to those who believed the Cold War to be at heart a contest between religion on the one side and ferociously antireligious ideology on the other. To understand just how dramatic that collapse appeared, it helps to bear in mind that many intelligent people thought for decades that the West might ultimately lose that struggle. Sixty years ago, for instance, at the height of the Cold War, no less an experienced observer than the American reformed Communist Whittaker Chambers could still believe that in rejecting Marxism and embracing the free West, he was "leaving the winning world for the losing world."[4] Nor was Chambers alone. Other informed Western observers believed that Communists and non-Communists were indeed locked in a life-and-death struggle, the outcome of which was anyone's guess.

In retrospect, of course, such misgivings seem almost perverse.

As ground zero of the struggle against the Soviets in the late 1980s became pious Catholic Poland; as Karol Wojtyla, aka Pope John Paul II, became so integral to the struggle against Communism that some historians would later give him great credit for the thing's ultimate implosion; in sum, as world events seemed practically to conspire on the side of religious believers, the contrary idea of a religious "end of history" seemed less defensible than before.[5] Thus did the fate of Communism, for one, come to be taken as a reverse verdict of sorts on the fate of the churches.

Other kinds of evidence for Christianity's continued potency also abound. One can see, for example, that constant engagement with hostile ideologies has inadvertently served here and there to empower Christianity's apologists even more—that modernity's relentless and multidimensional attacks on the churches have had an unintended jujitsu effect all its own. As Catholic scholar Robert Royal has put it, "Three centuries of debunking, skepticism, criticism, revolution, and scorn by some among us have not produced the expected demise of religion and are now contributing to its renewal."[6] Certainly that same effect also followed ideological attacks on Christianity by the wave of best-selling new atheists in the mid-2000s. For all their commercial success, these authors also provoked counterattacks high and low across the secular as well as religious Western media.[7]

To quote Peter Berger once more, these and other pieces of evidence for our "furiously religious world" in turn "means that a whole body of literature by historians and social scientists loosely labeled 'secularization theory' is essentially mistaken."[8] Pointing in particular to American religiosity which is anomalous by the standards of Western Europe, as well as to the energetic global religious scene, Berger argues that secularization theory has been confuted by both phenomena. "While secularity is not a necessary consequence of modernization," as he has put the point elsewhere, "I would argue that pluralism is."[9]

Once again, he is plainly right that religion continues to write the scripts of history quite without the permission of the world's secularists. In addition to the towering example of the demise of Communism, consider also just a few other transformative global events fueled by religious fervor in the past few decades: the rise of the Ayatollah Khomeini's in Iran, and of other fundamentalists across the Islamic world; the Islamicist terror attacks of 9/11; the abiding political influence in the United States of a coalition of Catholic and Protestant evangelical conservatives; the enduring and unexpected political saliency including in the West of abortion and other "social issues": all these and other examples could be piled up to prove that it may be secularism, not religion, for whom the bell of history really tolls.

Surveying these and related examples of religion's staying power, sociologist José Casanova has argued further for what he calls the "deprivatization" of religion, meaning "the fact that religious traditions throughout the world are refusing to accept the marginal and privatized role which theories of modernity as well as theories of secularization had reserved for them."[10] Once again, he and others who point to the unexpected tenacity of religious belief—including in particular Christian belief—have an impressive array of facts on their side. It is no wonder, given the historical staying power of the sacred, that some argue it is the *irreligiosity* of Western Europe, rather than the apparent religiosity of the rest of the world, that needs "explaining."

To all this one might add that on the stage of the world—as opposed to just that of the European Continent—Christianity has lately spread to many more millions. In 1900 there were roughly ten million African Christians; today there are some four hundred million, almost half the population. Pentecostalism, founded just over one hundred years ago in Los Angeles, now claims at least five hundred million "renewalists" worldwide. In the largely unknown example of China, government figures alone show the number of Christians increasing from fourteen million in 1997 to twenty-one million in 2006—and most Christians themselves believe that these are underestimates. These are just a few of the facts about Christianity's ongoing global advance to be found in John Micklethwait and Adrian Wooldridge's highly informative 2009 book, *God Is Back: How the Global Revival of Faith Is Changing the World*—one more work that goes to show the unexpected vibrancy of the Christian creed, at least when judged by secular standards.[11]

And yet despite such flourishing among followers of the Nazarene elsewhere on the planet, the logical problem of Western secularization remains. The *relative* religiosity of the rest of the world, however fascinating in its own right, does not answer the question before us: *Why and how did Christianity come to decline in important parts of the West?*

That question remains a problem independent of any appeal to the rest of the world. To answer by pointing to the robust nature of Islam on the Continent, say, is to compare apples and oranges. Similarly, the advances of Christianity in Africa and Asia in recent years may be intriguing in their own right, as well as comforting to those who welcome evidence that Europe is a special case; but those gains obviously don't tell us how and why Christianity elsewhere has come undone where it has. As contrarian theorists rightly point out, modernity is not causing religion always and everywhere to collapse—but that is different from addressing the question of whether Christianity specifically *has* collapsed in parts of the West, and if so, why.

In sum, the fact that religion has not withered away as predicted by a variety of secular theorists—critical though it may be, and a point to which we will return—does not tell us why or how it *has* withered, where indeed it has.

*"The West hasn't really lost God, because the idea of secularization depends in turn on the idea of a prior 'golden age' of belief. In fact, though, people were no more believing or pious in the past than they are today. Therefore, there has been no religious decline."*

Other people staring at the puzzle of secularization make a different point that they think argues against the fact of Christian religious decline. They say that we modern observers erroneously assume that the men and women who came before us were more religious than the men and women of today. If they are correct, of course, then there is really no such thing as "secularization," in the sense that many people think there is—and without secularization, there is no need to explain how secularization came about.

As the distinguished observer Owen Chadwick put the point in his 1975 Gifford Lectures, subsequently published as a much-noted book called *The Secularization of the European Mind in the Nineteenth Century*, "We cannot begin our quest for secularization by postulating a dream-society that once upon a time was not secular."[12] It is a deep point. Embedded in the Western psyche is a story about the arc of Christianity, according to which it rose from the low historical point of the apostles to reach an apex sometime in the Middle Ages—after which it slowly, but surely, began curving down again.

It is a story we all believe unthinkingly, to some degree, as contrarians about secularization correctly point out. Just about everyone in the Golden Age of Christianity attended church, we think; just about everyone lived in fear of heaven and hell; and the village atheist was just that—a singular rather than plural force; a social anomaly. The deceptively simple question that contrarians ask about this story is: Is it true?

Consider, Chadwick observes, the sharp increase in illegitimate births in Toulouse, France, between the seventeenth and eighteenth centuries. If people who believe in the Christian God take their beliefs seriously, they believe that sex outside of marriage jeopardizes their very salvation. Hence, illegitimacy may arguably be used as one possible proxy for the influence of Christian belief on personal practice (in this case, marriage or lack thereof). And so it is interesting indeed that according to Chadwick's statistics, one out of fifty-nine births were to unmarried women in 1668–75—whereas by a century later, in 1778, fully *one in four* births occurred to unmarried women.[13]

What the numbers show is that—at least in a significant area of France—a distinctly un-Christian practice was proceeding apace far earlier than most people would have guessed it did. One cannot blame state-enforced secularization for this change; the rise in out-of-wedlock births was apparently well under way before Robespierre and his fellow murderers would make the streets of Paris run with blood. No, the fact that more and more people were having babies outside of marriage in an ostensibly overwhelmingly Christian place tells us something else: either that not all Christians took their theological beliefs as seriously as we tend to think they did; or that the church was weaker in governing the behavior of its members than is commonly supposed—or both. In any event, is this example not evidence, as some would suggest, for a prior age that was not so much "golden," from the point of view of religiosity, as just *prior*?

To broaden the point considerably, it is also a fact that many other such examples could be produced to suggest that what we think of as the "good old days" of religiosity—or the bad old days, depending on one's perspective—were not as pious as the formidable statuary and paintings and other artifacts of the Middle Ages might lead one to suppose.

In a particularly compelling essay published in 1999 called "Secularization, R.I.P.," another outstanding sociologist of religion, American Rodney Stark, exuberantly compiles several pages of empirical and historical evidence testifying to what he calls "the nonexistence of an Age of Faith in European history."[14]

His *tour d'horizon* ranges impressively: from medieval historians who dispute that such an age ever existed; to religious men and women from across the centuries and languages and cultures of what is now Europe, complaining about the lack of practice and belief among the people; to rural parish churches far too tiny to have held more than a small fraction of the population at any given time—which suggests to Stark that the expectation of weekly attendance was not only unlikely, but impossible; to primary sources indicating that not only the mass of men and women, but also many of the clergy, were plumb ignorant of the rituals and even basic prayers of the church; and so on. The "conception of a pious past," he summarizes, is "mere nostalgia," a "once-upon-a-time tale."[15]

Stark also notes, as have others, that some empirical evidence about churchgoing in fact affirms rather the opposite point: namely, that later centuries of Christians were in fact *more* pious than previous ones, depending on which chunks of the timeline we examine. Church membership in Britain by 2000, he reports, was higher than it was in 1800 (in 1800, only 12 percent of the British population belonged to a specific congregation; and since 1950, a stable 17 percent has reported such[16]). Also affirming Stark's point here are other studies—for example about the impact of World War II on religiosity—that have similarly found apparent boomlets of churchgoing, professions of belief and affiliation, and other indicators.[17]

This larger point—that religiosity does not in fact show a steady downward decline only, but is marked instead by outbursts of piety unexplained by conventional secularization theory—is another interesting one to which we will return.

In sum, the contrarian theorists have obviously uncovered something important. It is that "the secularization thesis is incompatible with either stability or increase; it requires a general, long-term pattern of religious decline," again to quote Stark.[18] In their important 2000 book *Acts of Faith: Explaining the Human Side of Religion*, among other places, Stark and Roger Finke discuss a new paradigm to counter the secularization thesis: rational choice theory, or the notion that "religious choices are guided by reason to as great an extent as are secular choices."[19] It is a theory developed over the years as an alternative to conventional accounts of secularization.[20] That theory has in turn given rise to a great debate continuing into the present over the reasons why people might rationally choose religious belief.

Nevertheless—and despite the intuitively appealing truth that everyday Christians of yore almost certainly did not have their eyes as fixed on heaven and their hands clasped in prayer quite as constantly as moderns looking back through time tend to think they did—the specific argument against a Christian "golden age" goes only so far toward refuting the agnosticism and secularism of the present. The evidence accumulated by these critics, interesting and at times ingenious, does mitigate the more simpleminded paradigms of secularization; but it does not refute the claim that Christianity has declined measurably in some of its former Western strongholds.

First, the dichotomy being insisted upon here—between a strict Age of Faith on the one side, and an Age of Unbelief on the other—is too inflexible. As one prominent defender of secularization theory,

British sociologist Steve Bruce, has sensibly pointed out, "Nothing in the secularization paradigm requires . . . a 'golden Age of Faith.' It merely requires *that our ancestors be patently more religious than we are* [emphasis added]."[21] As Bruce also goes on to summarize, a number of commonsense measures comparing pre- and post-Reformation Britons demonstrate just such a disparity. "Can we really believe," he asks, "that people whose lives were organized by the calendar of the Church, whose art, music and literature were almost entirely religious, who were taught the basic prayers, who regularly attended church services, and for whom the priest was the most powerful person after their temporal lord, were untouched by religious beliefs and values?"[22] Bruce thinks the answer to that question is obviously no—meaning that there is ample reason to believe that the men and women who came before today in the Christian tradition were indeed more believing than our own, whatever isolated snapshots such as illegitimacy in Toulouse might otherwise suggest.

It is a point powerfully buttressed by another major work that appeared first in 1992: Eamon Duffy's *The Stripping of the Altars: Traditional Religion in England 1400–1580*.[23] This heavily documented study advances an account of the English Reformation that is profoundly subversive of received wisdom. Duffy argues that contrary to the widely accepted story line—according to which the Reformation breathed new life into what had become a decaying and discredited Catholic Church that had lost the support of the common people—the weight of evidence proves something very different: that "late medieval Catholicism exerted an enormously strong, diverse, and vigorous hold over the imagination and the loyalty of the people up to the very moment of the Reformation," and that "when all is said and done, the Reformation was a violent disruption, not the natural fulfillment, of most of what was vigorous in late medieval piety and religious practice."[24]

This is an arresting thesis for several reasons, in the first place because it amounts to nothing less than a rewriting of the standard account of English Reformation history. According to that account—to simplify and parody only a little—benighted and superstitious Roman Catholicism eventually fell of its own dead, corrupted weight, to be replaced by a kinder, gentler, more enlightened English Protestantism. In all these particulars, Duffy argues, the standard account is wrong. It was violence and property seizure and persecution, he argues, rather than sweet reason and literacy and sophistication, that ultimately succeeding in driving the people of Britain away from the Roman Catholic Church. "Medieval English Catholicism," he proposes in a nutshell, "was, up to the very moment of its dissolution, a highly successful enterprise, the achievement by the official church of a quite remarkable degree of lay involvement and investment, and of a corresponding degree of doctrinal orthodoxy."[25]

To be sure, Duffy's purpose has nothing to do with establishing whether and how the West lost God; it is rather to mount a serious challenge to a nearly unbroken line of historical thinking on the part of the British themselves about how to understand the Reformation. For our business here, however, what is of particular interest can be found in that phrase, "the remarkable degree of lay involvement and investment." Duffy invokes a great deal of evidence in his nearly seven-hundred-page book to support his claim that generally speaking, ordinary people in the late Middle Ages in England were indeed pious—measurably, variously, irrefutably so.

His list includes, for example, the multiplication of vernacular religious books (especially books aimed at teaching people how to pray); the intricacy and prevalence of church iconography in painting, carving, and stained glass, all of which suggested a population educated in the minutiae of Christian belief; the cult of saints, which spread nationally and regionally, and similarly suggested widespread fealty to the belief of intercession; the observance of the Christian calendar's many feast days and other rituals; the use in carols of whole Latin phrases taken from the liturgy, which would only make sense if a large part of the population knew them and understood what they meant; the way that mortuary alms and masses were embedded in almost all wills of the period, obviously suggesting that people believed such posthumous practices would hasten their time out of purgatory; and many other fascinating details that testify to the notion that late medieval Christians—at least in the England so painstaking documented here—were indeed religiously more literate than people are today, and also more observant, and (by implication, given the extent of their observation) more believing.

To this scholarly analysis one might add another observation that appears to refute the notion that Christianity is the same as it ever was. That point has to do with one simple way of measuring religious loyalty: attendance.

Consider some of the numbers available that make the point. Economists Raphaël Franck and Laurence R. Iannaccone, who have done extensive work in this area, have drawn on a large international database stretching over decades to analyze church attendance across the West using polls conducted by the International Social Survey Program (ISSP).[26] They summarize simply that "the ISSP data unequivocally show that church attendance decreased in the West during the twentieth century" and that "the decline in church attendance was particularly pronounced after the 1960s." Both the latter point and the authors' own interesting hypothesis—that the welfare state itself caused the decline in religiosity—are items to which we will return. Meanwhile, however, their work suffices to make the point that the decline in Christian practice in the West is not merely an anecdotal tale of empty churches here and there. It is rather a statistical fact.

Nor is the United States, for all its vaunted religiosity relative to Western Europe, exempt from the slide in attendance. Robert D. Putnam and David E. Campbell write in their important 2010 study of religion, *American Grace: How Religion Divides and Unites Us*, "independent streams of evidence suggest that Americans have become somewhat less observant religiously over the last half century."[27] Most of that decline is generational: Gen-Xers and Millenials both exhibit less religious attendance than their elders. This is one more demographic fact pregnant with implications for the future, as those generations become parents who do or do not choose to share their already attenuated religiosity with their children.

The matter of attendance is also obviously connected to another point demonstrating decline: observance of church rules. From the beginning, Christianity regulated via ritual and doctrine the fundamental matters of birth, death, and procreation. In fact, some might say that in its attentiveness to these matters, Christianity (like the Judaism from which it drank) was perhaps even more focused on such matters than other faiths—all of which raises the critical question of compliance. As is often pointed out, the church is nothing if not a collection of sinners. But are they sinners who fall short of the rules that they believe in—or people who don't believe they are bound by those same rules at all?

In that question lies all the difference, I would argue, between the Christianity of yesteryear and much of Western Christianity today. For it is surely the case in large stretches of the advanced West today, many sophisticated people do not believe that the churches have any authority *whatsoever* to dictate constraints on individual freedom.

This same point about the reduced gravitational pull of the churches on personal morality has also been documented repeatedly by those advocating the secularization thesis. In his influential book called *The Death of Christian Britain: Understanding Secularization 1800–2000*, for example, British historian Callum G. Brown assembles a formidable barrage of statistical information to make just this point about the decline of Christianity there, ranging from the decline in church marriages and baptisms to changing attitudes toward all aspects of sexual behavior.[28] "Secularization," he argues, "is to be located, in part at least, in the changing conditions which allowed previously regarded Christian and social 'sins' to be regarded as acceptable and moral, at least by many, in British society in 2000."[29] Practically an identical definition could be given for American society in 2000—and Australian, and French, and Canadian, and in every other corner of the West where practices once forbidden by the church under penalty of hell are now not only legal, but in a growing number of cases also objects of special social and legal protection.

In sum, Brown has the better part of the argument against contrarianism here: If "secularization" is not the name for the replacement of a Christian ethos with an ethos that explicitly rejects Christian thinking, then what *do* we call that phenomenon? He also makes a compelling empirical case for his claim that Christianity entered an especially steep decline as of the 1960s. "From 1956," he concludes toward the end of his study, "all indices of religiosity in Britain start to decline, and from 1963 most enter free fall."[30]

*Why* did faith in the Christian God stop mattering for so many right around that point in time ("in our lifetime," as Brown notes, at least for many people reading these words)? What was it about that historical moment that explains how, in much of Western Europe,

Christianity went into free fall after that? I believe the shorthand answer is: the Family Factor, and the chapters after this one will spell out the reasons why.

For now, however, the point made earlier in this section, and bolstered by Brown's study of Britain among other sources, stands unmolested. In the manifest willingness of so many men and women in the West to live in defiance of long-standing Christian doctrine on any number of points—whether or not they even intend that defiance as a public act—we have more evidence for the loosening hold of the Christian creed on the way more and more people begin, live, frame, and finish off their lives.

Another objection raised by scholars who disagree with the idea that many Western people are becoming more secular is this:

*"The West hasn't really lost God, because human nature itself does not change; it remains theotropic, or leaning toward the transcendent, and it always will."*

Here again, critics of the secularization thesis make a valid and intuitively appealing point: believing in God is just something most human beings *do*. It is a point plumbed with enormous subtlety by Émile Durkheim, who argued that religion is "real" in the sense that it arises out of and also reinforces the human need for moral community—which is another way of saying it is a permanent feature of humanity.[31]

Nor was Durkheim the only one to notice that people who believe in god(s) appear to be doing what comes naturally. Well before the new atheists made their appearance, religious apologists were deploying the ammunition of human religiosity against secular battering rams storming the churches. Consider as emblematic one engaging statement of the case, a book by sociologist (and Catholic priest) Andrew M. Greeley called *Unsecular Man: The Persistence of Religion*. First published in 1972, at the height of what was called "death of God" theology, it is a confident and informed statement of the author's case—sharpened further by a new introduction in 1985—that "the basic human religious needs and the basic religious functions have not changed very notably since the late Ice Age."[32]

Somewhat ironically perhaps, these key points made by Greeley and other thinkers who stress the theotropic nature of human beings have lately acquired increasing force from a quite opposite quarter fascinated by this same durability of religion: i.e., nonbelieving evolutionists and evolutionary psychologists. These theorists, too, seek to account for the observation made by no less an authority than Charles Darwin—that "a belief in all-pervading spiritual agencies seems to be universal."[33] Unlike some contemporary theorists following in his shoes, Darwin did not think that belief in the Western God *per se*—that is to say, in a "beneficent and universal Deity"—is innate to human beings; he appears instead to have viewed that particular belief as arising only relatively late in human culture, though he does not explain why.[34] Yet the universality of belief in a spiritual realm of some sort appeared to him as a puzzle that evolutionists needed to solve, whether or not his own thoughts amounted to a solution.

So remains the case today as Darwin's heirs examine the near ubiquity of some God or gods in human history. "The universal propensity toward religious beliefs," echoes evolutionary psychologist Steven Pinker, "is a genuine scientific puzzle."[35] In fact, with the benefit of today's technology—DNA sequencing, brain imaging, and the like—scientists interested in that puzzle are contributing more hypotheses than Darwin himself could possibly have foreseen.[36] Some even now argue that religious beliefs serve some sort of beneficial adaptive purpose—that we humans are home to some sort of "God gene" that explains the religious dimension of human history.[37]

Several points germane to our argument arise from these ponderings on the enduring nature of religiosity, whether they are by believer-friendly authors such as Greeley or by secularists whose thought is dominated by evolution and evolutionary psychology.

One such benefit is atmospheric. Unlike the triumphalism of much new atheist writing, for example, or the less overt but nonetheless palpable sense on the part of some secularization theorists that the witch—ding dong!—is finally dead, approaches that instead emphasize the mysteriousness of human belief by contrast show the virtue of epistemological humility. We modern men and women are not a different breed from all the humanity to have come before; and the twentieth-century ideologies premised in one way or another on exactly that—i.e., the supposedly malleable clay of human nature— have one by one bitten the dust of history.

After all, as we saw earlier in the case of Communism, the death of some of Christianity's most bitter rivals has come to hearten its embattled defenders. Greeley's own list of the "isms" that Christianity has outlived includes socialism and historicism—not exactly an inconsequential pair. It is they, and not Christianity, which now tend to their ailing old flocks and attract few young lambs.

The second valuable thing about this form of dissent from the secularization thesis is that it attacks the thesis where it is most vulnerable: its claim that secularization is *inevitable*. Thus, for example—citing with approval the late sociologist Robert Nisbet's influential work *Social Change in History*—Greeley argues alongside Nisbet that the very idea of humanity somehow "evolving" out of religion is suspect, because the fixity of human institutions, rather than evolutionary change, is the historical norm. Secularization theorists assume, sometimes unconsciously, that the human race evolves sociologically as well as biologically; but these assumptions are not substantiated by data or other facts. (Interestingly, this same distinction has been invoked by former Archbishop of Canterbury Rowan Williams, who has argued similarly that Darwinian arguments have been wrongly used to interpret culture, rather than simply biology.[38])

Andrew Greeley, Robert Nisbet, the archbishop of Canterbury: as these and other critics questioning the evolutionary model of religious change rightly argue, the so-called "necessity" of the demise of Christianity has been proven wrong time and again. Similarly, Rodney Stark opens his lengthy essay "Secularization R.I.P.," mentioned earlier, with an entertaining review of predictions of the demise of Christian faith dating back to 1660 during the Restoration period and continuing on up to the present day—a list including but hardly limited to such leading lights as Thomas Woolston, Frederick the Great, Thomas Jefferson, Auguste Comte, Fredrich Engels, A. E. Crawley, Sigmund Freud, anthropologist Anthony F. C. Wallace, sociologist Bryan Wilson, and other notables. As Stark wryly notes, all seem not to have grasped the irony that their own obituaries would be written long before the rest of the world stopped believing in God.[39]

Yet useful though the contrarian approach has been in exposing the faults with the conventional story line about the demise of the Christian God, it faces the same challenge discussed earlier in this chapter: the empirical reality of the decline in attendance, sacraments, schooling, religious rituals, and other measures of religious fealty—especially, though not only, in Western Europe.

One can take the point further. In many parts of the West today, religiously influenced personal behavior of the kind mentioned earlier—pertaining to such major decisions as life, birth, and death rituals—is so far reduced as to barely exist in large segments of the population. In *God's Continent*, professor of religious studies

Philip Jenkins summarizes the numbers as follows: "The precipitous decline in practice in several nations that . . . would have been regarded as heartlands of the faith"; "the number of seminarians has plunged"; "orders of monks and nuns have contracted"; and so on. He also cites "abundant anecdotal evidence, supported by opinion surveys, [that] suggests the depth of ignorance about even the most basic Christian doctrines. *One British poll found that over 40 percent of respondents could not say what event was commemorated by Easter* [emphasis added]."[40]

In sum, if God *were* to be dead in the Nietzschean sense, one suspects that the wake would look a lot like this.

Another, related problem with settling for the notion that "human beings are born theotropic, and therefore will turn to God eventually," is this: if that is so, then certain societies in the world today that are notably nontheotropic loom as large question marks over the theory.

Ironically, once again, this fact is not only a problem for those who would infer from the universality of belief the notion that nonbelievers will come round sooner or later. It is no less a problem for the evolutionary psychologists now busying themselves with speculative explanations for how and why religion might be "hardwired." The fact that some people—specifically, some people in secular regions of Europe—now seem to be able to live without God altogether thus becomes a fact in need of explaining, and neither religious thinkers attacking the secularization thesis nor antireligious evolutionary psychologists are there yet.

An interesting 2008 book called *Society without God: What the Least Religious Nations Can Tell Us about Contentment* illustrates just this point, though again inadvertently.[41] Author Phil Zuckerman, another sociologist, spent a year in Scandinavia and conducted over 150 in-depth interviews in two of the least religious nations on earth, Denmark and Sweden. Only 10 percent of Danes and Swedes believe in hell, for example, which the author reports are the lowest percentages in the world; the rate of weekly church attendance in both countries is also lower than any other; almost no one he surveyed believes the Bible was divinely inspired; and so on.[42] "I have come to seriously question the innateness or naturalness of religious belief," the author concludes.

To acknowledge that Zuckerman obviously has a point about Scandinavia is not to deny that a religious instinct or "theotropism" exists. But it is to say that a belief in divinity *alone*, of the sort elemental to Judeo-Christianity, lately looks to be significantly less universal than either conventional secularization theory or its critics have so far understood—which is to say, once again, that something seems to be missing from the prevailing accounts of secularization both pro and con.

One final fact that points to secularization as a real phenomenon is that the leaders of Christian denominations themselves—from the Continent on across to the New World—see the diminishment of their flocks as an enormous problem.

Both Pope Benedict XVI and former Archbishop of Canterbury Rowan Williams, for example, have made a point of attacking secularism and atheism in their public addresses—proof that those at the top of religious ranks see the diminution of Christianity not as a secularist ruse but as a fact of overwhelming importance. This is particularly true of Europe, where the falloffs in attendance and participation have been calamitous from the point of view of Christian shepherds. A special report issued in 2011 on which the archbishop signed off, for example, called upon Christians to confront the new atheism, and also drew attention to what it portrayed as the increasing intolerance of secularist society.[43]

Weighing in on the Catholic side, Pope Benedict has similarly made the combating of secularization a top priority not only for his papacy, but throughout his career as a theologian. He has also tried repeatedly marked attempts to engage those outside the Catholic Church in philosophical dialogue, among them leading German philosopher Jürgen Habermas.[44] Benedict has further spoken openly of the "de-Christianization of Europe"—a phrase that surely signals his personal conviction that the Continent is, at a minimum, less Christian now than in times past.[45] In 2010 he even took the step of inaugurating a Pontifical Council for Promoting the New Evangelization, citing explicitly the "phenomenon of the detachment from the faith, that has progressively manifested itself in societies and cultures that for centuries appeared to be impregnated by the Gospel."[46]

Hence it is not only secular sociologists who speak of Christianity having gone over a cliff in certain precincts but also Christian leaders themselves.

The reality, it seems, is that the specter of secularization can be seen by a great many people peering across history from different points of view. The difficulty of pinpointing exactly *when* so many men and women lost sight of God remains just that—an empirical and historical difficulty that will open to criticism anyone who attempts it. But that stumbling block *per se* does not change the fact that today's Western men and women are, generally and measurably speaking, considerably less governed by Christian beliefs and rituals than were their ancestors of five hundred years ago—any more than, say, the difficulty of charting a navigational course changes the fact that it is still on water.

To put the matter another way, to say that secularization theory has problems is not to say that secularization hasn't *happened*. Yes, a majority of Europeans identify themselves as Christians, as is often pointed out by people searching for a bright side of those same attendance numbers; but so what? Jeffrey Cox, an American historian, has sharply contested this very point: "An unwillingness by most Europeans to declare themselves entirely atheistic, or to abandon irrevocably all hope of life after death, is not persuasive evidence that Berlin and Amsterdam are throbbing with a hidden Durkeimian numinosity."[47] To cite one more scholar weighing in on this side, David Voas of the University of Manchester, the "fuzzy fidelity" of many modern Western people, especially in Europe, does not mitigate this critical point: data from the first wave of the European Social Survey show "that each generation in every country surveyed is less religious than the last" and that "although there are some minor differences in the speed of the decline (the most religious countries are changing more quickly than the least religious), the magnitude of the fall in religiosity during the last century has been remarkably constant across the Continent."[48]

It is the accumulation of data like those that makes it hard to avoid the conclusion that Christianity exerts far less gravitational pull over today's Europeans and many other Westerners than it did over their grandparents and their grandparents before them.

*"Secularization theory is mistaken, because what people call 'secularization' is really the death of Protestant Christianity; the Catholic Church isn't in the same straits."*

A number of distinguished Catholic thinkers have made this argument one way or another; and therefore I submit it here for consideration alongside the other serious objections to the idea that Christianity, at least in Europe, is in permanent decline.[49]

Let us start with the fat grain of truth embedded in this interesting hay bale of an idea.

It is indeed historically demonstrable that the societies that have moved closest to "society without God"—in the words of the book by Phil Zuckerman mentioned earlier—are overwhelmingly Protestant. Scandinavia, as we have seen, might fairly be described as ground zero of secularization; and Scandinavia as a matter of history has been Protestant almost through and through. Denmark, Finland, and Iceland—more countries remarkable for secularism—similarly embraced Lutheranism earlier in their histories; Great Britain, likewise, is far more Protestant than Catholic, and the Church of England, as noted earlier, seems to be evaporating before its clergymen's eyes. Is there in fact a larger lesson lurking somewhere in this cluster of historical facts—i.e., that the first societies to send the Catholic Church packing are *ipso facto*, down the road, the first to lose God?

Here are some more facts of possible relevance. It is also surely true that certain Protestant churches elsewhere—what in the United States are called the "mainline" churches of the Episcopalians, Presbyterians, Lutherans, and others—are in dire straits.[50] Note that we are not talking here of Pentecostalism or evangelicalism, both of which are on the rise outside the West and retain healthy numbers of adherents within it. No, in a fascinating turn, it is not the Protestant churches such as those that are floundering—i.e., the churches with the lightest institutional mooring. It is rather the best-off, those that were hitherto financially and socially strongest, that are lately diminishing most even as relative institutional underdogs continue to prosper.

It is a fact to which we will later return that this phenomenon is to be found across the Western world—one codified in 1972 by Dean M. Kelly, an American legal scholar and defender of religious freedom who was also an executive with the National Council of Churches. His influential book called *Why Conservative Churches Are Growing* remains the template for understanding which churches are prospering—and why. His argument was also given extra force in 1994 by Laurence R. Iannaccone, who deployed rational choice theory to demonstrate "Why Strict Churches Are Strong."[51]

To repeat, such is true not only in Western Europe, but also in America, once again of those churches known as the mainline. Whether one looks at Pew numbers or Gallup polls, the latest budget of Washington National Cathedral or that of the smallest rural Congregationalist church, the story remains much the same: traditional American Protestantism appears largely over. As essayist and poet Joseph Bottum has observed in an seminal essay summarizing the American Protestant religious scene:

> The death of the Mainline is the central historical fact of our time: the event that distinguishes the past several decades from every other period in American history. Almost every one of our current political and cultural oddities, our contradictions and obscurities, derives from this fact: The Mainline has lost the capacity to set, or even significantly influence, the national vocabulary or the national self-understanding.[52]

Is Protestantism really the cause of secularism, as the incomparable Max Weber would have agreed? Or to put the matter more boldly, does this marked decline of certain major Protestant churches in turn spell historical victory of some kind for the Catholic Church—thereby invalidating or at least mitigating the secularization thesis?

*Pace* those who might reduce the decline of Christianity to the decline of Protestantism, I think the answer to both questions is *no*, for two reasons.

The first concerns the definition of what is meant by "Catholicism." In Italy, among other countries, for example, most people when asked in surveys will identify themselves as Catholics. But how many are Catholic in anything but name only?

Consider just a few particulars about the current gap between profession of faith and practice. The Catholic Church teaches that attendance at Sunday Mass is a weekly obligation, and that failure to do so for any but the most serious reasons is a mortal sin (i.e., one that could send the bearer to hell, were he to die without having confessed and repented it).

Attendance numbers suggest that a great many Italians (among other Catholics) either do not believe that threat, or fail to act on it if they do believe it.

The Patriarchate of Venice, in a study between 2004–5, for example, found that only 15 percent of that Catholic city was attending Mass on Sundays.[53] Another survey by Italian political scientist Paolo Segatti for the University of Milan, whose results were published in the magazine *Il Regno*, found especially marked decline in religious practice among the young. "The youngest Italians are the ones to whom religious experience is most foreign," he observed. "They clearly go to church less, believe in God less, pray less, trust the Church less, identify themselves as Catholic less, and say that being Italian does not mean being Catholic."[54]

When one dispenses with stereotypes and looks at the actual numbers, "Catholic" Italy does not appear terribly different from the rest of the god-forsaken Continent.

Much the same could be said of the other historically Catholic nations in Western Europe, too. In Ireland, estimates Philip Jenkins, roughly half of Catholics still attend Mass on Sunday—down from some 85–90 percent of that same population a quarter century ago.[55] Attendance numbers for other Catholic countries are even lower. In France, the percentage of those who say they never or almost never visit church was recently clocked by Jenkins at 60 percent (by way of comparison, in the United States it is 16 percent).[56] So bleak is the situation in France, at least from the Vatican's point of view, that John Paul II plaintively remarked during his first visit there in 2000, "Eldest daughter of the Church, what have you done with your baptism?"[57]

And then there is the related question about what it means to be "Catholic" in the relatively religious United States. Consider what numbers from the Pew Forum on Religion & Public Life tell us about actual religious practice—as opposed to self-described Catholic "identity." Analyzing the Pew 2010 attendance numbers for thecatholicthing.org, for example, an online magazine dedicated to traditional Catholicism, columnist Brad Miner observed that "among America's nearly 80-million Catholics, only a smidgen more than 40 percent is actually, well, *Catholic*, in the sense that they recognize the *obligation* to attend weekly Mass."[58] Moreover, "65 percent are pro-choice," "the figures for all Catholics come out 45/45," and that "among all Catholics: 46 percent favor [same-sex marriage], [and] 42 percent oppose, an exact flip from just a few years ago."[59]

Miner's point and Pew's numbers are plainly germane to the question of whether the trouble with Christianity is just Protestantism. According to traditional Catholic moral teaching (as in Protestant theology too, until very recently), sexual relations apart from traditional marriage—whether same-sex, opposite-sex, multipartner, or interspecies—are all regarded as varieties of adultery, which is to say behavior that Christians are supposed to frown upon. To be sure, there is a great deal more to Catholic teaching than issues of sexual morality. On the other hand, the church since its earliest days has made those selfsame teachings a theological centerpiece of Christian thought. So if large numbers of "Catholics" in the West today are disregarding teachings as freighted with seriousness as these, what are they *not* disregarding?

Rather obviously, the fact that this moral code is so widely flouted—when it is not being openly questioned including by those in authority, a theological situation known as "scandal"—remains a grave, long-term problem from the institutional point of view. Whether one loves that code for its consistency or—as is more often the case these days—hates the thing for its interference with sexual freedom is here beside the point. The issue here is not whether one sinner or a billion of them falls short of that code. It is rather whether a sizable majority of those calling themselves "Catholic" do not believe in that code *at all*. That, surely, is a change from the Christianity of the past.

One final reason to believe that the decline of Christianity involves the decline of Catholicism and not just Protestantism, is this: fertility rates and family size—surely two indicators of religious health, from the point of view of Catholic theology at least—are not only changing in a secular direction, as we saw in the examples of Italy and Spain. They are also actually *lower* in the Catholic countries of Europe today than in the Protestant ones.

In the 1970s, women in Catholic European nations had the equivalent of "half a child" more, on average, than women in the Protestant nations. Yet by the 1990s, writes Philip Jenkins, Catholic countries showed the lowest rates of fertility on the entire Continent. So marked is this change that German sociologist Ulrich Beck has quipped: "in western Europe, there is a rough rule of thumb according to which the closer one gets to the Pope, the fewer children one has."[60]

Demographers and other scholars, for their part, differ wildly on the question of what Europe's tanking birthrates mean for the Continent's social and economic health. To some, the graying and declining population of the greater West is emblematic of a decaying civilization. Others point instead to increased longevity and better health as engines of a new cultural vitality just waiting for ignition. Once again though, these differences in prognostication are here beside the point. What matters for our purposes is something else: there is abundant evidence that religious practice is declining among the West's Catholics as well as among its Protestants—an empirical outcome contradicting the idea that the decline of Christianity in the West is somehow just a Protestant thing.

Judging broadly by history, and by the current state of their societies, it appears true that the Protestants have gone secular first—a point we will revisit in chapter 6. "Generally," Jenkins summarizes, "decline has been far more marked in formerly Protestant areas, such as Britain or Denmark, than in nations with a strong Catholic heritage, and that difference is as marked within particular nations." But as he also notes—surely correctly, in view of the evidence— "Catholics can take little comfort from this distinction, which might indicate not a qualitatively different fate, but rather a cultural delay of a decade or two."[61]

To put the point another way, one way of understanding "secularization" is this: it is the phenomenon through which Protestants, generally speaking, go godless and Catholics, generally speaking, go Protestant.

*"Secularization theory is mistaken, because the world is not really growing less religious; it is diversifying spiritually instead."*

The idea that the West is not so much abandoning God as morphing him into new shapes and sizes is another argument sometimes invoked to challenge the idea of Christianity's demise in the West. It is an idea closely associated with professor of philosophy Charles Taylor, whose previously mentioned opus *A Secular Age* is widely considered to be the best history of the idea of secularism yet written. There and elsewhere, Taylor advances the commonsensical point (albeit in luxuriously scholarly language) that religion in our world is a complicated, protean, multifaceted thing—that, as he puts it, "We shouldn't perhaps speak simply of the loss of a neo-Durkheimian identity, or connection to religion through our allegiance to civilizational order, but rather of a kind of mutation. The religious reference . . . doesn't so much disappear, as change, retreat to a certain distance."[62]

After all—to translate the observation into homely examples—it is not as if the elites of the West have ceased altogether in believing in *anything* transcendent. Where Christianity once was, varieties of other spiritual practice now abound—from the outright paganism of the modern-day Druids to what might be called the stealth paganism of New Age practices. There is also the deep respect for yoga and meditation, say, and the zeal that many now bring to greening the earth, and other evidence testifying to a continued search for connection to a realm beyond self alone. Given the abundance of these and other forms of "alternative" spirituality, it makes sense to spy, as Taylor does, a "nova" of spiritual diversity rather than simply a black hole of secularization. There is much that is attractive about this line of reasoning. Plainly, "alternative" movements are indeed filling a vacuum once filled for many Europeans (and Americans) by traditional religion; the devotion and moral seriousness which people bring to them are unmistakably quasi-religious in character. This is especially true, perhaps, of the embrace of environmentalism, a worldview that dictates cradle-to-grave morality among its believers as assiduously as did the medieval village church—from choices about ecologically correct diapers to questions about the environmentally proper way of scattering of ashes at the end of life. The question of how that movement, especially, came pouring to the shores of what was once the Sea of Faith—and how much residual Christianity lies buried in it—is a fascinating one, and one more digression deserving of further attention elsewhere.

There is also the wider fact that politics more generally operates for some people as a secular religion—especially politics dictated by a worldview professing to cover all aspects of life, such as Marxism. One compelling statement of that case has been offered by social scientist and journalist Stanley Kurtz, who locates just such a widespread transmutation in today's passionate embrace of political liberalism—what Kurtz calls the "collective defense of the individual's sacred rights"—by many Western people.[63] "A certain form of liberalism," he argues, "now functions for a substantial number of its adherents as a religion: an encompassing world-view that answers the big questions about life, dignifies daily exertions with higher significance, and provides a rationale for meaningful collective action."[64]

Moreover, even without the New Age or millenarian political substitutes, Christianity itself still commands more of the Western mind and heart than many secularists understand. This is an argument made convincingly by British sociologist Grace Davie, who has coined the phrase "believing without belonging" to describe that very phenomenon.[65] Davie points to numerous paradoxes arising from the current European religious scene—for example, that many people still consider themselves to be Christian, whether or not they go to church; that the churches continue to perform vital public functions, even as their numbers shrink; that Europeans, including in Scandinavia, pay taxes to keep their churches going. Her point, as she put it in an interview, is that people want "vicarious religion"—that is, a situation that "upholds the values that many Europeans don't very often live by but still would like to be there."[66]

These are indeed fascinating brakes on the notion of galloping secularization. Even so, and taking such vital nuances into account, the apparent fact that secular people in the West may not be quite as secular as they think is once more of limited relevance to the question insisted on here: *How and why did and does Christianity decline in the West?*

As political scientist Eric Kaufmann points out in his fascinating 2011 book, *Shall the Religious Inherit the Earth? Demography and Politics in the Twenty-First Century*, there are problems with equating spiritual diversity with traditional religion. People drawn to what are now considered to be "alternative" forms of spirituality are "inspired by earthly desires for health, meaning and wellbeing rather than a connection to the supernatural."[67] The instrumental nature of such "diffuse religion" is also a point made well by aforementioned sociologist Steve Bruce, who outlines the problems with using New Age beliefs as evidence of religious revival—including the fundamental problem that New Agers, unlike traditional believers, tend not to inculcate their children in the same beliefs.[68]

In sum, at some point, positing Christian religion as existing on a continuum with more nebulous forms of "spirituality" becomes problematic. Consider that modern forms of "spirituality" repudiate essential items of the Christian creed—sin, heaven, hell, the Trinity, the Incarnation, and the Resurrection just for starters. How many doctrinal particulars can be jettisoned before any given individual can fairly be called un- or even anti-Christian, un- or antireligious? At what point would St. Paul, say, find this modern syncretic "Christianity" altogether unrecognizable?

To summarize what we have learned by sketching the arguments and counterarguments of this chapter, the contemporary critics of secularization theory—the scholars of what I have dubbed, appreciatively, the so-what school—have managed to do two things, and those very well. First, they have brought eagles' eyes to the problems associated with the notion that Christianity, when faced with the forces of modernism, would somehow inevitably just dwindle away.

Their second accomplishment is even more profound—and has implications for the pages that follow. By emphasizing that religious practice and belief upon inspection do *not* follow straight downward declines, but rather wax and wane in different times and places, the critics of secularization theory have drawn attention to the same problem at the heart of this book—the felt need for a "theory of variation," as Stark has put it. What has gone missing, again, is a persuasive explanation of why Christianity has thrived in some places and times and not others. The hypothesis spelled out in the rest of this book is an attempt to fit that bill.

Perhaps the pithiest formulation with which to summarize our investigation so far belongs once more to Eric Kaufmann. He confronts the critics of secularization theory with the observation that "an employee of the Holy See who went to sleep in 1500 and awoke today would be depressed by what he saw. Spinoza and other freethinkers would be elated."[69] About that he is surely on target. In the end, and despite the creativity of contrarianism, the mystery of *why* parts of the West went secular remains—and that mystery is the reason why a new theory should be entertained.

As the great British historian of Christianity Owen Chadwick put it in 1975, in the final sentence of his classic work *The Secularization of the European Mind in the Nineteenth Century*, "What happened, and why, must still be matter for much enquiry by students of history and religion and society."[70] In the following chapter, we will take him up on that challenge by reviewing briefly but with real concentration the current going explanations for the "why" of secularization—with particular attention to why conventional ways of arranging the puzzle pieces seem to leave something out.

What Is the Conventional Story Line about How
the West Lost God? What Are the Problems with It?

THE PURPOSE of the previous chapter was to convince readers
that the great puzzle described at the outset of this book does
indeed exist—i.e., that parts of the West are indeed significantly
more secular, and significantly less influenced by Christianity in
particular, than they have been for much of the past two millennia
including even in the relatively recent past.

Many readers may not have needed convincing, of course. "Secularization" rings intuitively true, say, to those who toil in certain
Western cultural institutions where God has long since been sent
packing with a vengeance—such as the secular media, for example;
or the raunchier reaches of Western popular culture; or the many
elite colleges and universities that sport, for example, "Sex Week"
but never "God Week."[1] Still other readers may have seen the secular writing on the wall in images from contemporary Europe—the
hostility in some places toward any religious figure in the public
square; the continuing political attempts to minimize or rewrite the
influence of Christianity on European history; the many churches
home to no one in the pews below the age of sixty or so; and the rest
of the über-secular portrait presented already in the introduction
and chapter 1.

Nonetheless, and as the arguments in the chapter past have gone
to show, it was necessary as a logical matter to establish *that* Western
Christianity is in decline before examining the arguments about *why*

that change has occurred. And so, having (I hope) concluded this necessary logical detour, we return here to our opening question.

How did it come to happen that the cultural burden of proof, as it were, shifted in large part from unbelievers to believers—in other words, that Christians have increasingly played defense, while their adversaries have increasingly commanded the offense?

Now, *that* God has been banished—and/or that he ought to be banished—from large and hardly insignificant territories of the West is a notion that many urbane men and women no longer even think to question, so self-evident does it appear to them. As we have seen, the idea that religion would inevitably decline has been shared by almost every titan of modernity, including Émile Durkheim, Max Weber, Charles Darwin, Sigmund Freud, G. W. F. Hegel, Karl Marx, and Herbert Spencer, among others.[2] In fact, so familiar is their collective story of how the West lost God that it is now taken for granted by a great many educated people—including many who have never stopped to ponder the finer points of secularization theory because they just "know" that the Christian religion will sooner or later become a thing of the past.

As people across the West become more educated and more prosperous, the reigning collective story goes, they also come to find themselves both more skeptical of religion's premises and less needful of its ostensible consolations. Hence, somewhere in the long run—perhaps even the *very* long run; Nietzsche himself predicted it would take "hundreds and hundreds" of years for the "news" to reach everyone—religion, or more specifically the Christianity so long dominant on the European Continent, will die out. Exactly *which* feature of modernity would do the trick has been much disputed, but a representative list would include, at a minimum, technology, education, material progress, urbanization, science, feminism, and rationalism, among others cited for the withdrawal of the Sea of Faith.

Over the years, as indicated, many learned and influential people have bent their powers to tracking the receding God. Our purpose in this chapter is to listen to what they have to say and to see whether it all adds up. As before, the arguments for the hows and whys of secularization can be distilled into a series of arguments united by family resemblance. Let us now look at these related ways of putting the pieces together—in effect, at what might be called the "creation stories" of secularization itself—and consider briefly but carefully their various strengths and weaknesses.

*"What caused secularization? People stopped needing the imaginary comforts of religion."*

Embedded deep within modern thinking about secularization is an almost entirely unremarked-upon religious anthropology—that is, an implied view of human beings that purports to account for how and why people believe in the Christian God (and, by extension, in religion generally). Let us call one such particular creation story "the comfort theory." Widely accepted though this view may be among modern, sophisticated Westerners, it is also a font of some of the deeper problems with secularization theory itself, for reasons that will become clear during the following discussion.

Why is it that so many millions of people throughout history have been drawn to the Christian God—or again for that matter, to other gods as well? Some armchair theorists have offered one or another variation of the same answer to that question. People believe in God, they suppose, *because it comforts them to do so.* Religion is akin to "opium," as Marx put it.[3] It is an "illusion," in Sigmund Freud's word, one that "derives its strength from the fact that it falls in with our instinctual desires."[4]

More quotes could be produced to prove the point: from the perspective of anti- or un-Christians who have paused to think about it, Christianity is rooted in fear and superstition. Its purpose is to serve as a giant pacifier against the hunger pains of mortality.

This is also the explanation offered, more or less, by those toiling in the fields of modern atheism. Michel Onfray, for example, who is perhaps France's most prominent atheist apologist, opens his best-selling book *Atheist Manifesto* with these words: "In Flaubert's novel, Madame Bovary relieved her despair by pretending. Many people do the same. . . . Better the faith that brings peace of mind than the rationality that brings worry—even at the price of perpetual mental infantilism."[5]

Again like the baby with the pacifier, so are religious believers thought to suck comfort from their creed. Believers, says Sam Harris similarly in *The End of Faith*, "draw solace and inspiration" from what they do.[6] Both Richard Dawkins and Christopher Hitchens also explain religion by drawing attention to the gullibility of its followers—a dismissal that clearly implies some imagined consolation on the part of the believers.[7]

In sum, for the new atheists—as for others standing outside the tent of belief, and wondering how it ever got put there—the most common answer to the question of "why religion?" seems to be that there is something about that tent that is comforting to those inside it. *It is something that people have somehow devised to make themselves feel better* about elemental matters like mortality, suffering, deprivation, and the rest of the unfortunate human lot.

To begin to see what is problematic here, look for starters at the unstated premise behind this account of how religious belief enters and exits the world. According to that premise, the people who are comforted in this way are by definition more primitive or less intelligent than certain others; otherwise, presumably, they would not keep reaching for that ultimate pacifier. (As inadvertent confirmation of this condescension, consider that new atheists prefer to designate themselves as "Brights"—a word plainly implying that believers are by contrast either "Dims" or "Dulls.")

Every once in a while, the lordliness of this largely unexamined premise breaks through to the surface—as in a notorious example from 2008, when President Barack Obama referred to benighted people who "cling to their guns and their religion," only to have to backtrack mightily when faced with public wrath over that sublimely snobbish characterization of believers. That kind of arrogance is one problem with the comfort theory. Even so, it is not, technically speaking, an *insurmountable* problem; after all, it is *possible* that the theory could still be true, however much its superciliousness might annoy the rest of the world.

No, the main problem with the comfort theory is that as a strictly empirical matter, it fails. The fundamental problem with this widespread explanation for how Christianity comes and goes in the world is this: *as a description of how people choose to believe what they do, this one is falsified by economic and other empirical fact.*

For one thing, the notion that Judeo-Christianity is "comforting" to individual men and women is thoroughly subverted by a reading of either the Old or New Testaments—to say nothing of both sets of books. It is true, of course, that immortality, and at times even earthly benefits, are promised to the ones who keep God's laws (adamantly so in the New Testament, more obliquely in the Old). And granted—since nearly all human beings love their own lives, as well as the lives of some others—the promise of more life is indeed a weighty consolation, as modern thinkers like to point out, and hence on its face, an undeniably attractive one.

But that attractiveness, I would argue, is outweighed by something that those who think along these lines have *not* thought to emphasize, because it undermines their argument: namely, the heavy strings attached to that same offer of ultimate salvation, as verified by a quick checklist of Judeo-Christianity's other and profoundly burdensome claims on those same individual souls.

There are, for starters, the constraints that the Judeo-Christian moral code strives to place upon human free will. Consider sex. Pagans in ancient Rome could have their concubines, same-sex lovers, orgies, and could otherwise engage without religious penalty in an expanded notion of sexual enjoyment; but practicing Christians (and practicing Jews) could not. Similarly, modern pagans and secularists can freely ignore, say, the commandments to attend religious services on Sundays and Holy Days; practicing Christians (and practicing Jews) cannot. People living outside the Judeo-Christian universe can decide whatever they like about any number of the most personal and far-reaching decisions they make in life—when to have their children, how to raise them, where to send them to school, what to eat on any given day, what to do about their parents, what (or whether) to give to charity, and so on. But the Judeo-Christian rulebook, at least in theory, circumscribes each and every one of these activities from the everyday to the exotic—and more, to boot.

To put it more bluntly: Do you really want to tithe, in addition to paying your taxes? Do you want your workweek disrupted by the demands of observance, and your social or romantic life circumscribed by rules that many of your friends think ridiculous? Do you want to drag your kids to religious education for years on end, often missing things they'd rather do in the meantime? Do you want to be laughed at in the secular Western public square? Do you want to be peppered constantly with fund-raisers and requests for volunteer-time, food donations, funding drives, and the rest of the institutional reality of religion? Then get yourself to synagogue/church.

In sum, the idea that people turn to Christianity as some kind of easy way out is subverted by the demands of putting that creed into practice.

Second, the hardly inconsequential history of Christian saints and martyrs also contradicts the comfort theory. No doubt—as the late Christopher Hitchens and Richard Dawkins and like-minded souls have enthusiastically emphasized—the Christian cup overflows with hucksters and con men and criminals and hypocrites. No doubt it also always has. But even a casual acquaintance with history makes clear that alongside such exploitation, there also runs a tradition of individual martyrdom and self-sacrifice that is far more interesting—because it is impossible to explain the depth of self-denial it exhibits using the anthropology of the comfort theory.

From the beginning of Judeo-Christianity, hale and hearty and ostensibly sane men and women—and some children—have suffered and died rather than renounce their faith. In the book of Daniel, rather famously, three young Jews (Shadrach, Meshach, and Abednego) suffer prison and then risk death in a fiery furnace rather than accede to the demand of the King of Babylon—a fate they are rescued from only by divine intervention. It is a story that has resonated throughout the centuries of a Christianity put often to similar trials and tests. Among the twelve apostles, for example, and leaving aside Judas Iscariot for obvious reasons, only one is believed to have died of natural causes. Christians were persecuted under every Roman emperor up until Constantine, and Diocletian alone is credited with the creation of 20,000 martyrs. On through the centuries, and following the example of those early martyrs, Christians here and there would scatter martyrdom to every corner of the globe.

Even more intriguing and problematic, at least for the comfort theory, the twentieth century itself—one into which enlightenment and modern technology were supposedly seeping and changing mores everywhere—appears as the very high-water mark of martyrdom, with the number of Christians killed for their faith a positively staggering weight against the notion that Christianity is for suckers seeking a false fix from human reality. According to the International Bulletin of Missionary Research, for example, which delivers an annual "Status of World Christians Report" attempting to quantify what is happening worldwide, "The number of martyrs [in the period 2000–2010] was approximately 1 million."[8] This is compared to some 34,000 in 1900.

Of course one can quibble with the numbers, and a precise body count may be out of conceptual reach. But what if the real tally is "only" half that? The point is not to ask whether millions of human beings have been right or wrong to throw their lives at their religious cause. But their situation in the history of Christianity does raise this provocative question: How can so many manifestly suffering people scattered across human history be squared with a theory that says their attraction to their faith was . . . to make themselves somehow feel *better* about life? Similarly, what about the everyday martyrdom of many other Christians—the Catholic priests denying themselves in principle the consolations of family; the missionaries throughout history serving lonely and uncomfortable time among the wretched of the earth; the towering religious figures, among whom John Paul II stands as the latest example, who dedicate their lives to serving the church?[9] Are we really supposed to believe these people too took up their crosses because that burden made them feel good?

In short, champions of the comfort inadvertently illuminate all over again the difficulty squarely before us: upon reflection, *there are obvious problems with the going explanations for why Christianity has diminished in parts of the West.*

To summarize, the notion that people turn to Christianity as a kind of consolation prize for the slow of wit is deeply flawed when one considers what living by the rules of Christianity actually *entails* if put into practice—which is sacrifice, self-sacrifice, and the acceptance of some unambiguously heavy limitations on individual freedom. And since that same deeply problematic conception of religion as a consolation prize is deeply embedded in the prevailing story line for secularization, it ends up calling into question that theory itself.

The problem before us is this: *If we don't have an adequate explanation for why people believe in religion in the first place, how can we have one for why they stop?* This is the first of other reasons to wonder whether some other explanation for the weakening of Christianity across the West might offer a more plausible account of what has happened.

*"What caused secularization? Science and the Enlightenment and rationalism."*

Now consider another common explanation for today's levels of secularism, one that focuses on seminal historical events as the engine of religious change. This is another widely accepted explanation for the disappearance of God from some Western precincts—and like the foregoing one, it requires a closer and harder look.

The creation story from the Enlightenment, capital "E," runs more or less like this. Beginning in France in the 1700s or so—particularly with the often scathing works of the pseudonymous Voltaire and the other *philosophes*—certain specially gifted and bold men of letters came to understand that there was no God.[10] Over time, and bit by bit, their understanding of the fraudulent nature of Christianity and the mendaciousness of Christian leaders trickled down via various routes, including politics and the law. As a result of the power of their ideas and the increasing (albeit unexplained) ability of other human beings to see through the superstition of religion, today the secular worldview of the *philosophes* and of the scientists who followed them is widespread among the masses of people, especially in Western Europe.

Certainly this account of how God disappeared from parts of the West is widely held, at least casually, among modern secularists. The late Christopher Hitchens, for example, closes his 2007 manifesto *God Is Not Great: How Religion Spoils Everything*, with a chapter calling for "The Need for a New Enlightenment"—one that "will not need to depend, like its predecessors, on the heroic breakthroughs of a few gifted and exceptionally courageous people."[11] The clear implication is that the Enlightenment, by asserting that the proper study of humanity *was* humanity, started men and women down a path toward deliverance from religious bondage.

Similarly, historian and secular humanist Charles Alan Kors argues that the changes ushered in by Enlightenment science ultimately transformed not only science, but the entire theological world as well. Writing of Kepler and others, he summarizes: "There was, as a matter of historical fact, a religious awe in the new science, but it was one that located God's providence far less in the history of miracles and prophecies and far more in the natural mechanisms around us. . . . Such a change in understanding . . . made possible a reconceptualization and revaluation of nature with profound implications for religion, for thinking about human nature, and for ethical theory."[12] The Enlightenment led to what Kors calls "the secularization of values"—one which in retrospect could not help but weaken the church by changing the way people conceived of evidence for a supernatural realm.

All this might seem intuitively obvious. But is it empirically so? Is there really a straight causal line from the ideas of the Enlightenment to today's continuing falloff in Christian observance?

In his authoritative book with Werner Ustorf, *The Decline of Christendom in Western Europe, 1750–2000*, British historian Hugh McLeod identifies three problems with this way of explaining secularization. First, he observes, the masses were not part of the Enlightenment. Second, eighteenth-century elites were actually more likely to be rational Christians than they were atheists or free-thinkers. Third, he notes, "those who seek to trace a continuous line from Voltaire to twenty-first-century atheists also tend to overlook the fact that the first half of the nineteenth century saw a revival of more conservative forms of Christianity both among intellectuals and among the aristocracy and bourgeoisie more widely."[13] In other words, the top-down theory from the French Enlightenment does not fit so well with the historical facts.

What McLeod has his finger on here is more than a historical nuance. It is a gaping hole in the theory that the Enlightenment banished God. If such were true, then we would expect that sophisticated people—educated people and those highest up the socioeconomic ladder—would one by one fall into line behind secularism. If such were true, there would be no room in our theory for revivals of the more conservative Christian variety, at least at the higher levels of society.

Embedded in that argument from Enlightenment is a related and also problematic idea that similarly demands close attention: namely, that individuals become less religious as they become more personally enlightened, small "e." Less-educated people are more likely to believe in the Christian God; better-educated people are less so. This too is a causal notion about secularism that many people accept without qualm—if they even stop to think about it at all.

Like the notion that the Enlightenment caused secularization, this related idea that personal enlightenment leads to the same outcome has a surface plausibility. Everyone knows that the phenomenon of losing one's faith during the college years, for example, is commonplace. A secularist would argue that this trend is proof of the fact that the smarter or more educated or other enlightened one becomes, the less likely one is to believe in God, attend church, and the rest of the Christian religious requirement. Everyone also "knows" that rich people have less use for God than do poor people, and that smart people have less use for religion, frankly, than do those with duller heads. Don't we?

*Everyone* "knows" these things—yet in actual fact few people, especially those people advancing these notions as explanations for the weakening of Western Christianity, seem to know the empirical truth. Once again, if the theory from enlightenment were true—if it correctly predicted *who* was religious, and why—then we would reasonably expect that the poorer and less educated people are, the *more* religious they would be. Certainly that is a stereotype that many people hold—one flagrantly displayed, for example, in a subsequently infamous observation by a *Washington Post* reporter in 1993, describing the followers of leading American evangelicals as "largely poor, uneducated and easy to command."[14]

Conversely, if the theory from enlightenment were true, we would also expect from the theory that the better-off people are, the *less* likely they are to practice religion. This is also a social and economic stereotype to which many people would likely agree.

So are these two stereotypes backed up by the evidence available to us—or are they not?

No, they are not. In fact, the data heap here testifies to the opposite fact: i.e., that Christian religiosity, in at least some significant places and times, has in fact been more concentrated in the *upper* classes than in the lower, and more likely among the educated than among those who are less so.

Note that we are not attempting here to gather data for all social classes and all places and times—nor do we need to. We have enough already to make this point: *Christianity does not wax and wane in the world in the way the theory from Enlightenment or enlightenment says it does, because Christian socioeconomic patterns of belief do not look the way the theory says they should.*

Hugh McLeod—again, a major analyst in Great Britain of secularization both there and in Western Europe—has among other contributions performed painstaking work on historical London between the 1870s and 1914. One correlation he emphasizes is that "the poorest districts thus tended to have the lowest rates of [church] attendance, [and] those with large upper-middle-class and upper-class populations the highest."[15] In other words — and in contrast to the perhaps Dickensian image of the pious poor morally and otherwise outshining a debauched and irreligious upper class— reality among the populace seems to have been the opposite. "Only a small proportion of working-class adults," McLeod points out by way of example, "attended the main Sunday church services" (Irish Catholics being the sole exception).[16]

Historian Callum G. Brown, another expert on the numbers, cites McLeod along with observers from the mid-1800s. All make the same point about religiosity in Britain during those years: that contrary to common wisdom, "the working class were irreligious, and that the middle classes were the churchgoing bastions of civil morality."[17]

Are educated and better-off people actually *more* likely to believe in the Christian God and to practice the Christian faith than poorer and worse-off ones? Counterintuitive though it might appear, there is evidence for that proposition well beyond Victorian England. In fact, much the same pattern characterizes the United States today— one more socioeconomic subversion of the idea that economic and intellectual sophistication are somehow the natural enemies of Christian faith, or that personal enlightenment and sophistication explain the falloff in Western Christian practice today.

Robert D. Putnam's and David E. Campbell's *American Grace*, mentioned earlier, similarly refutes the notion that religiosity in the United States is a lower-class thing. During the first half of the twentieth century, the authors observe, college-educated people participated more in churches than did those with less education.[18] This pattern changed during the 1960s, which saw church attendance fall off most among the educated. But following that "shock" there emerged another pattern, according to which attendance tended again to rise faster among the educated than it did among the less educated (or depending on how one looks at it, the falloff in attendance then became more dramatic among the less educated than it was among those with college degrees—another way of saying the same thing). As Putnam and Campbell observe, "This trend is clearly contrary to any idea that religion is nowadays providing solace to the disinherited and dispossessed, or that higher education subverts religion."[19]

Similarly, in research summarized in another wide-ranging book on American social class called *Coming Apart: The State of White America, 1960–2010*, political scientist Charles Murray analyzes recent data on churchgoing, marriage, and related matters to conclude that "America is coming apart at the seams. Not the seams of race or ethnicity, but of class."[20] Most interesting of his proxies for our purposes here is that of religion.

The upper 20 percent of the American population, he summarizes using data from the General Social Survey, are considerably *more* likely than the lower 30 percent to believe in God and to go to church. Among the working class, 61 percent—a clear majority—either say they do not go to church or believe in God, or both; among the upper class, it is 42 percent. "Despite the common belief that the white working class is the most religious group in white American society," Murray summarizes, "the drift from religiosity was far greater in Fishtown [his imaginary working-class community] than in Belmont [a better-off suburb]."[21]

Such numbers also track with recent data on the state of American marriage—and once again, it seems safe to use marriage rates as *some* kind of proxy for the health of Christianity, insofar as all Christians are enjoined to marriage as an alternative to cohabitation. Of course people marry for reasons other than religious ones. But given that believers marry for the primary purpose of receiving a religious blessing on their unions, we can infer that religious people have more incentive to marry than do secular people or people antagonistic to religion. Thus, it surely tells us something about the condition of marriage in America that the better-educated and better-off people are, the *more* likely they are to be married as well.[22]

Related findings on religion and social class have also been documented independently by sociologist W. Bradford Wilcox at the University of Virginia, one of the country's leading authorities on American marriage. Wilcox has documented the "faith gap" between the better-educated and the people who are less so. Americans with a high school degree are more likely to get divorced than they used to; those with a bachelor's degree or higher are less likely. Americans with college degrees are more likely than those with high school diplomas alone to attend church on Sunday. Moreover, the researchers also found that the statistical likelihood of attending church varied inversely with the social ladder from bottom to top—in other words, that "the least educated have experienced faster rates of decline than even the moderately educated, and they began at an even 'lower' starting point . . . meaning the gap between the least educated and most educated is even larger than the one between the moderately educated and most educated."[23]

Why is this social pattern concerning marriage a problem for the going theory about how and why many Westerners stopped believing in God? For this reason: because if religion is indeed Marx's "opiate of the masses," as certain seminal modern thinkers seem to agree, then one would expect to see the *opposite* of the social pattern from the one just described. That is, one would expect the worse-off members of society to be consuming *more* of the Christian Kool-Aid—including, say, participation in marriage—than people in the better-off classes, not *less*. As a written report for msnbc.com put the matter pithily in a piece summarizing work by Wilcox et al., "Who Is Going to Church? Not Who You Think."[24]

Less pithily, there is an obvious problem in all this for secularization theory. After all, one would expect from conventional thinking about secularization that Christianity would wither away from the top down. Yet plainly, in at least some places and times that have been closely documented by experts, this is not what has happened. Yes, there are elite territories today where secularism is the unquestioned coin of the realm, and where religious believers appear to be few and far between—Ivy League campuses, certain subgroups of scientists, and academics generally.[25] But in the big picture of the United States today—as in Victorian England of yesterday, it appears—the reality of who believes and practices Christianity is the social and economic opposite of what is commonly supposed. Religious affiliation and attendance actually *increase* as one climbs the socioeconomic ladder.

Consider one more proof of this same significant trend—significant not least for what it tells us about the shortcomings of the reigning accounts of secularization: the Church of Jesus Christ of Latter-day Saints in the United States.

In 2011, the Pew Forum on Religion & Public Life published a major study of the beliefs and practices of America's Mormons—the largest one yet to be commissioned by an organization not affiliated with the LDS itself.[26] The report contained a number of findings testifying to the prevalence and strength of religious belief in the LDS community. Most germane for our purposes was this one: once again, in this community as in others discussed above, religiosity *increases*, not decreases, as one climbs the social and economic ladder. Thus, for example, "Mormons who have graduated from college display the highest levels of religious commitment (84%) followed by those with some college education (75%). Mormons with a high school education or less exhibit substantially lower levels of religious commitment (50% score high on the scale) than their more highly educated counterparts."[27] Once again, and contrary to popular belief, literacy and money do not drive secularism.

The mere fact of the existence of worldly, sophisticated men and women who nevertheless persist in their faiths goes to show that *something* is missing from the current story line about how and why God came to be discarded by many modern, secular human beings.

In short, the ebb and flow of Christian religiosity does not appear to be a function of personal enlightenment, small "e," *per se*, any more than they do of the Enlightenment proper. As with the problems inherent in the comfort theory, the empirical shortcomings of the enlightenment thesis point once again to this conclusion: *something else must be going on to account for the way religious belief, or at least Christian religious belief, comes and goes. Pace* received wisdom, and seen from today's end of the telescope, rationalism and sophistication and literacy and the like, simply in and of themselves, do not suffice to drive out God—and may even open extra windows for him.

*"What caused secularization? The world wars did."*

This is another idea about what caused the decline in Christianity that makes more sense the less it is inspected.

Like the answer about the Enlightenment, this one has an intuitive plausibility—and like that other answer as well, it cannot be *all* wrong. Surely some of the people who lived through those uniquely catastrophic events of history found their religious faith shaken and at times destroyed by the horrors they witnessed and experienced. Many must also have found it arduous to reconstruct their lives after years during which husbands and wives were separated on a mass scale and when the rhythms of ordinary life, whether those surrounding home or family or church or anything else related to human gathering, were disrupted as never before. So, yes: that the two world wars and their massive dislocations had enormous fallout for many millions of people is easily granted.

After all, Western Europe in the twentieth century was devastated by war as no other territory had been in history. Over twenty million Europeans died in the First World War, and some fifty to seventy million in the Second depending on the estimate. The horrors of the Holocaust alone, the deliberate murder of six million Jews, including by people who also called themselves Christians, would seem to more than justify despair about the incorrigible darkness of the human heart—to say nothing of calling into existential question a God who promised after the Flood that he would never again abandon his people. The Holocaust in and of itself might also explain a subject beyond the reach of this book, though obviously related to it, which is the falloff in religious practice among postwar Jews across the world (the most religious singularly excepted).[28]

The ways in which the wars seared world consciousness, especially European consciousness, has also been a constant theme of art ever since. Postwar British and European literature, not surprisingly, mourns a world never to come again—from the poems of Wilfred Owen and other members of the Lost Generation in England to the fictions of Heinrich Böll and Günter Grass and others in the shattered world of postwar Germany. *The Diary of Anne Frank* and other works memorializing the Holocaust are similarly grim literary windows onto catastrophic Europe in the mid-twentieth century. Across the board, whether in fiction or nonfiction, the portrait of the wars is one of a world shattered violently to bits and peopled by broken characters, devoid in equal parts of innocence and hope and pockmarked throughout by savagery.

Under the catastrophic circumstances of those wars and the horrors of that world, one might ask, how on earth could reasonable men and women *not* have lost their faith?

Yet once again, an intuitively appealing answer does not, indeed, seem to fit the empirical facts about the shrinkage of Christianity in Europe, for several reasons.

For one thing, the timeline of secularization is not the same in all places and times. Staying home on Sunday mornings happened faster in France than in England; it did not happen in Ireland until just about two decades ago. If war was really the engine driving secularization, why would it take decades to get from one country in Europe to another? The world-wars theory of secularization also does not account for secularization *before* the wars—and plenty of scholars would argue that Christian practice was already trending downward well before that fateful day in 1914 when Archduke Franz Ferdinand of Austria survived one assassination attempt via grenade in the morning, only to be felled by a revolver later in the day.

Second, one might reasonably expect that if the wars were in fact the reason for secularization, then the victorious nations might somehow look different from the vanquished ones; but this is not the case, either. By the yardstick of declining Christian practice, shattered Germany measures up much the same as victorious Great Britain. Catholic Spain—riven by its own civil war, which included the murder of an estimated one-fifth of its Catholic clergy—remained ostensibly religious, albeit deeply divided, until very recently, and has apparently been making up for lost time by galloping toward secularism at a faster rate than most. Neutral Switzerland is as secular and free of Christian fervor as any other country in Europe. Why should nations with such disproportionate burdens of wartime suffering all experience a decline in religious faith?

The theory of secularization invoking the wars does not say— which suggests that this theory is ultimately not going to shed much light on our great puzzle.

Third—and what is perhaps the insurmountable problem for the world-wars theory—at least some intriguing evidence suggests that in fact, the *opposite* may be true: that as mentioned in the previous chapter, the catastrophe of war may at times call forth greater faith, not less. World War II, at least, by wide agreement of secular experts, seems to have been followed by a boomlet in religiosity in different parts of the West.

In an intriguing essay alluded to earlier, for example, reviewing the role of religion during that war in the British, American, and Canadian armies, historian Michael Snape concludes that the soldiers of all three nations "were exposed to an institutional process of rechristianisation during the Second World War, a process that was widely reinforced by a deepening of religious faith at a personal level."[29] This experience, he concludes, further "reinforce[d] a religious revival that was stirring in the war years and which was to mark all three societies until the religious ferment of the 1960s."

Callum G. Brown agrees with this assessment. As he has put it, summarizing evidence from across the West of a religious boomlet in the mid-twentieth century:

> Between 1945 and 1958 there were surges of British church membership, Sunday School enrollment, Church of England Easter Day communicants, baptisms and religious solemnization of marriage, accompanied by immense popularity for evangelical 'revivalist' crusades. . . . Nor was Britain unique. . . . In Australia, the period 1955 to 1963 has been described as a 'modest religious boom' which affected every denomination across all the measurable indices of religious life, characterized by the same crusading evangelism and social conservatism as in Britain and the United States. In most regions of West Germany between 1952 and 1967 there was a modest rise in churchgoing amongst the Protestant population, whilst in France, Spain, Belgium and the Netherlands in the 1950s a resilient religious observance underpinned confessionalist politics. Nationalist experiences varied greatly, and there were exceptions (notably in Scandinavia), but *there is clear evidence that in the mid-twentieth century there was a significant resilience to Christianity in Britain and much of the Western world* [emphasis added].[30]

This apparent renewal of Christianity on the part of men and women across the West following the war was not merely an individual affair, but also a matter of public practice. In some countries, in fact, the language used by political leaders reached to Christianity itself in a way that would be considered shocking today. And this religiosity of public vocabulary following the war is one more bit of evidence that the war alone didn't kill God.

This was especially true in Germany. Immediately after the war, as the eminent German Protestant theologian Wolfhart Pannenberg has observed: "Germany was eager to reclaim its place in Western culture and to distance itself from the ruins of Nazism. Cultural reclamation included affirming Germany's specifically Christian heritage, which was helped by the fact that the churches had been less morally compromised than other institutions during the Third Reich."[31] From Konrad Adenauer on down through the newly created Christian Democratic Union (CDU) party, German politicians and other leaders forged new links to the Catholic Church, and found in the Christian tradition a usable moral past on which to try and rebuild the vanquished country. In fact, at a famous speech at Cologne University in 1946, Adenauer not only urged the refounding of Germany on a Christian ethic, but also blamed Nazism itself on the weakness of Christianity in Germany before the world wars.[32]

Of course it is impossible to imagine any such words issuing from the mouth of any European leader, anywhere, anytime, today; Germany today is as characteristically secular as any other countries of Western Europe, including in the public pronouncements of its leaders. Indeed, the speed of the Christian collapse in Germany may be especially interesting for just this reason—because it is one more example of how a society with an explicitly Christian public ethos could watch so much of that ethos evaporate in a matter of mere decades, rather than over centuries or millennia.

Taken together with the other evidence, however, the postwar public religiosity of Germany suggests the same conclusion: the argument that the world wars traumatized the modern West into secularism simply doesn't hold up as a sufficient explanation for what really happened to Christianity after 1914—or 1945.

It may well be—and would surely make sense—that many people shattered by the war lost their faith in a benign Creator. It may also be that the loss of their faith was not evident for some mysterious reason until later on in history. But why, generations later, should so many of their children and grandchildren who knew nothing but relative postwar prosperity be secular too?

Once again, a piece of the overall puzzle seems to have gone missing.

*"What caused secularization? Material progress did. People got fat and happy and didn't need God anymore."*

This is a colloquial way of summarizing one more explanation for secularism and secularization that many people instinctively accept.

It is also a thought that pops up frequently in the pastoral literature created by contemporary religious leaders seeking to rein in their wandering flocks. Thus, for example, Arthur Simon, evangelical pastor and founder of the charity Bread for the World, is also author of a book called *How Much Is Enough? Hungering for God in an Affluent Culture.*[33] There he sounds a theme of concern to many a minister and priest: namely, "the supremely difficult challenge of living faithfully for Christ in a culture that is more alien to our faith than we may realize."[34] By "culture," he specifically means the pursuit of material accumulation—that the unprecedentedly high standards of wealth in the advanced nations (recessions notwithstanding) are the chief force standing between modern Westerners and God.

Many Catholic leaders, too, have similarly connected the dots between increasing affluence on the one hand, and increasing secularism on the other. A series of papal encyclicals and related commentary have warned against the temptations of commercialism and accumulation, further attempting to stake out the answer to Arthur Simon's question—i.e., how much may be too much?[35] Pope Benedict XVI has vigorously and repeatedly condemned what he calls the "idol" of consumerism, noting for example before 150,000 young people in Sydney, Australia, that "in our personal lives and in our communities, we encounter a hostility, something dangerous; a poison which threatens to corrode what is good, reshape who we are and distort the purpose for which we have been created."[36]

Certainly here, too, everyone has grasped some piece of the truth. God and Mammon, at least according to the holy books, have been at odds from the very beginning; so why *shouldn't* the unprecedented prosperity of modern times drive men and women away from the pursuit of heaven? The Old and New Testaments, for their parts, do not stint on the idea that storing up riches on earth rather than in heaven is inimical to following God. Jesus tells parable after parable in which the rich man is made the unenviable villain of the piece—and that passage about camels and needles' eyes can still induce uneasiness, maybe even more among well-off modern people than their forebears. Following this tradition of regarding material wealth with judgments ranging from healthy skepticism to frank enmity, Christian leaders generally have regarded warnings against materialism as a critical part of their religious message.[37]

Perhaps the most nuanced version of the relationship between money and God, at least as it pertains to secularization, comes from political scientists Pippa Norris and Ronald Inglehart. They have explored in fine detail the connections between privation and religious belief. According to their model, the poorer and less secure people are, the more they "need" religion.[38] Once again, this is a theory bolstered by the numbers; across the world, broadly speaking, better-off countries are less observant than poor ones (this despite the fact that, as we have seen, in some advanced countries it is the better-off people who appear more religious). It is almost certainly also true, as they suggest, that affluence appears to erode some of the bonds between individuals and church in this specific sense: people who can rely more on themselves financially are by definition in less need of the traditional social-service functions that have helped to make Christianity go round—like soup kitchens, shelters, and the rest of the charities and good works that churches perform.

Yet while the fat-and-happy argument surely contributes to our understanding of secular*ism*, or the ways in which comfortable modern people live more of their lives outside the religious sphere, it seems limited as the overriding explanation for secular*ization*.

First, it shares the same limitations as the argument reviewed earlier from rationalism and enlightenment. If the "material progress" explanation were all we needed to know about secularization, then one would expect religiosity to *decline* as one climbs the social ladder in the advanced West—and instead, as we have seen, the opposite appears to be the case, in at least some significant quadrants.

Second, as a related point, the "material progress" theory implicitly advances the notion that—to put it colloquially—more stuff equals less God. Yet in fact, Christianity has coexisted comfortably, even exuberantly, in materially comfortable surroundings from ancient Rome to Renaissance Florence to the gated communities and megachurches of the United States today. At times, in fact, rather infamously, bearers of the Christian message have proven so at home with first-class surroundings that scandal has been the result. One can scarcely stroll through the gardens and astonishingly sculpted fountains of Villa D'Este in Tivoli, say, without wondering how Cardinal Ippolito II D'Este viewed his odds of jamming one of the

most sumptuous estates ever commissioned through that proverbial needle's eye—or by extension, how the ostentatious artworks
and monuments of Christianity can possibly be squared with the
founding message of abstemiousness, moderation, and self-denial.

But the ultimate limitation of the explanation from material
wealth is one shared by the other going theories for secularization:
i.e., there are too many exceptions to be explained—in other words,
too many pieces left over once the problem is supposedly "solved."
It is this list of questions, finally, that clinches the case for an alternative theory of where the Western God has gone—a list that amounts
to puzzle pieces yet to be fitted together in one place.

Why is the United States of America, by any measure, more
religious than the economically comparable nations of Europe—a
problem known in the specialized literature as "American exceptionalism"? Why are women more religiously observant than men?
Why is 1960 such a pivotal year for religious observance and practice, as nearly all observers agree; what is it that makes Christianity
seem to go off a cliff after that point? Current theories of Christianity's decline cannot answer these questions—meaning that the truths
of each going version of the theory are partial, and not complete.

As will be argued in chapter 5, each of these subsidiary puzzles—
and a couple of other loose pieces—are better explained by a theory
that takes the Family Factor into account.

Finally—if any more proof is required by now of God's not having
exited the scene on the timetable predicted by secular soothsayers—
consider also this intriguing piece of subsidiary evidence suggesting
that the current story line about religion and secularization needs
revising. That is the constantly expressed frustration on the part of
nonbelievers and anti-believers at Christianity's apparently unfathomable persistence in the modern world.

Frustration with one's fellow humans for not having absorbed

Nietzsche's message by now is a continuing preoccupation of the new atheist genre, for example—and one that indirectly tells us something interesting about just how limited the standard secularization script has turned out to be.

Michel Onfray, for example, seems to blame the plodding majority of humanity for just not getting it. "The explosive nature of his [Nietzsche's] thought," he opines, "represents too great a danger for the earthbound clods who play the leading roles in real-life history."[39] American atheist Sam Harris seems similarly to believe that most other people are inferior to atheists in understanding what is, at least to him, the obvious truth of the cosmos. Hence he ends his *Letter to a Christian Nation* on this doleful note: "This letter is the product of failure—the failure of the many brilliant attacks upon religion that preceded it, the failure of our schools to announce the death of God in a way that each generation can understand, the failure of the media to criticize the abject religious certainties of our public figures—failures great and small that have kept almost every society on this earth muddling over God and despising those who muddle differently."[40]

Plainly, despite broad agreement among themselves on the perils of religious faith, today's atheists remain in the dark about what exactly it is that has kept so many human beings believing in God anyway. In this the new atheists are markedly inferior to the great thinkers of modernity, whose understanding of the impulse toward religiosity was immeasurably more nuanced and empathetic.

Let us take a brief tour of their thoughts here. Émile Durkheim, to make a long story ridiculously short, believed that religion contained deep truths. In particular, as he argued in a seminal essay on "The Dualism of Human Nature," Durkheim held human beings to be dual creatures with both an individual and social side.[41] Religion, he argued, was created by the social side; it is an institution through which human beings embody and celebrate and reinforce underlying social truths.[42] Durkheim, unlike certain modern superficial critics of religion, would have understood as they do not the history of martyrdom and religious sacrifice. In fact, he argued that sacrifice was necessary and to be expected. It is part of the price that the individual pays for belonging to the social group.[43]

Sigmund Freud, for his part, argued similarly in *Civilization and Its Discontents* that society requires sacrifice on the part of individuals and repression as the price for civilization.[44] Thus, though he was also a signatory of sorts to what has been dubbed the "comfort theory" of the origins of religion, he understood as critics of Christianity today seem not to that religion is more than "just" an illusion—it is a practice that gives something back to practitioners.

Max Weber—whose immense work on the sociology of religion defies summary, but will be mentioned here anyway because it is impossible to omit—believed in the original variant of the "Protestantism" explanation for secularization visited earlier. That is, he held that certain features of Protestantism, especially Calvinism, were essential to modernity and its concomitant "disenchantment of the world."[45] He also believed that societies follow a progression from magic to polytheism, and finally, to ethical monotheism.

As even this brief tour makes plain, there are riches in the tradition of the sociology of religion that are lacking in the new atheists and other contemporary skeptics or adversaries of Christianity. The classicists understood in their own ways what most thinkers today do not—namely, where religion might come from—without the signature condescension that marks so much anti-theist writing today. But even the classicists did not, any more than contemporary thinkers, explain the question we are rounding over and over in this chapter: *What causes God to come and go?*—in all likelihood because most of them did not believe that religion could wax as well as wane.

Plainly, and to repeat, Christianity does just that. Surveying the past two decades' statistics on the growth of unbelievers in America, for example, Ronald A. Lindsay, president of the Council for Secular Humanism, recently made a point with which this book is in whole-hearted agreement: that the increasing number of Western people who reject belief in anything transcendent is indeed "unprecedented in the history of the world."[46] Even so, and correctly, he warns that secularists would be wrong to celebrate prematurely—because to judge by human history, the next rise in religiosity might be just around the corner.

After all, as he notes, "I doubt whether many Romans in the early second century would have predicted the rise of Christianity, whether many Americans in the mid-nineteenth century would have foreseen the survival and prospering of Mormonism, or whether many Americans in the early twentieth century correctly conjec-tured there would be a simultaneous decline among mainstream Protestant denominations and a rise in Protestant fundamental-ism." These failures of prognostication are also failures of some-thing larger—namely, the inability of secularization theory in all its forms, popular as well as erudite, to deliver a coherent explanation of why religion rises as well as falls.

In sum, and as we have had occasion to observe before, what is missing is an adequate "theory of variation." But the fact that such a theory does not yet exist only inadvertently emphasizes the con-clusion of this chapter: we have by now not one, but many, reasons to believe that not all of the pieces of the secularization puzzle have been put on the table.

The pages in this chapter have given us an opportunity to con-sider the main lines of thought about why parts of the West have gone secular—including the comfort theory, the theories from

Enlightenment and enlightenment, the wars theory, the fat and happy theory, and variations on same. In each case, scrutiny of these theories points beyond them to this conclusion: whatever else has happened in the world, the projected diminishment of the Christian God appears either not to have happened for exactly the reasons it was supposed to, or not on the timeline that was set for it—or both.

Of course we have not considered these large matters in anything like the depths plumbed by academics who spend their careers tracking the baptismal records of French provinces in the 1600s, say, or conversely via gargantuan Pew research surveys or other massive statistical undertakings. In a way, though, the relative brevity of this inquiry is exactly the point. For as the general reader can see, even considering these theoretical issues in the relatively finite length of a chapter makes clear that there is something missing from the explanation we currently have for secularization.

Having established that doubt in the reader's mind, or so I hope, we can now turn to more circumstantial proof that something is amiss with our current way of seeing things—and that an alternative invoking the Family Factor, as outlined later in chapter 7, will throw new light on which pieces really belong where.

Circumstantial Evidence for the "Family Factor," Part One:
The Empirical Links among Marriage, Childbearing,
and Religiosity

Now LET US summarize where we are in this puzzle-hunt so
far. Our review of the pros and cons of secularization theory, in conjunction with certain empirical evidence about the persistence of religious belief and other relevant matters, has pointed
to two overall judgments. First, conventional secularization theory
has been correct in identifying a decline in Christian practice and
belief across large swatches of the West. Second, it has not managed simultaneously to deliver a convincing "theory of variation,"
to quote Rodney Stark once again—that is, an adequately developed
understanding of why religion, or more specifically Christianity, has
flourished in some times and places and declined in others.

Similarly, the critics of secularization theory, for their part, have
illuminated significant flaws within the theory's edifice, sometimes
brilliantly. What they have not dedicated themselves to is a satisfac-
tory account of why religious decline took hold in the first place—in
part because many of them deny that religious decline itself exists.
Once again, as noted in the introduction, everyone staring at this
puzzle appears to have a piece, or pieces, of the truth in hand; but
still the picture before us looks somehow incomplete.

At this point in our investigation, a change of metaphor may be
helpful to understanding where the argument is going.

Forget for a moment about that giant jigsaw puzzle. Imagine instead that we are district attorneys, prosecuting someone for murder. All of the evidence we have before us is circumstantial—which, as anyone addicted to crime dramas will already know, may or may not be sufficient to convict, depending upon just how compelling it is. Bit by bit, we are able to show, say, that the gun was fired at a certain time; that our defendant was the owner of the gun; that he cannot account for his whereabouts the minute it was fired; that the person killed had been the object of threatening texts issued by the defendant for several weeks prior to the deed; and so on.

To be sure, we do not have a proverbial smoking gun, i.e., incontrovertible and conclusive evidence for our case (in today's terms, this would be the equivalent of a YouTube video of the crime being committed by the defendant). Still, it is our hope that we can convince the jury even without evidence meeting that highest standard. We have instead what is known as a *smoldering* gun—evidence that falls short of being conclusive, but that remains significant evidence nonetheless. Bit by bit, we mean to force those rational men and women of the jury to the conclusion that the *only* reasonable inference to be made is that our defendant committed the crime.

In a similar spirit, this chapter and the next present what I believe to be compelling empirical evidence that something like a Family Factor is missing from the conventional story line about secularization, and that something like a Family Factor does a better job of making sense of the circumstantial evidence surrounding secularization. Like our imaginary murder case, this one does not depend on a single piece of evidence, or a single "aha!" moment turning all that has gone before upside down. But as in that imaginary scenario, the evidence bit by bit compels us toward the conclusion that something like a Family Factor should be added to our understanding of how and why the West loses God, when and where it does and has.

Let us begin to consider that circumstantial evidence for a Family Factor via this opening question: Where *is* the institution of the family in the current accounts of secularization? The answer is everywhere and nowhere—but mostly nowhere, and that fact alone demands more scrutiny than it has so far received.

"The family" is everywhere in the literature that has gone before, in the sense that many thinkers pondering this subject *do* often end up mentioning the family for one reason or another—but almost always, especially in the scholarly and technical literature, the family appears as an afterthought.

Sociologist David Martin's book *On Secularization*, for example, a rich and dense study, brims with erudition about the people and ideas and history of the last few centuries, which he argues amount to "successive Christianizations followed or accompanied by recoils."[1] Yet the word "family" does not so much as appear in the book's index, and the wider discussion of its otherwise very interesting pages similarly omits consideration of that institution. The same is true of sociologist Steve Bruce's robust defense of secularization theory in his also-influential and also-impressively detailed book *God Is Dead: Secularization in the West*.[2] Like other academic theorists, Bruce sees and emphasizes the importance of "community" in understanding Christianity's decline—but without zeroing in on the very atoms of which the primary human community itself is built, i.e., those of family.

To the extent that academic experts *have* considered the role of the family in secularization, what most have taken for granted is that religious belief or the lack thereof have *consequences* for family life. In other words, family formation is seen strictly as a *by-product* of belief. Religion is the horse; the family sits in the cart. Theorists have simply assumed that religious belief comes chronologically first for people, and that they then tailor their actions accordingly—including their personal decisions about family formation.

Consider for starters the relationship—much studied over the years—between religion and one aspect of the family: decisions about having babies. That the two things have *something* to do with one another is easy enough to see; statistical correlations abound. But what exactly is the nature of their relationship? Modern sociology says, once again, that religion comes first. "Secularization and human development," to take a representative example of this line of thought, "have a profound negative impact on human fertility rates."[3]

Let us italicize this common formulation for emphasis: "*Secularization and human development have a profound negative impact on human fertility rates.*" Again, this way of connecting the causal dots is a commonplace of the academic literature—and for that matter, among many general readers as well who have given even a little thought to the matter. More God means more babies; less God means fewer of them. These are unthinking, uncontroversial formulations, and to the best of my knowledge they are accepted by every party to this discussion, living and dead—by the deniers of secularization, as well as the leading experts in the field. So far, this unanimity may seem unremarkable.

But now look at that italicized proposition more closely. Embedded within it is an unexamined assumption—a profoundly radical, ungrounded assumption about an important matter of cause and effect. Our job is to question that assumption, and to propose a new way of looking at this relationship between Christian religious belief on the one hand, and family formation on the other.

*Faith and family: Which really comes first?*

Let us begin with some well-established empirical truths about the conjunction of these two things. Vibrant families and vibrant religion go hand in hand. Conversely, *not* having a wedding ring or a nursery means that one is less likely to be found in church.

Scholars have demonstrated these related propositions repeatedly. Beyond question, being married and having children is linked to higher levels of churchgoing and other types of religious practice. Sociologist W. Bradford Wilcox, cited earlier, recently summarized the data on church attendance and secularization in the United States as follows: "The recent history of American religion illuminates what amounts to a sociological law: The fortunes of American religion rise with the fortunes of the intact, married family."[4] From 1972 to 2002, according to Wilcox's reading of the numbers in the General Social Survey (GSS), the percentage of American adults attending church or synagogue fell from 41 to 31 percent—and almost a third of that drop, he argued, could be "explained" by the fact that fewer adults are now married with children.

Similarly, the late sociologist Steven L. Nock observed in his 1998 book, *Marriage in Men's Lives*, that "changes in the number of children in the married couple's household have large consequences for men's church attendance. . . . With each additional child, men increase their attendance at services by 2.5 times per year."[5] More children, in short, mean more God. Similarly, marriage as a statistical matter increases the likelihood of belonging to a religious organization—whereas cohabitation, by contrast, has what other researchers have called a "strong, negative effect on the probability of religious activity."[6]

In other words, what you decide to do about your family—whether to have one, whether to marry, how many children you will have: all these are strong *predictors* of how much time you do (or do not) spend in church.

The data also corroborate this same phenomenon from the other end of the demographic telescope. They show that unmarried people without children are less likely to go to church than are married people, or married people with children. A married man with children, for example, is over twice as likely to go to church as an unmarried man with no children.[7] Charles Murray, mentioned earlier, has lately documented similar links between churchgoing and family formation. "The central fact about American whites and religion since 1960," he summarizes, "is that whites have become more secular across the board"—with the proviso that they are now significantly more so in the working class.[8] Once again, where there is more marriage, there is more religion; where there is less, ditto.

Now comes the critical question of this chapter: Exactly *why* does there appear to be such a tight connection between churchgoing on the one hand, and married people with children on the other?

Interestingly, and once again, almost no one seems to have given that question much thought. One can search the literature on secularization—for that matter, one can thumb the pages of Durkheim and Comte and Weber and Nietzsche and other giants of modernity—and still find little serious attention given to this very interesting question: *Why are married people with children more likely to go to church and to be religious than are single people?*

One notable scholarly exception to this general lack of commentary on the connection is in the work of aforementioned W. Bradford Wilcox. He has suggested three reasons for why churchgoing is so tightly bound to being married with children: because they find other couples like themselves in churches—i.e., those who are similarly navigating family life, which gives them something in common; because children "drive parents to church" in the sense of encouraging them to transmit a moral/religious compass; and because men are much more likely than women to fall away from church on their own.[9]

All of these sound like plausible explanations for the well-established ties between family and faith, and all further exhibit the virtue of resonating with common sense. Of the three, however, I would like to zero in on his hypothesis that children "drive parents to church" by needing instruction that parents feel may be more efficiently done by an institution. What is fascinating here is his conjecture that something about the *family* is driving faith—not vice versa.

Why is that remarkable? Because it is one of the few examples available in which someone has thought to reverse the standard causality of faith and family. In this case, Wilcox does not have the "fact" of faith driving family decisions; instead, he reverses the common story and says that *something about the way people live in families makes people in those families more inclined to church*.

My purpose in belaboring the point is to ask what happens if we radically expand Wilcox's insight. Why, after all, should we assume always and everywhere that married people with children go to church because that's just what married people with children "do"? To put the causal matter that way renders it obviously tautological. Yet that is just what conventional thoughts about secularization seem to do. But why should we not believe the reverse is true instead—that *there is something about being married, or having children, or both, that is making the adults in those situations more inclined toward Christianity in the first place?*

Let us now consider some other interesting circumstantial evidence for the notion that there is more going on in the relationship between faith and family than is commonly understood.

*Faith and fertility: What really drives what?*

As intimated earlier on, it is beyond dispute and an empirical matter well documented by social scientists that religious people have larger families than do secular people. In fact, orthodox believers of *all* major faiths are more likely to have children, and to have them in greater numbers, than are unbelievers. So tight is the connection between faith and fertility that such differences in birthrates—between religious believers on the one hand, and secular people on the other—are common across the world.

As Eric Kaufmann, an excellent authority on faith and demographics cited earlier, has put the point: "The religious tend to have more children, irrespective of age, education or wealth. . . . In an analysis of data from 10 European countries for the years 1981–2004, I found that next to age and marital status, a woman's religiosity was the strongest predictor of her number of offspring."[10] This is, in fact, practically an iron law of demography, and it applies both across the West and beyond.

In Israel, for example, the overall total fertility rate for nonultraorthodox women 1994–96 was 2.26 (relatively high in the advanced West)—but for the ultraorthodox it was 7.57 during those same years.[11] In other words, the ultraorthodox have over twice as many children as the average for the rest of Israel. Likewise, as Eric Kaufmann also documents, religious Muslims in different cultures have higher fertility than do less religious Muslims; religious Turks have more babies than nonreligious Turks, and so on throughout the Muslim countries.[12] In a particularly intriguing finding of his, support for Sharia law as the law of the land—surely one interesting measure of religious devotion—also goes hand in hand with higher fertility.[13] This is another fact commonly observed that speaks to the link between religiosity and childbearing.[14]

Similarly, to pluck another example from another religious culture, practicing Mormons in the United States are significantly more likely to be married, and married early, than non-Mormons, and they average one child more per woman than Americans of other religious groups.[15] And so on the tally goes. The hand that rocks the cradle is more likely to go to synagogue/mosque/church.

But exactly *how* religiosity might cause higher fertility is by contrast a matter of dispute. In one particularly interesting tour of that territory, American demographer Conrad Hackett begins with the observation that there is "no consensus about the causal mechanisms involved." He goes on to propose what he calls the "reference group hypothesis"—meaning the idea that fertility ideals and fertility both increase in accordance with the intensity of congregational participation.[16] On this careful reading of the statistics concerning the faith-fertility relationship, theology counts for less than does one's religious peer group and frequency of exposure thereto in a given church.

In another noteworthy work, a fascinating working paper for the Max Planck Institute in Rostock, Germany, published online in 2006, demographers Tomas Frejka and Charles A. Westoff pore through a great deal of demographic and other expert literature concerning the United States and Europe, including the World Values Survey, the European Values Survey, and the Pew Forum on Religion & Public Life. In so doing, they hope to discern the answer to a fundamental question in this book: namely, what is the real nature of the relationship between religiosity and fertility— because the two trends are so closely aligned that they are obviously related *somehow*.[17]

What Frejka and Westoff turn up are two findings that track with other well-established results: first, that fertility in Europe as a whole is lower than it is in the United States (though they emphasize that there are some nations in Europe where the rates are similar, depending on what kind of comparison is used); and second, that "there is no doubt that religiosity is high in the United States compared to Europe as a whole."[18] "Fertility," they note of the numbers, "is fairly consistently negatively related to the frequency of attendance at religious services, both in the U.S. and throughout Europe." In other words, women who don't go to church have fewer children than those who do. Once again, faith and fertility appear joined at the hip.

At this point in the academic fine-tuning, the patient reader may be tempted to object that the exact mechanism at work here is beside the point; after all, religious people have larger families—so what? But look carefully at that common formulation, because it contains the same hidden assumption pinpointed earlier—i.e., it assumes that *because* people are more religious, *therefore* they have larger families.

To be clear, I am not saying that cause and effect *never* flow in the way that preceding sentence describes. I am making a different point: Where is the evidence for putting our variables in that conventional order, every single time? Why should we believe—since no one has given us empirical reason to believe—that personal, atomistic religious belief always comes first and decisions about family come second? It is at least as plausible—in fact, given the evidence ahead, it is *more* plausible—to assume the opposite: *that something about having larger or stronger or more connected families is making people more religious, at least some of the time*.

Of course it is undoubtedly true that some people seek to have more children because they feel religiously "called" to do so. As serious Christians know, there is ample biblical evidence suggesting that fecundity is both pleasing to the Creator and also that the promise of future fecundity is deployed in certain instances as a divine reward. "Go forth and multiply," the command given in Genesis, may be the most familiar example of God's stated interest in procreation, but others abound. Later in that same book, for example, God promises Isaac that he will "make your descendants as numerous as the stars." Psalm 127 notes that "happy is the man whose quiver is full" of sons; Psalm 128 says the blessed man has a wife "like a fruitful vine."[19] The message in full is unmistakable: Creation is good—including and especially the creation of human beings.

Even so, the axiom that religion is always and everywhere dictating family size is *assumed* rather than proven by the evidence—and this critical fact opens the door to a new way of understanding the relationship between family and faith.

Now contemplate another, related difficulty that calls the standard purported causality into question.

It is commonly assumed that religious Catholics have larger families "because of" the prohibition against birth control. (Never mind, for the moment, all the problems of deciding just what a "Catholic" is, or that "Catholic" rates of childbearing closely resemble Protestant ones unless we are talking about the very most observant Catholics; we are just sticking here to the stereotype to see what it reveals.) Such may well be true, again, some of the time; the argument here, recall, is not that our current ways of understanding secularization get *everything* wrong.

But if the prohibition against birth control is supposed to be the *exclusive* reason or even the *main* reason why religious people have larger families, then we can make no sense of this fact: evangelical Christians, most of whom do not similarly have theological injunctions against birth control as such, have a higher fertility rate than do secular people. Orthodox Jews in America, as well as in Israel, have far more children than secular Jews—even though orthodox Judaism also allows contraception within marriage for certain, quite broad purposes, and even though it does not wholly proscribe abortion. And members of the Church of Jesus Christ of Latter-day Saints have a high rate of natural family formation compared to non-Mormons too, even though abortion is not wholly proscribed for them either, and couples are also allowed to use artificial contraception (if they determine after prayer that it is best for them—rather a large theological loophole).[20]

In other words, the idea that having large families is just something that religious people "do" begs the question of the real causal relationship between those two things—especially since, apart from the Catholic Church, no absolute restrictions on artificial contraception exist any longer almost anywhere in the religious world.

To put the matter another way: if secularization theory and the conventional way of understanding faith's relationship to family were correct, then *we would not expect to see religious people continuing to have larger numbers of children than do nonreligious people, even when their religion allows them the option of contraception.* Yet we do see exactly that connection repeatedly across different Christian denominations in different places and times—which fact strongly implies that something in our current causal thinking requires a second look.

In sum, the surface explanation that people have families just *because* they are religious is problematic—because it does not explain why those other Christians with theological *carte blanche* to use abortion and contraception nevertheless persist in having larger families too. So here is one more piece of circumstantial evidence strongly suggesting that cause and effect are in fact working the other way, at least sometimes—i.e., not only that religious people are inclined toward the family, but *also* that something (or more than one somethings) about the family inclines people toward religiosity.

That is the element of doubt that I want to instill here—that conventional sociology of religion, or at least sociology concerning the disappearance of Christianity in parts of the West—has missed something important about the very nature of religious transmission. The idea that readers are being asked to entertain is this: the family is not merely a *consequence* of religious belief. It can also be a *conduit* to it.

Consider two more pieces of tantalizingly suggestive evidence for this claim, necessarily speculative though they may be.

As many with adult children will know—and as sociologists of religion can also verify—the late teens and early twenties are years during which many young Christian people either stop going to church or go to church less frequently than they did as children. David Kinnaman, president of the Barna Group, recently devoted a book to documenting why this age group often leaves God behind, including six broad reasons for the decline as it is explained by subjects themselves.[21] Indeed, the long godless gap between the teenage years and the married years is a source of constant concern to pastors, especially. Sociologist Mark Regnerus, among academic experts to have pondered these numbers, has argued in a widely debated piece in *Christianity Today* that this ever-expanding, irreligious adolescence of young American adults amounts to "The Case for Early Marriage."[22]

I would like to advance as a friendly amendment to such analyses one other thought: maybe these young people are not *only* irreligious because they are away from home for the first time, sowing their proverbial oats and reaping their colloquial hookups and otherwise following the standard script of how young adults lose their faith. Perhaps they are *also* skipping church and prayer and the rest because they are no longer living with families. Perhaps *something about living in families makes people more receptive to religiosity and the Christian creed*.

We will continue such speculation in more detail in chapter 7.

Once again, it is being introduced here for the purpose of raising doubt about whether our current understanding of a loss of faith during the college years is really all there is to it.

Another such doubt also arises if we consider the flip side of this demographic coin: As is well known among sociologists of religion, religiosity on the whole increases with advancing age. Putnam and Campbell, among others, have documented the fact that in the United States, "Religious observance is highest among older Americans."[23] The same is true across the Western world. The National Opinion Research Center (NORC) at the University of Chicago recently issued a fascinating document called "Beliefs about God across Time and Countries."[24] For the year 2008, the report says, "In 29 of 30 countries certain belief in God increased with age." The comparison is especially vivid if one looks at, say, a forty-year interval: "The average increase from those 27 and younger to those 68+ was 20.0 points."[25] In other words, even though belief in God had declined modestly in almost every country, according to this report, "belief in God is especially likely to increase among the oldest groups."[26]

But why is this so? The going thought seems to be the one provided in the NORC study—that the age gap is "perhaps in response to the increasing anticipation of mortality occurring." Once again, causality is seen as a one-way street: aging inclines people toward God, it is supposed, *because* moving closer to death makes one more eager for the (presumed) consolations of religion.

Once more, it is not the point of this book to dispute what might seem obvious. It may well be the case that the likelihood of increased religiosity among older adults is indeed explicable in just such terms—at least sometimes.

But *all* the time? Why could we not supplement that theory with another one, according to which at least part of what goes on in the religious age gap is something else—the fact that older age for most people means more experience of the rhythms of birth and death and family? Couldn't we imagine that at least some of what makes older people more religious is the Family Factor? Is it not at least possible that the increased experience of age, including the accumulated familial experience, might incline people who live in families toward a more expansive, transcendental idea about the religious order of things?

These are speculative rhetorical devices, to be sure. But speculation is intrinsically part of this book. The question is whether it is effective in raising doubts in the reader's mind about the limitations of the theories currently available.

To summarize, the empirical links between religiosity and families have typically been construed as a one-way street—a street on which religiosity is assumed to be driving decisions about family formation. In all likelihood, at least some of the time, that one-way street is indeed the way traffic is running. But it is also clear, or should be by now, that the assumption that *faith drives family* is far more problematic than it appears on first glance—and that the contrary notion, according to which at least some of the time *family drives faith* instead, is one that makes superior sense of the facts and thus demands a place at our figurative table.

$\approx$4

Circumstantial Evidence for the "Family Factor,"
Part Two: Snapshots of the Demographic Record;
or How Fundamental Changes in Family Formation Have
Accompanied the Decline of Christianity in the West

T HE LAST CHAPTER went to show that the connection between family and faith *can* be seen as a two-way rather than one-way street. Now let us consider another set of circumstantial evidence— more evidence suggesting that at least sometimes, it *should* be understood that way.

This is probably as good a place as any to note that the preceding chapter and this one are most likely to provoke cries of "foul" from academic and other experts. It is probably inevitable that one social scientist or another will hurl the ultimate charge of methodological heresy at my thesis: that "correlation does not prove causation." In other words, some may respond, the mere fact that family decline has *paralleled* religious decline in the West does not tell us anything meaningful about what caused what, or which came first.

More often than not, this charge is used to dismiss any new proposed way of looking at things. To be sure, the theory suggested in these pages is open to objection, expert and otherwise. Nevertheless, it is worth emphasizing that the phrase "correlation does not prove causation," as commonly deployed by experts against nonexperts, remains a slogan and not an argument.

So let us consider that charge preemptively. First, I would

respectfully point out that there already *is* a causal theory embedded in the conventional secularization script. According to that theory, people *first* have their religious beliefs, and *then* they change their personal behavior (specifically, in the matter of family formation). The fact that this is an *unacknowledged* or *unspoken* theory does not invalidate the point that it is just about universally assumed. If we are going to allow causal theories to sneak under the tent this way, then we might as well have them roaming around more openly where we can see them better and study their habits, or so it seems to me.

According to that hidden theory, as reviewed, something like this causal chain is supposed to be true: *first* people lost their religion, *then* they stopped having children and families. To clarify once more, there is no point in making any claims larger than the ones that can be sustained by the evidence. Surely some of the time, as noted in the chapter just ended, the going theory does describe how people do what they do in these matters.

On the other hand, there is also ample evidence, all things considered, for reading the facts the other way—which is essentially upside down. In this chapter, readers will be offered additional arguments for why family and faith should be understood, say, as a double helix rather than as independently occurring linear processes. Here we will try and clear a place through the dense academic forest surrounding this subject, the better to see how people in the West really get from abstractions like *urbanization* and *industrialization* to the individual reality of just plain not going to church anymore.

This chapter will try and map that terrain by means of a sweeping yet (I hope) effective question: *If* the Family Factor were in fact part of the reason for secularization—that is, if something about family drives people to faith, and not just vice versa—then *what* kinds of large trends would we expect to see? Interestingly enough, we see patterns that corroborate the thesis.

*If the Family Factor were part of the explanation for secularization,
we would expect to see family decline accompany religious
decline. This we see.*

Once again, consider what the historical facts suggest if we use fertility as one (albeit only one) proxy for the state of the family.

What demographers call the unprecedented and overall "sustained fall" in birthrate that characterizes the West today started earlier almost everywhere than is widely understood. One gold standard for measuring this change is the European Fertility Project conducted at Princeton University under Ansley J. Coale and Susan Cotts Watkins during the 1970s and early 1980s. It documented the profound demographic change of the fertility transition in Europe—the decline of 50 percent or more in the number of children the average woman would bear (the timeline running from the late eighteenth century to the mid-twentieth).[1]

Again keeping our eyes fixed on the forest, what are the largest trends to emerge from the project? They are that fertility began dropping in the late 1700s in Europe and kept dropping within marriage, with variations in different countries, but always with the same overall arc. Now crosshatch that trend with another—the later rise in cohabitation, which can arguably be used as a proxy for religious decline, insofar as Christianity rather famously frowns on sex outside of marriage. Cohabiting is not something that most Christians in good standing "do." And what do the numbers on cohabitation look like in Europe? According to the OECD, as authoritative a source as any, "Over the last decades, patterns in partnership formation and living arrangements have changed significantly in most OECD countries." For the OECD as a whole, roughly speaking, among adults aged twenty to thirty-four, over a third living in partnership households are cohabiting. There are of course variations on the theme; in Denmark, for example, more people cohabit than marry, whereas in Poland, say, the ratio of married to cohabiting households is 20:1. Nevertheless, what Christians once commonly called "living in sin" continues to grow across the board.[2]

Again, putting this trend together with the demographic transition numbers makes the growth of relative parts of the forest pop out. Over time, *many people stopped having babies AND they stopped getting married AND they stopped going to church.* I am not trying to establish that any one of these trends came first in any particular case, nor is that necessary to the argument. Think again of the double helix and how it looks in three-dimensional space. The very point is that the spirals reinforce one another and become impossible to straighten into two-dimensional lines. What we see, again, is that family decline and faith decline operate in lockstep.

Changing metaphors yet again, let us now look at some of the individual historical trees to see particular examples of this dynamic.

In France, for example, the decline in births started in the late eighteenth century—earlier than in any other country of Europe.[3] Looked at broadly, the example of France would seem to bolster reading the causal connection between family and faith in the way being suggested here. The natural family began to decline as people stopped having babies earlier in France than in the rest of Europe. Illegitimacy rose also—from just over 1 percent in the early eighteenth century, according to the historian David Garrioch, to between 10 and 20 percent by the 1780s—and 30 percent in Paris.[4] The family decline signaled by such changes then accelerated under the "reforms" of the French Revolution, which liberalized marriage laws to an unprecedented degree and further persecuted the institution hitherto most closely identified with defending "the family" as such: i.e., the Catholic Church. The French family as an institution was weakened by all these disparate trends. How could it not be?

Once again, we must lay the two large phenomena—family decline and religious decline—side by side if we are to grasp their organic connection. In the work cited by David Garrioch in the preceding paragraph, for example—a fascinating 2002 book called *The Making of Revolutionary Paris*—the author paints a vivid and careful picture of the decline of Christianity in that city during the eighteenth century. As evidence of that decline, he cites a variety of evidence ranging from the obvious to the more subtle. Confraternities, for example—religious organizations dedicated to a particular saint or cult—saw their membership drop dramatically across the century. Religious bequests in wills declined sharply. Religious symbols became markedly less important in public life; by 1777, the city of Paris could decide that voters would no longer have to swear on the crucifix in electing city councilmen. By the 1750s, accusations of blasphemy, or using God's name in vain, were rare, whereas before they had been ubiquitous.[5]

And so on the historian's litany goes—a compelling and detailed account of how Christianity lost public and private power in the course of that particular century, as well as a tacit case study in the empirical difficulty of disputing the fact of the historical decline of that faith in Europe. Yet alongside this dramatic portrait stands another that is obviously related to it: the portrait showing what *family* trends were doing at the same moments in French history.

For as Garrioch also documents, French family trends were heading in the same direction throughout that century—i.e., downward. In addition to the sharp rise in illegitimacy already discussed, Garrioch also notes the decline in fertility, "clear evidence," as he says, "of the adoption of birth control, in direct defiance of Church teaching."[6] The *fermiers généraux*, or tax collectors, for example—in other words, relatively wealthy people—had a mean number of 3.5

children in 1726, down to 2.6 by 1786.[7] Across the social spectrum, he reports, women stopped having children earlier than they had previously. And so on this litany goes too.

Garrioch connects these dots, to the extent that he does so, in the conventional manner. That is, he views the changing family trends as instantiations of religious decline—in other words, as changes that could only take place if Christianity exerted less of a moral and social hold over people than it had before. Once again, our purpose is not to dispute that the causal arrows might indeed point just that way, at least some of the time. But also once again, why should they not point the other way too? Why shouldn't the dramatic decline of the family in eighteenth-century France—which as Garrioch and others have documented was unique in Europe at that time—*also* power the religious decline so well documented by this historian and others?

After all, the big picture is very simple—and very suggestive. People stopped having babies in France earlier than elsewhere in Europe; they stopped getting married as often as they did elsewhere in Europe; *and their religiosity declined earlier than elsewhere too.*

To put the matter differently, look at what did *not* happen here. French religiosity did *not* decline in the absence of family decline. Obviously—to invoke the image of the double helix again—their spiral fates were historically joined. In sum, the French case in and of itself is dramatic circumstantial evidence for a "Family Factor" as a key engine in the decline of religiosity.

Now let us look at another portrait of the Old World landscape painted with broad strokes. In Britain, which was then richer than France, the decline in births started a century later—i.e., at the very height of Victorian England, which (as we have already seen) was for its part associated with trends that amounted to religious revival or religious strength.[8] Bit by bit over time, however, the same family trends already established in France—fewer births, more divorces, more out-of-wedlock births—also began reshaping the world of Britain. By our own time, over half of all children in Britain are born to unmarried people, and the fertility rate stands at 1.91 children per women.[9]

Are we really supposed to believe that the widespread diminution or watering down of such family links is just *incidental* to the widespread loss of religious faith? On Sundays at this moment in time, some 15 percent of the population in the United Kingdom now shows up for church *monthly* (not weekly).[10] Aren't both declines rather obviously connected—just as obviously as in the case of eighteenth-century France? Or to put the point another way: Doesn't it make more sense to think that British families are less religious today because they are also less *familial*—and that this generalization appears to apply across the advanced nations of the West?

Now consider one more example taken from the other extreme: Ireland. Some countries would not see their fertility decline until much later in what experts call the "demographic transition," and Ireland was a particularly compelling example; fertility-wise, it did not begin resembling other European countries until well into the twentieth century. But as the Irish case demonstrates, whether early or late to the party of demographic decline, and with or without the occasional "baby boom" blips, the pattern remains the same: no matter which end of the spectrum one looks at, European fertility collapse and other proxies for family decline appear closely connected to religious collapse on the timeline.

Essentially, the Irish stopped having babies and families—and Irish religiosity went over the Cliffs of Moher. This change in public religiosity came much later than it did in, say, France; in fact, it has been most dramatic just in the past generation. The decline in weekly Mass-going, for example, is reported to be one of the steepest in Europe—from 91 percent of Irish Catholics in 1973 to 34 percent in 2005.[11] Irish culture, it is routinely reported by natives and visitors, has changed more in the past generation than in the hundreds of years preceding it. And while sociologist Andrew Greeley, true to his contrarian work cited earlier in this book, is among a handful of people to dispute the notion that Ireland is secularizing, he is surely overruled by the stark facts about attendance and practice.[12] Seminaries house few seminarians. In 2005, for the first time, the archdiocese of Dublin—*Dublin*—ordained no one.[13] As Archbishop Sean Brady put it, summarizing the one thing on which most of those both for and against these developments would agree: "The influence of secularism has struck Ireland with great speed and intensity."[14]

Plenty of explanations have been offered for this especially speedy collapse in religiosity: rising prosperity (at least pre-2008), lowered taxes, urbanization, and the rest of the secularization script. Some have also hypothesized that recent priest sex scandals, more widespread in Ireland than elsewhere in Europe, have also played a leading part in that collapse.[15] No doubt each of these explanations touches some part of the truth; to repeat, few social phenomena would appear powered by just one force, secularization included.

But what these explanations overlook is perhaps the most obvious contributing cause of all. Not only has Irish religiosity been anomalous in the speed of its collapse; *so too has Irish fertility*. Ireland's twentieth-century baby boom came markedly late—the 1970s, during which births were roughly double replacement level. This boom was followed by a dramatically steep decline of fertility such that by 2000, total fertility rate was 1.89. In essence, Ireland went through this demographic change in one generation rather than two.

Once again, as in the case of France, where the chronology is equally clear albeit more spread out, why is it not more fitting with the facts to suppose that the dramatic collapse of fertility, used again as just one proxy for the state of the family (because it is easiest to measure), has been helping to drive the collapse in religiosity, rather than just vice versa? That not having babies any more made people less likely to bother about—or hear, depending on your point of view—God?

Look again at what did *not* happen in Ireland: dramatic religious decline did *not* transpire in a vacuum, but was plainly accompanied by also-dramatic family decline.

Once again, we are not reaching here for a way of explaining secularization that discards all the explanations that have come before. In zeroing in on the causal role that weakened families appear to play in weakened Christian faith, I do not mean to slight other and supplemental ideas with which this theory is wholly compatible.

For example, in his classic book *Bowling Alone: The Collapse and Revival of American Community*, Robert D. Putnam examines minutely the decline in American "social capital," or the weakening of various bonds of association during the past few decades in particular.[16] He identifies several independent forces contributing to that decline, among them individualism, commuting, and the change in women's roles. Also of interest is his linking of the phenomenon of declining association with television watching. "This massive change in the way Americans spend our days and nights," he writes, "occurred precisely during the years of generational civic disengagement." And though Putnam is careful to note that these are correlations only, other readers might well think the evidence fairly screams for a causal inference here: "More television watching means less of virtually every form of civic participation and social involvement."[17]

The point is that more than one factor appears to have been powering the decline of Western community, including the community of the Western family. How could it be otherwise? Modernity, it seems safe to say, is a large and swirling sea fed by many a stream and river. But stepping back from such individual currents, and contemplating at more distance the timeline over the past few centuries of both Western family decline and Western religious decline, it makes most sense to think of these developments as causally connected both ways.

This is just some of the circumstantial evidence suggesting that a "Family Factor" demands a larger role in the explanation of secularization than it has so far been given. There is more.

*If the Family Factor were part of the explanation for secularization, we would expect to see other trends associated with family decline accompany religious decline. This we also see.*

Scholars and other experts agree that secularization in the West has been associated with two powerful and related trends—urbanization and industrialization. What's missing is an explanation of the nature of those links in language that the rest of us can understand. How does one get from abstractions like these—these mass movements of people and things—to the human reality of one man and woman after another ceasing to attend Mass or pray to God or baptize their children?

Here again, something like the Family Factor would seem a critical way of bridging the conceptual gap. Recall historian Peter Laslett's evocative words about "the world we have lost"—that is, the world of the West before industrialization, the one in which "the whole of life went forward in the family." Such was quotidian reality for almost all human beings up until the Industrial Revolution—that great event marking the break between the past and the present. Like no single force before it, the Industrial Revolution also contributed to family decline, upending families across the world as wage earners from the countryside left for cities to find work.

To repeat, almost all scholars would say that the Industrial Revolution was one engine of secularization. As Eric Kaufmann summarizes, "Industrialisation explains a good deal of the astounding slide in church attendance across Europe."[18] After that Revolution, religious belief, practice, and the rest of the measures of religiosity appear to career downhill—with upward blips here and there, to be sure, as in the postwar years; but overall, the trend since the Industrial Revolution points down.

Again, scholars have done a fine job of establishing that A and B go along with C. But just how do the correlations work? Put differently, invoking industrialization to explain secularization does seem to answer a "what?" question—as in, "*What* historical force appears closely linked with secularization?" But it does not in and of itself answer what might be called the "why?" question before us. That one is, "*Why, i.e. in what way*, did industrialization contribute to the decline of Christianity?"

Now let us see how that question is answered via the Family Factor. Adding that to the equation allows us to see that it is not the Industrial Revolution *per se* that is sufficient explanation for the falloff in Christianity in Western Europe. It is rather the destructive effect that the Revolution had *on the family* that somehow made it harder for people to believe and practice their Christian faith.

So, for example, a nineteenth-century farmer moves to London from the British countryside for the promise of a more secure existence. (Legendary though Charles Dickens may have made the factories and mores of industrialization, we must nevertheless remember: human beings ran to the cities from the villages because many saw that as the economically *better* of their alternatives.) Here, our farmer discovers several truths about life in the city as opposed to in the countryside. Real estate is more expensive. Material possessions, at least for those with means, are more luxurious and varied. Anonymity is vastly easier to come by in the city than it is on the village green. As a corollary, temptations toward all manner of things—gin, prostitutes, drugs, thefts—are arguably easier to indulge.

What even this brief sketch shows us is that at every turn, our imaginary factory worker finds that family formation and religiosity are both more difficult in the city than in the boondocks from where he came. Children are more expensive to take care of, if one tries to take care of them, and they are housed as are all people in more crowded conditions. He may or may not even have a family; many migrating men who moved to cities for work left their women and children back on the farm. Family breakup, for its part, is definitely made "easier" in the city because the bonds of a small town, however constricting, also come with a kind of enforcement power: knowing everyone's business makes it harder to get away with all kinds of things that are arguably inimical to family life (alcoholism, prostitution, bigamy or "double life," etc.). It is at least a challenge in the village to be a good man on one end of the green, and a bad one on the other; in the city, by contrast, a double life is easier to come by.[19]

Now add to this discussion one other, related fact. People also appear to be more religious in the countryside than in the city. It is well known among historians of secularity that the "larger the town," as Owen Chadwick has put it in the case of England, the "smaller the percentage of persons who attended churches on Sundays. This statistic is liable to variation and even exception, according to country, parts of the same country, or social conditions. Still, it is a proven statistic. . . . Whether or not decline in churchgoing is a sign of secularization (and it probably is), bigger towns were a cause."[20]

Though obviously any generalization this large is fraught with problems, as he acknowledges, other scholars would agree that the evidence we have from England affirms Chadwick's point. Moreover, what was true in England was also true in France. In *Awash in a Sea of Faith*, his landmark study of the history of Christianity in America between 1550 and 1865, Yale University historian Jon Butler opens with a lengthy survey of the European religious heritage. In France, he reports, "strong geographic variations . . . appeared by mid-[eighteenth] century." Only 60 to 70 percent of adults took Easter communion in rural districts surrounding Chalons, he reports, and "the rate plunged to less than 25 percent in Paris and Rouen."[21] Once again, broadly speaking, smaller towns equal higher religiosity, and larger towns less of it.

And what does the distinction between the God-fearing village and the godforsaken city tell us about how secularization happens? The answer is that if we put those facts about towns and cities together with some other evidence—namely, demographic evidence—then we may see this puzzle more clearly. The one thing that all scholars will attest is that as a general demographic rule, *urbanization leads to falling birthrates.*

To cite a United Nations paper from 1994 on demographic changes under urbanization, for example, is to find that "in the United States and practically all European countries in which the Survey was carried out, urban fertility is lower than rural fertility. . . . The result is consistent for different sizes of residence, both the village and the small town having nearly high and virtually identical fertility and both the large town and the city recording much lower fertility. *The conclusion, therefore, is that urbanization has been responsible for fertility decline in the developed countries* [emphasis added]."[22]

That sentence has been italicized for this reason: because it shows an obvious link between fertility—one of the proxies for the natural family—and urbanization. Putting the pieces together suggests once more that it is at least *possible* that people did not stop believing in God just because they moved to cities. The missing piece would appear to be that moving to cities *made them less likely to have and live in strong natural families*—and *that* intermediate, unseen step may have been what really started them down the road toward losing their religion, at least some of the time.

*If the Family Factor were part of the explanation for secularization, we would expect the most irreligious parts of the West to have the smallest/weakest/fewest natural families—and vice versa. This too we see.*

The Organization for Economic Co-operation and Development (OECD) among other organizations tracks marital and other statistics in Western Europe. One paper discussing such numbers in the period 1970–2008 notes characteristic trends: during that period, divorce increased in almost every country; marriage rates in almost all OECD and EU countries fell; age at marriage increased.[23] This is the demographic face of contemporary Europe—or to switch metaphors, it is the demographic forest that we are now hacking through with our figurative machete.

Other studies could confirm the same trends, and it would be easy to get lost in the leafy minutiae of their analyses. Once again, however, our eyes need to be focused on the forest.

Where is Christianity now weakest? Where is the natural family now weakest? If we ask for a longer chronology of these matters, what we find is the same pattern as that suggested by fertility rates. It is not *merely* the case that Europeans now divorce and cohabit more and marry less than they used to—though that is also true. More interesting, it appears to be the case that the more secular countries are those where the rates for these behaviors have been highest.

Again, it is instructive to use Scandinavia as a bellwether. Consider: marriage rates fell in Scandinavia before they fell elsewhere in Europe. In fact, the Scandinavian countries taken together now exhibit such a distinct form of marital and nonmarital relations that it is known as the "Nordic model."[24] This paradigm is characterized by high divorce rates (Sweden's is among the highest in the world); high rates of births out of wedlock (over half of all births in Sweden, by 1996); and high ages at first marriage (over twenty-nine years of age for women in 1996).[25]

In other words, Scandinavia and especially Sweden once again affirm the proposition that collapse of the natural family and collapse of Christianity are obviously closely tied. Sweden is also at the cutting edge of family trends in one other way: its families are simultaneously ever more atomized. Almost *half* of Swedish households now contain only one occupant. This is another aspect of the transformation of Western domestic life that reaches far beyond Scandinavia alone. According to sociologist Eric Klingenberg, who has written a book on the rise in solitary living, one out of seven American adults now lives alone—and half of American adults are single.[26] More families of one equal less God.

Once again, we see evidence that societies where fewer people live in families are societies where fewer people go to church. Is it not possible that the family is a bridge of sorts between its members and the transcendental world represented by church—and that burning this bridge also annihilates the main thing that once joined the two sides and made it possible for traffic to pass back and forth? Or to put the question in religious language, might it be possible that detachment from those people most closely related to oneself—those most evocative of one's personal creation—might somehow make it harder to see the Creator?[27]

To reiterate, scholars poring over the demographics of contemporary Europe have pointed repeatedly to the connections between faith and family. In 2004, for example, journalist and researcher Phillip Longman published a much-discussed book called *The Empty Cradle: How Falling Birthrates Threaten World Prosperity And What To Do About It*, arguing as its title suggests that the demographic state of Europe especially would turn out to have a dark side—including the fear that religious fundamentalists, because of their "relentlessly pronatal" message, would own the future.[28] In 2008, conservative best-selling author Mark Steyn published a satirical version of the theme called *America Alone: The End of the World as We Know It*, another popular treatment that repeatedly connected the dots between the loss of faith and the loss of families in the West.[29] In 2011, as mentioned earlier, *Shall the Religious Inherit the Earth?* by Eric Kaufmann argued persuasively and at length that the demographics of the secular West would be overtaken in the long run by those of religious fundamentalists.[30]

These and other scholars and pundits have grasped and examined a prodigious truth: that there is a fundamental connection between strong religion and strong families, or weak religion and weak families. We are just using their work to construct a more expansive conclusion.

As Phillip Longman once summarized the evidence: "The least likely to procreate are those who profess no belief in God; those who describe themselves as agnostic or simply spiritual are only somewhat slightly less likely to be childless. Moving up the spectrum, family size increases among practicing Unitarians, Reform Jews, mainline Protestants and 'cafeteria' Catholics, but the birthrates found in those populations are still far below replacement levels. Only as we approach the realm of religious belief and practice marked by an intensity we might call, for lack of a better word, 'fundamentalism,' do we find pockets of high fertility and consequent rapid population growth."[31]

Once again, a radical other possibility remains: that reversing the causality Longman spells out here might also describe reality.

*Conversely, if family decline was in fact helping to* cause *religious decline, we would also expect to see, for example, family boomlets accompanied by religious boomlets. This we also see.*

To recap a point visited before: it is one of the assumptions of this book that part of the strength of the natural family comes from children—more specifically, from the presence of children in the home.

This is not to suggest anything as simple minded as a one-to-one correspondence according to which, say, a family of a dozen is bound to be more religious than one with an only child. Nor is it to say that people without children biologically connected to them are people who cannot be devout. The entire history of Christianity, from the adoptive father St. Joseph through the monks and priests and nuns and popes stretching over two millenia, would confute such a view, as would ordinary experience of actual people. Such would be caricatures of the case being made here—along the crude lines, say, of Monty Python's caricature of Christian teaching about birth control in the song "Every Sperm Is Sacred."

But the insistence on using children as one particularly meaningful proxy for the strength of the natural family does make rather obvious and intuitive sense. And just as children can fairly be argued to be bellwethers of the natural family in decline, so, conversely, does the opposite appear to be true as well—i.e., *that the flourishing of children, at least as measured by numbers, appears closely linked to boomlets in religiosity.*

Recall, first, the evidence offered in chapter 1, where we weighed the arguments against secularization itself. There we encountered data from Callum G. Brown, demonstrating that the years after World War II were followed by just such a religious boomlet. Across the West, as he and others have observed, church attendance and affiliation shot up in the 1950s. In chapter 1, the reader will recall, we reviewed that evidence to shoot down an appealing but ultimately unconvincing argument about secularization—i.e., that it has been caused by the moral chaos of two world wars. But there is another way of considering that same evidence that speaks to the power of the Family Factor.

The outbreak of postwar religiosity across the West, one can argue, also amounts to powerful weight for the thesis of this book. For what happened in those societies in the 1950s was not *simply* a religious boomlet, period. What happened was a religious boomlet—*in conjunction with a much better known demographic phenomenon, the baby boom.*

Thus, for example, Callum G. Brown gives the following years as dates of postwar Christian revival: 1945–1958 (Great Britain), 1955–1963 (Australia), and 1952–1962 (West Germany). What is striking about this list is that the dates overlay almost perfectly with the postwar baby boom. This baby boom began immediately after the war and continued, depending on the country, on into the 1960s. As Tony Judt summarized in *Postwar: A History of Europe since 1945*: "Between 1950 and 1970 the population of the UK rose by 13 percent; that of Italy by 17 percent. In West Germany the population grew in these years by 28 percent; in the Netherlands by 35 percent. . . . The striking feature of Europe in the nineteen fifties and sixties . . . was thus the number of children and youths. After a forty-year hiatus, Europe was becoming young again."[32]

Exactly the same trend also characterized another important

petri dish, the United States. Before the Second World War, writes Charles Murray among others, Gallup polls suggested that religiosity declined slightly in the interwar era, reaching a low point in 1940. Then, "*suddenly and for no obvious reason*, membership and attendance both started to rise and continued to rise during the 1950s, reaching historic highs [emphasis added]."[33] What Murray calls the "membership apogee" was reached in the mid-1960s, and the "attendance apogee" occurred around 1936.

I have italicized those words, *suddenly and for no obvious reason*, for a purpose: because they signal the truth that there is currently no satisfying, going explanation for the boomlet in Christian religiosity that followed the war. But couldn't having more babies have been part of it?

Moreover—a point that arguably clinches the case—the baby boom in turn did not occur in a vacuum, but was accompanied as well by a sharp rise in marriage rates following the war. Once again, using marriage rates as another proxy of the strength of the natural family, we are led to the possibility that something about forming those families and living in them was driving up the level of religiosity—and not just vice versa.

Here is what social science has established: More children equal more God. More marriage equals more God. But why? Once again comes the chicken and egg question: Was it merely the case that postwar religiosity was driving people to form families during those years? Or was the formation of family *also* driving people to church, in more ways than one?

And once more, given the complexity of all that is involved, it seems most sound to see these two forces as a dynamic. In sum, given the weight of circumstantial evidence, the natural family does not appear to be *merely* an afterthought or consequence to religious belief. To study the timelines of faith and family is to see something else: that the family is also a *conduit* to belief, or at least—bearing in mind the limits established to this inquiry at the outset—to belief in Christianity.

The demographic and historical timeline, in which the strength of the natural family appears to wax *and* wane alongside that of Christian practice, is highly suggestive proof for that claim.

Circumstantial Evidence for the "Family Factor,"
Part Three: Because the "Family Factor" Explains
Problems That Existing Theories of Secularization
Do Not Explain—Including What Is Known
as "American Exceptionalism"

ANOTHER REASON to believe that we need to augment our understanding of secularization to include the Family Factor is this:
taking account of the role of families in transmitting religiosity does
a better job of explaining certain existing puzzles or problems than
does conventional secularization theory.

Specifically, by introducing the Family Factor, we can shed new
light on the largest problem that has bedeviled the theory all along:
i.e., the difference in religiosity between two of the most advanced
areas on earth, Western Europe on one hand and the United States
on the other.[1] As atheist Richard Dawkins has correctly posed that
problem, which is a constant of scholarly talk about secularization,
"The paradox has often been noted that the United States, founded
in secularism, is now the most religious country in Christendom,
while England, with an established church headed by its constitu-
tional monarch, is among the least. I am continually asked why this
is, and I do not know."[2]

Other scholars who have pondered the puzzle would agree
wholeheartedly. That is exactly why what is called the "problem
of exceptionalism" is such a problem. After all, if modernity is supposed to wipe away religion, how is it that the still largely Christian

United States—with its inarguably modern universities and its pre-eminent economy and extraordinary wealth —registers such different patterns of belief and churchgoing than do the also advanced yet relatively faith-free nations of Europe?

Or is it the other way around, as Rodney Stark has argued? Is it instead *Europe* that is the exception demanding explanation, whereas the United States is more the religious "norm"? This is a fascinating question. But whether one accepts the traditional version and calls America the exception to the trend, or inverts it so that Western Europe is the outlier instead, the fact remains that their divergent paths toward and away from church do seem to call for some kind of explanation.

This problem of "exceptionalism" is much larger than a dispute over how to read demographic statistics.[3] It is fundamental to our attempt to figure out what actually happened to Western Christianity, because it springs from that same hidden assumption—-i.e., since religious belief is unthinkingly assumed to come before family formation, "therefore" either America or Europe must be "explained." In other words, there is only the "problem" of American (or European) "exceptionalism" if one assumes what secularization theory assumes about the relationship between those two variables—namely, that belief comes first, and in turn drives personal behavior.

But if instead the supplemental theory being proposed here has merit—i.e., if changes in marrying and having babies and families *also* help to drive changes in religiosity—then the "problem" of American exceptionalism disappears. It appears instead to be perfectly adequately "explained" by the difference between today's American and Western European tendencies toward family formation—meaning that there are more families following the traditional model in America, even today, than in Europe. There are more marriages in the United States, even today, and more children per woman—both of which seem reasonable proxies for the *relative* strength of the natural family.

Once again, note that fertility is only one proxy one might cite in considering the difference between America and Europe in the matter of the natural family. What about marriage? Citing Tocqueville, who considered the American way of marriage fundamental to the national experiment, Charles Murray argues that American and European attitudes toward the wedded state have differed historically such that there is also an "American exceptionalism" concerning marriage. Reviewing what observers foreign and domestic had to say about the institution of marriage earlier in U.S. history, Murray summarizes, "American marriages were different from European ones (or so both Americans and foreign observers seemed to agree) in the solemnity of the marital bond."[4]

Part of that historical difference, of course, was that arranged marriages were uncommon in America compared to Europe (indeed, that way of doing things was largely stigmatized in the United States). But part of that difference, at least as Tocqueville saw it, also concerned the contractual nature of marriages on either side of the ocean. With American women far freer, generally speaking, and "perfectly free not to have contracted them [the burdens of marriage]," they were also more squarely on the moral hook for having assumed those same burdens when they could have done otherwise.[5]

If it is true that the United States, even today, remains more marriage-minded than Europe, then this is one more suggestive bit of evidence that what is called the problem of exceptionalism may not be a problem after all. In sum, looking more deeply into the "exceptionalism" issue unearths more evidence that families are a causal factor in religiosity.

*The Family Factor also helps to solve another puzzle about
religiosity that has yet to be satisfactorily explained:
the male/female religious gender gap.*

One other commonplace that has also been observed and documented by scholars (to say nothing of exasperated pastors) is this:
women are more likely—far more likely—to be found in, and
engaged in, church.

From yesteryear's caricature of the "Church Lady" on the television series *Saturday Night Live* to the realities of running bingo
games, school fund-raisers, and soup kitchens out of church base-
ments, the stereotype holds true: it is women, and not men, who are
the everyday backbone of the Christian churches.[6] As Putnam and
Campbell have summarized some of the most thorough numbers
available, "Women believe more fervently in God. They aver that
religion is more important in their daily lives, they pray more often,
they read scripture more often and interpret it more literally, they
talk about religion more often—in short, by virtually every measure
they are more religious."[7]

Moreover, this is true not only in America, where the gender gap
is the object of sometimes vigorous intra-Christian debate. It is also
true of European parishes and congregations, too.[8] Like American
women, European women also not only practice more, but also pray
more.[9] One 1990 review of the gender-gap literature in England
estimated that the overall ratio of women to men in church was
55–45—higher than that in the liberal nonconformist churches, and
lower in the evangelical ones.[10]

Buried somewhere in these and other data about the religious
gender gap is a question highly pertinent to the Family Factor—
and one that has not received the scrutiny it deserves. As sociologist
Tony Walter pointed out in his aforementioned study of England,

"There is as yet no generally accepted theory of why women in general seem to be more religious than men."[11] True enough. But *why*, if Nietzsche's parable and secularization theory are all that the world needed to know about the collapse of faith, should this gender difference exist in the first place? Why, if news of God's death is moving through Western society slowly but ultimately surely, should it be that one particular sex in one country and culture after another seems to be getting the news faster than the other?

It is less than persuasive to argue, for example, that women are more prone to belief because they are mentally inferior to men, or more inclined toward magical, superstitious thinking (though such admittedly would be one possible explanation for the gap). At one time assumptions about the cognitive inferiority of the human female were commonplace; but today, even if someone were privately to believe such a thing, the evidence would overrule him. As a matter of established fact, IQ is essentially evenly distributed between the sexes.[12] So of all the possible arguments about why women are more likely than men to be found in church, the notion that women are intrinsically intellectually less capable of grasping the Truth about Deep Things seems unlikely to be it.

Are women by nature, perhaps, more docile and easily led then? Is that why they seek out churches, with their preponderantly male leaders?

Once again, defending an explanation from female inferiority seems doomed to self-destruct. The widespread skepticism about Freudian ideas since the late twentieth century has surely taken the bloom off arguments about women searching for a "father figure." And the notion that women need men to lead them is an equally hard sell in an era when more women than men go to college.

No, some alternative explanation for the religious gender divide seems in order—and a theory arguing that religiosity, especially

Christian religiosity, is driven in part by the experience of family formation just might be it. In the differing dedication that men and women generally show toward religion, we seem to have another fact that fits the supplemental theory. Why?

One can only speculate. Perhaps women who are mothers tend to be more religious because the act of participating in creation, i.e., birth, is more immediate than that of men. Perhaps that fact inclines women to be more humble about their own powers and more open to the possibility of something greater than themselves—in brief, more religiously attuned. Or perhaps for both mothers and non-mothers, there is something about caring for the smallest and most vulnerable beings, which is still overwhelmingly women's work—after all, even "power mommies" employ other women to do it—that makes it easier to believe in a God who stands in a similar all-caring relationship to relatively helpless mortals of every age (or, as believers might have it, to hear him). In other words, maybe what separates men from women in the pews is that women have more hands-on experience of the Family Factor.

Isn't it possible that sex differences in religiosity, hitherto a puzzle, might have something to do with homely yet potent explanations like these?

Another puzzle addressed by the new theory is this: Why is religion stronger in the developing world than in affluent societies?

Several theorists have drawn attention to this disparity over the years. Perhaps most attentive have been political scientists Pippa Norris and Ronald Inglehart, whose book cited earlier, *Sacred and Secular*, is a meticulous attempt to revise the secularization thesis to take account of what they call "existential security." According to their model, the poorer and less secure people are, the more they "need" religion.[13]

Yet it is surely a friendly amendment to point out that there is another large difference between the developing world and the developed: generally speaking, *natural families in the developing world are stronger*, in the sense that individual human needs are more likely to be supplied within the confines of the family than they are in the modern developed West (which, as we saw early on in the book, has pioneered via the welfare state a host of substitutions for family ties and family obligations).

Similarly, to touch briefly on what is obviously a matter beyond the scope of this book, a theory that seeks to take the Family Factor into account also appears consistent with rational choice theory. For example, economists Raphaël Franck and Laurence R. Iannaccone, cited earlier, maintain that the Western welfare state has eroded religiosity "because churches offered welfare services which were not provided by the State."[14] More welfare, as their data show, means less God. Insofar as the welfare state usurps the family's historical tasks of seeing to the well-being of its members, their explanation of how the West lost God is consistent with this theory. In other words, everyone here has a different part of the same elephant. Everyone has a piece of the truth.

A fifth intellectual problem that makes more sense once we figure in something like the Family Factor is this:

*The Family Factor helps to explain something that comes up repeatedly in the scholarly literature, which is the mystery of why 1960 or thereabouts is such a pivotal year in secularization.*

Over and over in discussions among the experts, one finds near-consensus surrounding the notion that Western religiosity went over some kind of cliff in the 1960s. By just about any measure that makes practical sense—churchgoing, baptism, participation in religious education programs, and religious marriage, to name a few—numbers which had been declining in all these categories pick up the pace in the 1960s, especially across Western Europe.

Two particularly useful books examining that phenomenon are Hugh McLeod's *The Religious Crisis of the 1960s* and Callum G. Brown's *The Death of Christian Britain*. Both agree, as Brown puts it, that "From 1956 all indices of religiosity in Britain start to decline, and from 1963 most enter free fall."[15] McLeod provides a handy metaphor, noting that scholars see the 1960s as a "hinge decade" in Western Christianity. Even during the period from mid-1800 until World War I, he argues—where secularization was progressing on many fronts—it nonetheless remained true that in England, France, Germany, and elsewhere, "religion continued to provide a 'common language'" despite the overall decline in church attendance.[16]

But what *exactly* happened in the 1960s to turn that common language into a tower of Babel? Brown points to the changing role of women as the central cause. "The reconstruction of female identity within work, sexual relations and new recreational opportunities," he argues, "put not just feminism but female identity in collision with the Christian construction of femininity."[17] McLeod believes that there was no single cause, but rather "the cumulative impact of a number of smaller factors."[18] He outlines other forces that cumulatively served to weaken religiosity—the civil rights movement, the reformist mood of Vatican II, affluence, radical theologies, and above all "the weakening of collective identities that had been most important in the years before 1960."[19]

As before, it seems to me that both theorists—and for that matter, other scholars examining this question about what happened in the 1960s—make excellent points. But it is the Family Factor that unites those points as no other single explanation appears to do. Invoke that new factor for the purposes of explaining what happened in the 1960s, and the resulting changed explanation reads something like this.

Civil rights, Vietnam, rock music, a general weakening of authority—it certainly does make sense that all these social developments played a role in the diminishing appeal of Christianity. But one other large and perhaps preeminent change goes almost unseen in the academic literature. The underlying and underappreciated quantum leap toward irreligiosity in the 1960s, one can argue, owed most of its force to the approval in 1960 of the birth control pill, which would change relations between the sexes—that is to say, within the natural family—as never before.

To be sure, what we now call the "sexual revolution" was not a single event. As documented of late by Oxford historian Faramerz Dabhoiwala in *The Origins of Sex: A History of the First Sexual Revolution*, attitudes toward sexuality were changing dramatically, at least in the Anglo-Saxon countries, during the centuries before the Pill.[20] This was particularly true, the author observes, of the upper classes, whose alleged debauchery and immorality were perennial targets of reformers during the 1800s, especially.[21] Dabhoiwala also makes the interesting point that ideas about sexual morality, like other ideas, ebb and flow in Western history; for example, he argues, they tightened under the Reformation, then loosened in the eighteenth century.

The point here is that, as with any social change with massive consequences—whether it be the sexual revolution or, say, the subject of this book—humility and nuance must be understanding's constant companions.

Even so, it is surely another friendly amendment to observe that while a long-running sexual revolution predated the new contraceptive technologies, it was the technologies that turned that revolution into capital letters. Once the genie of the Pill was literally out of the bottle, extramarital sex became easier—freer of the immediate consequence of pregnancy—than ever before. And once again, however one feels about that change, it had an obviously seismic impact on family formation and the lack thereof. Divorce rates soared as never before. So did illegitimacy—in part because the sexual marketplace grew and grew with every woman who took the Pill or related technologies, which in turn made it ever less likely that men would marry simply for the sake of a sexual partner.

Some interesting works about the effects of the contraceptive revolution on men, especially, show something of the social metamorphosis brought on by those little pills. As early as 1973, for example, in a book called *Sexual Suicide* that was often called provocative at the time, George Gilder argued that the sexual revolution was driving men away from women and families—in part because, in a world where men no longer had to marry to assure their access to sex, many lost interest in marriage.[22] In another prescient book published in 1999 called *The Decline of Males*, secular sociologist Lionel Tiger argued similarly that in giving women complete control over reproduction, the Pill essentially rendered men obsolete.[23] The result, he observed, was that men existed in an ever-more attenuated relationship to women and children—one that began in what he called an "atmospheric anti-maleness."[24] Both Gilder's and Tiger's points would come to be made by others over the years, with or without crediting what were initially judged to be their controversial theses (including in the recent vogue for discussing "the end of men"). Plainly, there was—and is—a deep truth excavated by their work.

And what of the effect of the 1960s sexual revolution on women?

Initially, to judge by culture both high and low, the new contraceptive order rode in on a tidal wave of approval. Women's magazines like *Good Housekeeping* and *Redbook* embraced the new order, to say nothing of racier offerings like *Cosmopolitan*. Sisterhood was in, Ozzie and Harriet were out.

Not everyone concurred in the euphoria. In books like *The New Chastity and Other Arguments Against Women's Liberation*, as well as in her essays, social critic Midge Decter was among the first to warn that the new Garden of Eden was less enchanting from the point of view of women and families than liberationists claimed.[25] Following Decter, other skeptical women (and men) would come to make the case that the sexual revolution was more problematic for men, women, and children than it first appeared.[26] Precisely because the sexual revolution is a paramount social fact of our time, this ongoing battle over its legacy—i.e. over who shall write its final verdict, liberationists or skeptics—looks to continue for a long time to come.[27]

Whatever that ultimate verdict, however, the empirical record so far would appear to vindicate at least one subset of thinkers: those who saw that the Pill would increase sexual temptation for a great many people, thus adding new and unprecedented pressure to what was already one of the most demanding jobs on earth: keeping a family together. The Pill and its associated movement, the sexual revolution, contributed to the weakening of family bonds as no other single technological force in history—which explains as no other single factor why the 1960s are the linchpin of the change in Western religiosity.

Sociologist Robert Wuthnow of Princeton has laid out the connection between the Pill and the decline in traditional religiosity in his 1998 book *After Heaven: Spirituality in America Since the 1950s*.[28]

"During the 1950s," he writes, "the average time between confirmation class and birth of first child for U.S. young people had only been seven years; by the end of the 1960s, in large measure because of the new contraceptive technologies, this period had more than doubled to fifteen years. Since the time between confirmation and parenthood has always been one in which young people could drop out of established religion and turn their attention to other things, *the doubling of this period was of enormous religious significance* [emphasis added]."[29]

In other words, do the transitive arithmetic. More Pill equals less time in a family. More time in a family equals more time in church. Therefore more Pill equals less God.

In sum, it was the sexual revolution, then as now, that has done most to weaken the family and with it, the Family Factor. As Fr. Pablo Ghio of the Pontifical Council on the Family once put it during an interview, "The sexual revolution washed over the West like a tidal wave, and has yet to recede."[30] The more people had sex outside of marriage, the less incentive there was to form marriages in the first place—and the more reluctance to sign on to official Christian (or similar religious) teaching in these matters. With more people living without marriage, more men and women had profound new reasons to tell themselves that the Judeo-Christian moral code was out of date—and to be kindly inclined toward experts and even clergy purveying the same message, as more and more men and women of the cloth would come to do (see chapter 6). With more children growing up in one-parent (typically fatherless) homes, fewer parents had the resources, or, for some, the motivation to be sure the children made it to religious instruction classes or church.

And so on, and so on, and so on. The decline in religiosity—from what is taught at the kitchen table to what is taught in the pews—shares one common denominator: the family, which in the course of that tumultuous decade was battered as never before, chiefly on account of easily acquired and foolproof contraception. The religious decline of the 1960s so well documented by scholars is one more puzzle that looks less puzzling once the Family Factor is given a place at the table.

# ≈ 6

Assisted Religious Suicide: How Some
Churches Participated in Their Own Downfall
by Ignoring the Family Factor

T HE STORY OF how Christianity has declined in parts of the
West cannot be told in full without doing justice to one other
momentous and ironic historical fact that stands apart from the
Family Factor, but is also intricately connected to it. To invoke the
image of the double helix again, imagine those straight lines bridging the two spirals of family and faith. What are the short rods that
join them? Those can only be religious teaching and doctrine, or
church itself. The stronger (or more coherent) those rods are, the
better connected are the two spirals.

It will be helpful to keep that image in mind in this chapter, as
we trace the sometimes revolutionary changes in Christian doctrine that, I will argue, led inadvertently to even more weakening of the family as an institution across the West. Once again, we
must keep the different pieces of that helix before us to grasp how
interdependent these forces really are. Just as the shrinking and
weakening of the family across Western Europe was contributing to
religious decline, especially with the acceleration of that process in
the 1960s, so at the same time did many Christian churches behave
in ways that in retrospect appear to have been self-destructive, at
least from the point of view of holding onto their flocks. They initiated one doctrinal change after another that further weakened the

ties between family and church—a process that surely accelerated decline even more.

None of which is to say that anyone intended as much. These reform-minded religious leaders generally shared one goal that they thought of as humanitarian: they wanted to construct a Christianity with a kinder, gentler, more inclusive face. They were also up against hard pragmatic reality that only added to the pressure for change: many members of the flock, especially as of the 1960s, were already living in ways that amounted to tacit defiance of church teaching— and churches that frowned on them weren't likely to keep them. For these reasons, both reformers within the churches and laypeople and women outside of them independently sought doctrinal change. From the acceptance of divorce to the okaying of contraception to the embrace of active homosexuality today, these realities have been the engines driving most changes in Christian doctrine.

At the same time, however, these reformist efforts bit by bit contributed to an unwanted and unexpected denouement: they weakened both literally and figuratively the foundations on which those same churches depended—i.e., natural families. In their efforts to reach out to individuals who wanted a softening of Christian doctrine, the churches inadvertently appear to have failed to protect their base: thriving families whose members would then go on to reproduce both literally and in the figurative sense of handing down their religion. Here again, we see the powerful effect of the double helix of family and faith.

This chapter tells a brief version of the story of those changes that amounted to inadvertent neglect of the traditional family—and of the fate of the churches that initiated them. These were chiefly the Protestant churches of Europe, and those of what is called the Protestant mainline in the United States. The story of the rapid fall of these particular churches is one more proof that faith and family fit the double helix model. Pry one off the other, and the unit will be unable to reproduce as it used to.

To say that there is a story in this doctrinal weakening is not to say anything as simpleminded as that church moral teachings were strict in some imaginary Golden Age, after which each became more and more lax and went to hell in a handbasket. The historical truth is of course more nuanced than that kind of crude declinism can explain. As Faramerz Dabhoiwala, cited earlier, reminds us in the example of the sexual revolution, not all historical arrows point in the same direction. Similarly, as Charles Taylor notes of the course of secularization, "The actual road from here to there has been much more bumpy and indirect than a simple diffusion story can capture."[1] The course of church doctrine, similarly, is cyclical rather than linear. (One might add: as befits a helix, after all.)

Once again, the reader is asked to keep an open mind and consider the evidence. The question before us is not how anyone *feels* about the reforms worked over the centuries by Protestant churches on the traditional Christian moral code. Many people—at least, many modern people—would say that the world is a better place for the softening of that code over the centuries. They would say it is simple mercy to allow divorce to couples trapped in miserable marriages, for example; or to ratify contraception; or to overrule the sanctions against homosexuality; or otherwise to de-emphasize and sometimes abandon traditional Christian teaching about sexual morality.

Once again, though, personal opinions are irrelevant to our inquiry here. What we are trying to understand instead is the answer to this question: *Did* the doctrinal changes and reforms of modern Protestantism specifically further contribute to the weakening of family bonds in the West? Does that part of the historical record amount to more evidence that the health of the traditional family and the health of a given Christian denomination appear to go hand in hand? A review of what has actually happened to family and faith suggests that the answer is yes.

Begin with some historical perspective. From the beginning, Christianity carried with it a moral code—specifically, a sexual moral code—that was strict by most other religious standards, including even by those of the Judaism that it inherited.

In the largely pagan world where Christianity first took root, as Roman writers themselves reported, infanticide was common; abortion was hardly unknown; births to unmarried couples abounded; divorce was a rather obvious solution to marital unhappiness, at least for men; and in certain classes, homosexuality was a familiar fact of life. All of these were behaviors and customs that Christianity then pronounced to be sins. This dramatic disparity between what plenty of other people were doing and what Jesus and his followers told people they *ought* to be doing did not exactly go unnoticed, either by Christians themselves or by anyone else. From the first believers on up to our own time, the stern stuff of the Christian moral code has been cause for commentary—to say nothing of frequent complaint. "Not all men can receive this saying," the disciples are told when Jesus puts divorce off-limits. Observers throughout history, Christian and otherwise, have agreed: the teaching about the permanence of marriage is hard indeed, and so are some of its corollaries. From pagan Rome two thousand years ago to secular Western Europe today, the church's rules about sex have amounted to saying *no, no,* and *no* to things about which non-Christians have gotten to say *yes* or *why not.*

This code, in short, was always problematic from the perspective of people who resented its constraints. (It still is.) The historical surprise, therefore, is not so much that reformers would ultimately work to make it more user-friendly. It is rather that this code stood untouched at the center of Christendom for as long as it did—i.e., more or less until the Reformation. That was when churchmen first started picking apart the tapestry of Christian sexual morality— hundreds of years ago, long before the sexual revolution, and over one particular thread: divorce.

As the historian Roderick Phillips puts it in *Untying the Knot: A Short History of Divorce*: "The Reformation . . . represented a sharp break in the direction of divorce doctrines and policies. The trend toward a homogeneous and enforced principle of marital indissolubility that had begun in the ninth century was, 700 years later, arrested and reversed throughout much of central and northern Europe. Reformers, led notably by Martin Luther and John Calvin, rejected not just the Roman Catholic church's doctrine of marital indissolubility but virtually all aspects of its marriage doctrine."[2]

Henry VIII, as is often misunderstood, did not divorce any of his wives; he rather succeeded in obtaining three annulments which some in the Christian world, notably the Catholic Church, deemed to have been wrongfully got. Nonetheless, those annulments—so clearly similar to divorces in their plain intent to undo an ostensibly done marriage—prove with hindsight to have been the camel's nose under the theological tent. On the Continent, some other reformers at the time, such as Huldrych Zwingli, stood with Henry on the annulment question; others did not—yet. In the long run, of course, almost all Protestant churches would capitulate on the controversy; but in the short run, they did so at different rates.

For about two centuries, for example, and despite the fact that other Protestant churches were allowing divorce, the Church of England held fast to the same principle of the indissolubility of marriage on which the rest of Christian tradition insisted. According to Phillips again, "No bishop, archbishop, or incumbent of high Anglican office in the first half of the seventeenth century supported the legalization of divorce."[3] Even so, this early dedication to principle would turn out not to hold. Ultimately, and with increasing speed in the New World especially, it would erode, one clergyman and one churchyard at a time.

In the United States, Phillips reports, Anglican churches soon were relaxing the strictest restrictions, making divorce more or less easy to come by depending on where one lived. Meanwhile, although the Church of England lagged behind the Episcopalians, by the mid-eighteenth century divorce was theoretically and practically available by an act of Parliament—a recourse that, although not widely exercised, went to show that exceptions to the indissolubility principle could be made. Bit by bit, the numbers of people seeking to put their marriages behind them crept up, and the social as well as religious stigma once associated with divorce began to lessen accordingly. As of the General Synod in 2002, divorced Anglicans could now remarry in the church—one more wiping away of any remaining taint.

By our own day, divorce in the mainline Protestant churches is not only destigmatized; it has been almost entirely emptied of moral content, period. And in one more fascinating turn now visible in retrospect, the departure over divorce appears as the template for other, related doctrinal changes to come.

The Anglican attempt to lighten up the Christian moral code over the specific issue of divorce exhibit a clear pattern that appears over and over in the history of the experiment that I have elsewhere dubbed "Christianity Lite": First, limited exceptions are made to a rule; next, those exceptions are no longer limited and become the unremarkable norm; finally, that new norm is itself sanctified as theologically acceptable.[4]

Exactly that pattern emerges in another example of the historical attempt to disentangle a thread of moral teaching out of the whole: the dissent about artificial contraception. In that case, too, it was the Anglicans who took the historical lead. As many people today seem not to know, throughout most of its history, all of Christianity—even divided Christianity—taught that artificial contraception was wrong. Not until the Lambeth Conference of 1930 was that unity shattered by the subsequently famous Resolution 15, in which the Anglicans called for exceptions to the rule in certain carefully delineated marital (and only marital) circumstances. Almost two millennia of Christian teaching on that subject, in other words, did not begin to change until less than a hundred years ago.

Exactly as had happened with divorce, the Anglican okaying of contraception was born of compassion for human frailty combined with concern over keeping up with the times—and dedicated to the idea that such cases would be mere exceptions to the rule. Thus Resolution 15 itself—for all that it was a radical break with almost two thousand years of Christian teaching—abounded with careful language about the limited character of its reform, including "strong condemnation of the use of any methods of conception control from motives of selfishness, luxury, or mere convenience."

And also exactly as had happened with divorce, the effort to hold the line at such meticulously drawn borders soon proved futile. In short order, not only was birth control theologically approved in certain difficult circumstances, but soon thereafter, it was regarded as the norm.

Nor was that all. In a third turn of the reformist wheel that no one attending Lambeth in 1930 could have seen coming, artificial contraception went on to be sanctioned by some prominent members of the Anglican Communion not only as an option but in fact as the *better* moral choice. By the time of the outspoken American Episcopal Bishop James Pike, only a quarter century or so later, it was possible for a leading Christian to declare (as he did) that parents who should not be having a child were not only *permitted* to use contraception but were, in fact, under a *moral obligation* to use the most effective forms of contraception obtainable.[5]

And Bishop Pike was only one of many forward-looking Christian leaders to participate in this same theological process leading from normalization to near-sanctification of what had once been regarded as a sin. Although the Eastern Orthodox churches sided generally with Rome on the issue of contraception, most Protestant churches ended up following the same script as the Anglicans—moving one by one from reluctant acceptance in special circumstances, to acceptance in most or all circumstances, and finally (in some cases) to complete theological inversion.[6] No less an authority than the Baptist evangelist Billy Graham, for example, eventually embraced birth control to cope with what he called the "terrifying and tragic problem" of overpopulation.[7]

In just a few decades, in other words—following the same pattern as divorce—contraception in reform-minded churches went from being an unfortunate option, to an unremarkable option, to the theologically *preferable* option in some cases.

Now consider a third example of the same historical pattern holding in another area: dissent over traditional Christian teachings against homosexuality.

Although homosexuality may be the most explosive current example of the effort to reshape Christianity into a religion more congenial to modern sexual practice, it is actually new to that doctrinal party. Homosexual behavior has been proscribed throughout history, by Judaism as well as Christianity, until very, very recently—including in the same Protestant churches that have lately taken the lead in abandoning that same teaching. (Henry VIII, to name one prominent example, invoked the alleged homosexuality of the monks as part of his justification for appropriating the monasteries.)

Yet "extraordinarily enough," as William Murchison puts it in his book *Mortal Follies: Episcopalians and the Crisis of Mainline Christianity*, "a question barely at the boundary of general consciousness thirty years ago has assumed central importance to the present life and future of the Episcopal Church."[8]

Why this remarkable transformation? In part, because the reformers at Lambeth and elsewhere did not foresee something else that in retrospect appears obvious: the chain of logic leading from the occasional acceptance of contraception to the celebration of homosexuality would prove sound. That is precisely why the change in doctrine over contraception has been used repeatedly by Anglican leaders to justify proposed changes in religious attitudes toward homosexuality. Robert Runcie, for example, former archbishop of Canterbury, explained his own personal decision to ordain homosexually active men on exactly those grounds. In a BBC radio interview in 1996, he cited the Lambeth Conference of 1930, observing that "once the Church signalled . . . that sexual activity was for human delight and a blessing even if it was divorced from any idea of procreation . . . once you've said that sexual activity is . . . pleasing to God in itself, then what about people who are engaged in same-sex expression and who are incapable of heterosexual expression?"[9]

Similarly, former archbishop of Canterbury Rowan Williams has also connected the dots between approving purposely sterile sex for heterosexuals on the one hand, and extending the same theological courtesy to same-sex couples on the other. As he observed in a lecture in 1989, three years before he became bishop, "In a church which accepts the legitimacy of contraception, the absolute condemnation of same-sex relations of intimacy must rely either on an abstract fundamentalist deployment of a number of very ambiguous texts or on a problematic and non-scriptural theory about natural complementarity, applied narrowly and crudely to physical differentiation without regard to psychological structures."[10]

Put differently, the rejection of the ban on birth control was not incidental to the Anglicans' subsequent about-face homosexuality. It was what started it.

This same pattern of dissent over sexuality, followed by decline in both numbers and practice, also appears clearly in modern history of the Protestant mainline churches. Here, too, the speed with which both practice and principle have unraveled bears scrutiny.

In 1930, for example, the initial reaction among America's Lutherans to Lambeth's Resolution 15 was disbelief bordering on hostility. Margaret Sanger was denounced in an official Lutheran newspaper as a "she devil," and numerous pastors took to the pulpits and op-ed pages with blistering complaints about the Anglicans' theological capitulation. Nonetheless, by 1954, the Lutherans, too, were encouraging contraception in order to make sure that any child born would be valued "both for itself and in relation to the time of its birth."[11]

Also like the Anglicans, the Evangelical Lutheran Church in America has proven that one thread could not be teased out of the moral garment without pulling others out too. In 1991, a Social Statement found that abortion—regarded as a grave sin almost universally throughout Christian history—could be a morally responsible choice in certain circumstances. That same year, the Churchwide Assembly (CWA), the leading legislative body of the church, affirmed that "gay and lesbian people . . . are welcome to participate fully in the life of the congregations of the Evangelical Lutheran Church."[12] Less than two decades later, in 2009, official tolerance for individuals with homosexual tendencies had transposed into something else: official approval of the sexual practice of homosexuality, enshrined in the decision to allow noncelibate homosexuals to serve as pastors.

This leads to a third pattern arising from the attempt to knead the traditional Christian moral code into something softer and more palatable to modern sensibilities. That is the ongoing and inarguable institutional decline of the churches that have tried it. Today, the ELCA—the largest and most liberal of the Lutheran bodies of America—faces the same fate as the Anglican Communion: threats of schism, departing parishes, diminishing funds, and the rest of the institutional woes that have gone hand in hand with the abandonment of dogma.

The same fate also threatens the rest of the mainline Protestant churches—in addition to the Episcopal Church and the Evangelical Lutheran Church, the Presbyterian Church (USA), the United Church of Christ, the United Methodist Church, and the American Baptist Church. In December 2009, the Barna Group observed based on the latest round of numbers that all the mainline churches appear to be "on the precipice of a decline." Across the board, funding is down, numbers are down, numbers of the young are especially down, and missionaries—one particularly good measure of the vibrancy of belief—are diminishing apace. Even the kind of social work for which Christian churches have been renowned is also down: mainline volunteerism, according to the Barna numbers, had dropped a shocking 21 percent since 1998.[13]

This same pattern—relaxation of the traditional rules, followed by exit en masse from the pews—also obtained outside the United

States, as scholar Hugh McLeod documents in one chapter of *The Religious Crisis of the 1960s*.[14] McLeod charts the currents in Anglicanism and elsewhere during that decade, most of which sharply departed from the traditionalist sea of the immediate postwar years.

The "typical themes of 1960s Christianity," he observes, included "a critical view of the church (and indeed of institutions generally); an insistence that the best practical Christianity was often to be found outside the church; the rejection of a legalistic code of morality [i.e., the traditional Christian moral code] in favour of situation ethics; the claim that the true place of Christians is with the marginalized, and a consequent suspicion of any kind of respectability or recognized status; a horror of dogma."[15]

In practical terms, these changes trickled down to new emphases similar to those emerging in the United States—among them the studied abandonment of traditional images such as Christ the King, the preference for social work over traditional ministry, the replacement of traditional music with guitars and other innovative forms, the appearance of best-selling books traducing religious orthodoxy and arguing that the marginalized were closer to God than conventional worshippers, and other signs of the ascendency of a progressive spirit in Protestant Christianity.

Nonetheless, while some of these revisions in emphasis had more to do with atmospherics and arguments over aesthetics than with actual doctrine, in Great Britain as in America the most enduring theological changes were aimed at the same target: the traditional Christian moral code. Many Christians, argued some, had "a damaging and exaggerated sense of guilt."[16] Christianity, said Bishop of Woolwich John Robinson in his wildly successful 1963 best seller *Honest to God*, needed a "new morality" based on love and situational ethics rather than the legalism of yesteryear. "Nothing," said

Robinson, "can of itself always be labeled as wrong."[17] Many more examples could be adduced, as scholars have shown, to advance the proposition that the 1960s saw a widespread relaxation of traditional Christian dogma across the West.

The exception, of course, was the Catholic Church, whose issuance of *Humanae Vitae* in 1968 both famously and infamously affirmed the traditional moral code by upholding the ban on birth control. The church paid dearly—and pays dearly still—for its theological fealty in the face of pressure across the West to repeal that ban. Indeed, it is hard to think of any other document in modern times that has been the object of as much enduring and even enthusiastic revilement as that one.

Nevertheless, this excursion into the history of changing doctrine offers even more evidence of the potency of the Family Factor. *Relaxing the rules hastened the decline of the churches that did it*—and the reason can only be that relaxing the rules inadvertently meant failing to protect and nurture the natural families on whom churches have depended (picture that helix again) for reproduction.[18]

What accounts for this epochal, perhaps even counterintuitive outcome—one that surely would have shocked the original Christian architects of these reforms, most of whom longed only for what their congregations wanted too: i.e., Christianity with a happier human face?

Again, the answer is the Family Factor, which operated in tandem with the doctrinal revolution in several ways.

One is obvious enough—even prosaic. If enough people over enough time turn their backs on the injunction to be fruitful and multiply, eventually their churches will cease being fruitful and multiplying, too. The pastors who taught that the church was now indifferent to procreation all but guaranteed themselves thinning and graying ranks in the years to come—just as those who taught that procreation was positively immoral effectively wrote themselves out of a job.

Sociology, for its part, confirms this elementary if perhaps unwelcome point. In research published in 2005 in *Christian Century*, three sociologists (Andrew Greeley, Michael Hout, and Melissa Wilde) argued that "simple demographics" between 1900 and 1975 explained around three-quarters of the decline in mainline churches (Episcopal, Lutheran, Presbyterian, and Methodist).[19] By contrast, they pointed out, during those same years membership rose in more conservative Protestant churches (Baptist, Assembly of God, Pentecostal, and so on). The difference was that women in the former churches were using artificial contraception before or instead of women in the latter ones—in sum, that "the so-called decline of the mainline may ultimately be attributable to its earlier approval of contraception."[20] The claim here, note carefully, is not that women were using contraceptives *because* their pastors told them to. It is rather that women were *of course* more likely to use contraceptives once their church leaders stopped regarding that behavior as sinful.

A second way in which the Family Factor appears to have been on a collision course with these kinds of doctrinal changes is this: children, to repeat, drive people to church. In the following chapter we will consider in more detail the various mechanisms that seem to power that process. For now, though, let us merely note that the shrinking of the family also meant fewer reasons for some adults to find church—because they had no need of religious instruction, say, or to search for a wholesome peer group for their nonexistent young. Whether one is a Durkheimian, neo-Durkheimian, or anti-Durkheimian doesn't matter here. One can still plainly see that the social bonds forged by all that the churches traditionally do—from Sunday schools to soup kitchens to visiting hospitals to bingo—

are dependent in part on vibrant families who can engage in these communal ties on different levels. In this way, too, diminishing the family meant diminishing the church.

In sum, the churches that did most to loosen up the traditional moral code of Christianity are the same churches that have ended up suffering most for that effort—demographically, financially, morale-wise, and otherwise. Some are on the brink of actual extinction. As a recent article in the *Independent* put it, speaking the thought for many, "Will the last person to leave the Church of England please turn out the lights?"[21] It is a question into which other church names might soon be substituted, including those of the mainline.

It is *not* a question anyone asks about certain other churches that have not rejected the traditional moral code, but have instead held it fast—the Church of Jesus Christ of Latter-day Saints, for example; or the traditional-minded evangelical churches; or the Pentecostals; or the Anglican churches of what is now called the Global South, who tenaciously defend the moral teachings of Christianity against the paganism of their own societies and the secularized reform-minded Christians of the West alike.

And what of the Catholic Church? Despite sticking to its theological guns about the family, the Church too has also seen a significant falloff in practice, especially in Europe, as discussed in chapter 2. But it is also true that the most vibrant areas of Catholicism are the most orthodox. Opus Dei, for example, has spread from one man's vision to flocks in sixty countries, all in the modern period. Comunione e Liberazione, similarly, which was founded in the 1960s as an alternative to "soft" Italian Catholicism, has spread to sixty-two countries and holds massive meetings each summer of some 700,000 people.[22] Both within churches as well as between churches, it seems, what is traditional tends to be strong.

All of which is to say that one kind of fallout from the centuries-long tinkering with doctrine that began with the Reformation has had one clear consequence: it has weakened the churches that attempted it. It weakened them demographically, as removing the emphasis on the family and the injunction to be fruitful and multiply has resulted in graying parishioners and empty pews across the Western world. It weakened them financially, as the failure of worshippers to replace themselves has left those churches with an ever-shrinking base of contributors—the same problem facing the West's aging welfare states. And it has weakened the same churches in a wider sense of mission and morale.

Whether one cheers these results in the name of liberation or regrets the lost world they represent, there can be no doubt that the doctrinal changes have played their own part in the emptying of the pews. As a compelling confirmation of the Family Factor at work, that process is an important and ironic part of the story of how Christianity came to seep out of many Western minds and homes.

Putting All the Pieces Together:
Toward an Alternative Anthropology
of Christian Belief

I N THIS CHAPTER we will switch narrative gears once more.
So far we have zeroed in on the defects of conventional explanations of Christianity's decline and the proposal that a supplemental theory pivoting around the Family Factor is more consonant
with the facts. This chapter will try to answer the next logical question: If this alternative theory of the decline of Christianity is true,
*why* might it be true? That is, what is it about the natural family that
might make the specific religion of Christianity so dependent on
its vitality? What are the forces, the explanatory mechanisms, that
make the double helix go round and round?

This chapter attempts to answer those questions by way of a
series of hypotheses about the ways in which the natural family itself
seems to increase the likelihood of religiosity. These building blocks
of a new anthropology of religious belief are necessarily speculative.
Nonetheless, there is evidence to be considered for each.

*First, the experience of the natural family itself drives some
people to religion.*

As noted earlier on, children drive parents to church in various ways
—in part for reasons of seeking a community. But this does not mean
that parents *only* go to church for the sake of community. Other,

extra-communal experiences might also make them feel more compelled to explore questions of divinity than they did before they were parents. Just consider what the experience of childbirth itself does to almost every mother and father.

That moment—even that first glimpse on a sonogram—is routinely experienced by a great many people as an event transcendental as no other. This fact of epiphany hardly means that pregnancy and birth *ipso facto* convert participants into religious zealots. But the sequence of events culminating in birth is nearly universally interpreted as a moment of communion with something larger than oneself, larger even than oneself and the infant. It is an experience that many people describe as religious or sacred—or as close to those states as one can get.

Certainly humanity's artistic record verifies that nothing matters more to the vast majority of parents than their children. That most primal of human connections echoes throughout the masterpieces of human history. It is why *King Lear* is nearly universally recognized as Shakespeare's greatest tragedy, whereas, say, *Romeo and Juliet* for all its pathos is not—because the predeceasing by Lear of his daughter Cordelia is the perfect symbol of the worst tragedy life can present, at least as far as the mothers and fathers of the world are concerned.

It is why the story of Jesus is so similarly universal in its tragic appeal, whether told via that masterpiece of sculpture, Michelangelo's *Pietà* (whose primary focus, suggestively enough, is Mary, not Jesus), or just via the familiar story that begins with Mary and Joseph fleeing to Egypt to save their infant's life—one that has obviously resonated among literates and illiterates for two millennia.

Similarly, the theme of not only outliving one's children but symbolically profiting from their death repeatedly presents itself as the worst transgression imaginable in works that stand at the absolute pinnacle of Western literature. Consider Medea's unwitting devouring of her children as related by Euripides almost 2,500 years ago; Dante's portrayal of Ugolino, one of the most famous figures in the *Inferno*, whose punishment in hell is to watch his four sons die and then to eat their flesh out of his inability to stop himself; Shakespeare's sounding of the theme in *Titus Andronicus*, where the title character's ultimate revenge on the Goth queen who has destroyed his family is to engineer her unwitting digestion of her own two children, cooked like Medea's in a pie.

In all these literary cases, the meaning is clear across centuries and languages: nothing could be worse than losing one's children—unless it is the taboo of living off that which should never have died first.

What is it about the predeceasing of parents by children that has so captured the imaginations of the West's (though not only the West's) greatest artists across millennia and languages and cultures? The answer can only be that this theme resonates most deeply with the human heart—or at least the heart joined to children by family ties. As even Aaron, Shakespeare's moral monster in *Titus Andronicus*, cries upon seeing his illegitimate newborn, "This before all the world do I prefer; This maugre [pleasure] all the world will I keep safe / Or some of you shall smoke for it in Rome."

Now leave aside the literary evidence just offered for the proposition that having children is experienced by most as a transcendental fact like no other. Consider this in more colloquial terms. How many people do you know who have gone back to church or synagogue because of having children? It may seem so common as to be unremarkable, but *why* does it happen?

We have already seen that children "drive" parents to church in other ways—by needing education and involvement in a community, two social desiderata about which churches have a great deal of practical experience. The novel suggestion here is that this is one side of the religious coin, and that there is also another: children might also "drive" parents to church in the sense that *the experience of having them makes parents more willing to believe*. Perhaps something about children might make parents more inclined toward belief in the infinite—to a supernatural realm that is somehow higher and less well understood than this one.

The reasons for this might be several. For one thing, the love that most parents bear for their children is the strongest emotion many people will ever feel. Perhaps it is too intense for many parents to believe that the life before them has a cold, finite end. That might be one way in which children compel some parents toward religious belief. Also likely (and not mutually exclusive) is that many parents feel, and commonly say, that they did not themselves could not create any *particular* child; they experience the child as "created" by someone else. Many a mother and father staring at a newborn has had the sense that they are witnessing something that only a Creator could have made—a feeling captured powerfully in prose by the Cold War figure Whittaker Chambers, who writes in his memoir *Witness* about how studying his newborn daughter's ear ultimately led him to reject atheism and believe in God.[1] Once more, this is a literary example of something to which many other human beings, literary or not, could testify.

These are speculative claims, to repeat—but for the reason that no one has yet thought to document or test them with social science and not because they are implausible.

Thus does a complementary religious anthropology begin to emerge, grounded on the primal fact that the mother-child and father-child bond, as no other, appears to push at least some people toward an intensity of purposeful connection with the divine that they might never otherwise have experienced.

Now consider more ways in which experience of the natural family might incline some people to religious belief. After all, birth is not the only familial experience that has the transcendental effect of raising one's focus beyond the immediate individual horizon. So do other common family events that defy ordinary, atomized human pleasure-seeking or the calculating, coldly rational decision-making *homo economicus* demanded by theories that do not take account of the centrality of family in most people's lives.

These common events include, say, the selfless care of an ailing family member, the financial sacrifices made for those whose adulthood one may never live to see—even the incredible human feat of staying married for a long time. These kinds of sacrifice of self that are often part of family life are fully consonant with the emphatic Judeo-Christian call to die to self and to care for the sick and weak—meaning that Christianity might make more sense, or perhaps seem more appealing, to people engaging in those kinds of sacrifices. Further, in binding those alive to relatives both past and yet to come, the family is literally death-defying—another feature that might make it easier for those living in families to make related transcendental leaps of the religious variety.

Third, families and especially children also transform people in other ways that may incline people toward religious belief, including in what may be the deepest way of all. All men and women fear death; but only mothers and fathers can be counted upon to fear another individual's death more than their own, for almost all do.

To put the point another way: if the cataclysm of 9/11 drove to church, for weeks on end, millions of Americans who had not contemplated stained glass in years—as it did—imagine the even deeper impact on ordinary mothers and fathers of a sick child, or the similarly powerful emotions of a devoted spouse on the brink of losing the other. Surely family love gives individuals an extra incentive to contemplate eternity. Just as there are no atheists in a foxhole, so too are there fewer inside the nursery as opposed to out of it—and the same for the critical care unit.

None of these speculations, of course, bears on the "truth value" of Christianity or any other system of religious belief; they can only tell us *why* some people might be more inclined to believe than others, not *whether* they are right to do so. But bit by bit we can see in such meditations the beginnings of an intuitively resonant account of how Christianity (and likely other religions too) really waxes and wanes in the world.

A second principle of this complementary religious anthropology —that is, a second way of understanding how integral the family is to Christianity—is this:

*The Christian story itself is a story told through the prism of the family. Take away the prism, and the story makes less sense.*

It is a premise of this book that we Western men and women, whether inside the churches or not, are only at the beginning of understanding how the fracturing of the natural family has in turn helped to fracture Christianity. Evidence from all over suggests that understanding Christianity requires understanding the natural family—and a world where natural families are often weak is one in which the very language of Christian belief, literal and figurative, is destined to be less well understood than it was before.

Consider the work of Elizabeth Marquardt and Norval Glenn, whose work appears in a pioneering 2005 book called *Between Two Worlds: The Inner Lives of Children of Divorce.*[2] Based on interviews with over 1,400 adult children of divorced parents, it reveals among other findings one of particular fascination to this study.

Like it or not, the Judeo-Christian tradition has anthropomorphized the Deity in one particular way: by analogy to a wise, protective, loving, ever-present male parent. The fact that many children, in an age of broken or unformed natural families, do not associate those adjectives with their male biological parent makes for elemental, ongoing confusion and heartache among some of the subjects of the Marquardt/Glenn study. At one point, for example, Marquardt asks her subjects to reflect on the idea of God as a parent, elaborating on one:

> Will was mystified by the question. He had been angry at his father for years because of the way he treated Will's mother. When I asked Will if god is like a father or parent he looked puzzled. "Yeah, I think a father is somebody who is your last string of hope," he said slowly. "He'll watch over you, make sure everything is going to be okay." Then his voice faltered and he looked down at his hands in his lap. "I'm drawing a blank," he said. "I'm just drawing a blank."[3]

These are words that build a window onto a much larger world in which the receding of the sea of faith comes into clearer view. Surely Will is not the only one "drawing a blank" on understanding Christianity because of his limited understanding of the natural family. Surely a great many other people similarly find Christianity more distant these days precisely *because* of its insistence on the centrality not only of "the family" in the abstract, but also on understanding a *particular* family from two thousand or so years ago—one peopled by a mother, an adoptive yet loving father, and a child for whom all sacrifices would come to be made.

How could such a story *not* cause confusion these days, when the natural family is so fractured in some places as to render what is called the Holy Family unrecognizable? What, for example, might the sainted adoptive father known as St. Joseph mean to a modern child whose male "parent-figure" is a series of Mom's abusive boy-friends? How does Mary's profound obedience to God ("let it be done to me as You will") make sense to generations taught to regard birth itself as an act of "choice"? How, in short, does the highly individualized West—so individualized that its families are often in a state of permanent reinvention—make sense of a religious tradi-tion premised on such irreducibly familial, rather than individual, dynamics?

The artistic dimension of the Christian story buttresses this same case about the centrality of family in this religion. Some of the great-est paintings in the history of the world revolve around that family tale, replete with Madonnas and nursing infants and other images that painters could draw upon to link to the divine—because they were once commonplaces of ordinary human experience.

But how can those same paintings possibly speak to people today as they once did? How can someone without ordinary experience of teenagers grasp what is really sublime about Botticelli's angels? How do you explain the brilliance of any of Raphael's Madonnas— the way in which they convey Mary's unique place in Christian theology—to an adult who has never held a baby? How does the preternatural horror at the heart of the Christian story—the pre-deceasing of mother by devoted son, brought to almost supernatu-ral life by Michelangelo—even make sense in a world where more and more people have no children, and some have no close family members at all?

In this way, as in others, *family illiteracy breeds religious illiteracy*. This is a corollary of taking the Family Factor into account.

This brings us to yet one more way in which family decline has arguably furthered religious decline. The Christian story may not only be *inaccessible* to some people on account of living in nonnatural families. In an age when many people live lives that contradict the traditional Christian moral code, *the mere existence of that code becomes a lightning rod for criticism and vituperation—which further drives some people away from church.*

This fact is so prosaic as to have been overlooked in secularization literature, to my knowledge; but it is nevertheless true, as plain English goes to show. The decline of Christianity in the West is not just about people ceasing to attend church, or about burning bodies up after death rather than burying them in the ground, or about otherwise simply failing to observe what are judged to be inconvenient rituals. It is also about the increasing hostility that the mere existence of Christian beliefs attracts in an age when many people live in tacit or open defiance of church tenets.

This is a challenge, to put it mildly, that previous generations of Christians did not have to grapple with, at least not on today's scale. To put the conflict into plain English: if your parents are divorced, you might well find positively offensive Jesus Christ's injunctions against divorce. At a minimum, you will almost certainly find the judgment disagreeable, likely a disincentive to entertain the Christian faith. Similarly, if you have been adopted and raised by two lesbians, say, you may find simply unfathomable the church's traditional teaching (shared by traditional Judaism and traditional Islam) against homosexuality—and undoubtedly, to judge by the public record of what is said in cases like that, your adoptive parents are likely to feel the same.

Here we arrive at another unseen engine of secularization, and a crucial one. People do not like to be told they are wrong, or that those whom they love have done wrong. But Christianity cannot help sending that message, however tacitly *or* overtly, without abandoning some of the first and core precepts hammered out from Jesus and the apostles on down. In an age where nontraditional and antitraditional families and even nonfamilies abound, there are more and more people who are bound to take offense at certain teachings in the Judeo-Christian heritage. It is in this way that broken and frayed homes not only interrupt the transmission of the Christian message: in some cases, *they provide the emotional material for a whole new barrier wall to Christian belief.*

Again, there are times when plain English helps more than do abstractions about the "transvaluation of values" or "the disenchantment of the world" or even "secularization" itself. If you spend your alternate-custody weekends happily with your father and his new wife you may find intolerable the traditional Christian idea that so long as your mother is alive, your father is committing adultery and risking hell. Similarly, the very idea of being punished in eternity for fornication may strike you as bizarre under any circumstance—especially if you've been sexually active, and on the Pill since you were fifteen years old. In a hundred ways just like these, traditional teachings at the core of Christianity—teachings still held by the Catholic Church, and to a lesser or negligible degree in the churches of Protestant Christianity—are not only difficult when considered from the point of view of many modern people; they are positively puzzling to some and openly resented by others.

Consider the way this head-on collision—between traditional church teachings on the one hand and the fact that plenty of people today live in contradiction of those teachings on the other—plays out as a matter on the global stage. In September 2011, Pope Benedict traveled to Berlin in his home country of Germany (on what is formally known as an "apostolic" trip). In all, one might have expected this trip to be what well-wishers hoped it would be before the fact: a homecoming of sorts for the aging pope, a refreshing trip by an especially distinguished son to the country of his birth.

Yet it was not—and the main *reason* it was not is the distance between the way people live in secular Europe and the way that Christian doctrine teaches that people ought to live. Because of that conflict, the pope becomes a lightning rod for all that people resent about Christianity—as was inadvertently illustrated by that German excursion. As the *New York Times* noted, for example, the pope "was welcomed at Bellevue Palace by President Christian Wulff, a Catholic who divorced and remarried." He was hosted in Berlin by "the gay Catholic mayor, Klaus Wowereit." In Potsdamer Platz, crowds turned out to protest traditional church teachings on homosexuality and contraception. "His policies on condoms are as good as murder," one protester explained.[4]

To be sure—and this has also been true of Benedict's other European forays—the pope's visit had its upside as well, including in this case a Mass for seventy thousand in the Olympic Stadium, as well as diplomatic religious meetings and other work. Even so, the public fury directed at the Catholic Church for refusing to abandon the teachings about sexual morality that are now hated here and there across the Continent did not abate. As one German journalist issuing a rare defense of Benedict in *Der Spiegel* noted, "I am almost frightened by the rage that is greeting the pope."[5]

Much the same hostility has attended Benedict's other travels across Europe during the last few years, again for the same reasons. Once more, from the point of view of the faithful, the trips were successes in their own right and included record crowds, particularly of young people. But they also increasingly attract what is obviously a growing hostile sentiment toward Christianity—more specifically, toward traditional Christian doctrine.

In August 2011, to take another example, a trip to Spain for World Youth Day was greeted with violent protests.[6] Though the ostensible reason was economic—the cost of the papal trip was partially subsidized by the Spanish government—economics alone clearly didn't explain the reaction; as the government argued in its own defense, the trip was expected to generate more in tourist revenues than it cost. As had happened in Barcelona the year before, many of the protest signs concerned Church teachings on homosexuality. In London in 2010, similarly, some twenty thousand turned out to protest the pope, and leading atheists suggested that he be arrested.[7]

The unique fury that the pope—who is of course synecdoche for the Catholic Church—attracts across Europe today is not due to priestly sex scandals alone. Most likely, the fury is due instead to exactly what the noisy protesters say it is: the unwanted persistence of Catholic Church teachings about sexuality and the family. As the most visible proxy on earth for those teachings, the pope now cannot help but attract the anger of all those people who do not agree, do not want to agree, or simply fail to understand how anyone could believe what two thousand years of Christian teachers have had to say about these matters. Nor is the next pope, or the next, likely to escape the same fate.

Why should people who do not believe any of these teachings repudiate them so ferociously in public? Why not simply shrug and shake their heads over the backward and irrelevant teachings of an institution that (they think) is going the way of the buggy whip? What we might call (to riff on Peter Berger) the furious *irreligiosity* of today's anti-Christian sentiment is a deep mystery, and one that should be meditated upon at length somewhere else.

For purposes of understanding the Family Factor, though, the hostile reception greeting Benedict in many parts of the West these days is more emblematic testimony to this fact: *the decline of the family has contributed to the decline of Christianity in more ways than one.* It has rendered some people less capable of understanding what life with a protective, loving father could be like. It has left others feeling annoyed and on the defensive about church teachings, either on their own part or that of others near and dear to them (mothers, fathers, friends, etc.). And the simple ubiquity of the modern varieties of un- and anti-Christian behavior further erodes the traditional understanding of right and wrong in these matters by sheer repetition. After all, many people seem to reason, if there really is a hell for these sorts of things, isn't just about everyone they know going to end up there? It is a thought impossible for many people in a secular modern society to believe; and so they don't.

In short, the fracturing of the family combined with the sexual revolution has put a great many people in the West on a collision course with certain fundamental teachings of the Christian faith. Church officials often wring their hands about getting out the "positive" side of those teachings, and one can understand why. But what is less clear is how many understand the deeper reason for their difficulty: that the unprecedented proliferation of weakened natural families and nontraditional quasi-families has left a great many individuals resistant as they never were before to fundamental features of the Christian moral code.

What has been sketched in this chapter is an alternative theory of how Christianity has tended to come and go in the modern world—one that understands family and faith as a double helix.

The conventional causal chain, as seen earlier, runs something like this. One by one, and thanks mostly to the Enlightenment, a few brave souls in Europe came to recognize the charlatanry of the Continent's historic Jewish and Christian faiths. As they did, it became clear that more and more people would eventually come to their point of view—that such a transformation is ultimately inevitable and, once widespread enough, would usher in a new and better era of history. ("There never was a greater event—and on account of it, all who are born after us belong to a higher history than any history hitherto!" as Nietzsche's parable of the madman has it.)

Given the evidence we have seen about the family's role in faith, we can augment that story line as follows. As secularization theorists correctly point out, urbanization is closely linked with smaller families. Following the industrial revolution, many Western people started having smaller families and more chaotic families on account of their moves into cities.

Then came another series of shocks that further weakened family bonds: the legalization of divorce, the particularly momentous invention of modern contraception, the consequent increasing destigmatization of out-of-wedlock births, and the rest of the factors discussed at greater length in chapters 3 and 4. Many of these changes were then given even more force by related changes in Protestant theology, chapter 6, that unwittingly amounted to more blows against an institution already being roundly battered. Thus the severely weakened Western family ceased to transmit Christianity among its shrinking generations as it once had.

Of course this account leaves out other world-historical dramas playing out parallel to this one, including the historical struggles between church and state in Western Europe that also had some part in the de-powering of the Christian churches there. But if those de-powerings—beginning with the demise of the idea of the divine right of kings—had made secularism inevitable, then we cannot explain the enduring power of Christianity in the advanced United States, or its positive victories these days in what is called the Global South. Historical events in Europe, therefore—though obviously part of the great puzzle—go only some distance toward explaining how the West really lost God.

## The Future of Faith and Family:
## The Case for Pessimism

I F THE ARGUMENT of this book is correct—if the success of Christianity in the West is indeed dependent in large part on the success of the natural family, as well as vice versa—then there seems at first to be one way, and only one way, of reading the barometer of current times. That is to say, the forecast of further decline in both institutions, family and faith, practically makes itself.

After all, it hardly matters which proxy one uses for the overall health of the Western family. Nearly every one points downward, and some appear to be in free fall. Across the advanced nations, the intact married family with children is a diminishing percentage of households. Fewer people are having children; fewer people who *are* having children are able to sustain intact two-parent homes for them to grow up in; and institutional substitutes for the family, from day care in early life to nursing home care at the end, have syncopated and interrupted the familial rhythms of birth and dependence and death as never before in history.

Taken together, these and related indicators suggest a Sisyphean struggle for the natural family, both as a vibrant institution and as a social norm—and once again, as the family goes, so go the churches. Yet even that formulation does not do justice to the dramatic demographic landscape of the West's immediate future. Let us put some statistical flesh on that picture of current trends, the better to understand just how inimical to family revival the times really are.

*Fewer people are getting married.*

Recent work by American scholars in particular has lately added one other new and perhaps unexpected detail to the decline in the marriage rate: it has fallen most among the worse-off, i.e., the very people arguably most in need of the stability and other resources that marriage confers.

To quote Charles Murray once more, summarizing the last fifty years of U.S. statistics, "Over the last half century, marriage has become the fault line dividing the American classes."[1] Similarly, writes W. Bradford Wilcox in a report cited earlier in this book titled *When Marriage Disappears*, "In the last four decades, moderately educated Americans have seen their rates of divorce and nonmarital childbearing rise, while their odds of wedded bliss have fallen, to the point where their family lives look more and more like those of the least-educated Americans (defined here as having no high-school degree) who make up 12 percent of the adult population aged 25–60. By contrast, marriage trends among highly educated Americans have largely stabilized since the 1970s."[2]

Moreover, considering the economic advantages of getting married and staying married—particularly the beneficial effects on family income—the fact that marriage appears more and more to be a luxury item enjoyed by the uppermost classes will surely only exacerbate the sense that social and economic inequality in America are on the rise. This larger trend of exacerbated social tension also cannot possibly be of benefit to Christian churches, given their insistence on the value of every human soul and their consequent aversion both theological and pragmatic toward class warfare.

As for family trends in Europe, let us look only glancingly at what are said to be the more "traditional" Catholic countries of Italy and Spain. Though divorce was not ratified in Italy until 1974, and historically remained low by the standards of other European nations, the past ten years have seen a soaring of marital breakups; according to the research institute Eures, for example, divorce in Italy rose 45 percent from 2000 to 2002 alone.[3] Between 1995 and 2005, similarly, the number of nonmarital births doubled.[4] "Catholic" Spain, or at least large swaths of it, looks similar. As in Italy, nonmarital births more than doubled in the decade between 1995 and 2005.[5] Catholic Spain's divorce rate is the highest in Europe.[6] The family trends subversive of Christianity itself show no sign of abating anywhere in the West.

*Fewer people are having children.*

As is now familiar fact, generations of Europeans have decided against reproducing themselves. So few children are now being born into non-Muslim families that experts have coined the phrase "demographic winter" to describe the world to come.

But it is not only in Europe, as we have seen, that a great many people have voted with their pills against having babies. Apart from the most religious, the birthrate is trending downward almost everywhere—including well beyond the West itself. More babies, as we have seen, equal more God, beginning with the simple arithmetic according to which families with children are more likely to be in church than are single people or families without children. So will fewer babies mean less God? The corollary seems inescapable.

*Fewer people who are having children are sustaining intact two-parent homes for them to grow up in.*

There are many ways of bending and breaking the natural family, as seen here and there across the pages of this book. Consider all those single-mother homes. What used to be called "illegitimacy" is not only no longer stigmatized; across the West, it is so widespread as to be unremarkable in society both polite and otherwise. "In much of Europe and the Americas," Phillip Longman observed in a piece on what he called the "sustainable demographic dividend," "from the United Kingdom to the United States, from Mexico to Sweden, out-of-wedlock births are the 'new normal,' with 40 percent or more of all children born without married parents."[7]

That same "new normal" achieved another landmark in early 2012, much commented upon at the time, when over half of all births to mothers in their twenties occurred to unmarried women for the first time in the United States.

Again, it does not matter whether the reader regards that landmark as a "social catastrophe," as *National Review* editor Rich Lowry wrote, or alternatively whether one celebrates being "knocked up and proud," as a differently minded piece on the *Huffington Post* once put the point.[8] What does matter is that the spread of nontraditional families further weakens the traditional family in another way: because nontraditional and antitraditional families encourage skepticism and even mockery of the notion that the traditional family is a legitimate norm. Some do so inadvertently—as when, say, the sheer volume of fatherless homes leads people to treat all families with moral equivalence for the sake of politesse. Some, by contrast, attack the traditional family quite consciously, usually in an effort to compel acknowledgment of their own familial mutation. But whether intended or unintended, aided and abetted by the welfare state or not, nontraditional families and antitraditional families cannot help but serve as living contradictions of the principle that the natural family is any kind of ideal.

For purposes of pondering the future of faith and the family, therefore, the fact that the nontraditional home is here to stay spells problems for the vitality of Christianity in a number of ways—not least of which, to mention one more factor, is the antagonism that some people feel toward what they deride as the Ozzie and Harriet model. Look again at that quote from the *Huffington Post*, which is emblematic of the rhetorical belligerence that critics of the traditional family bring to this conversation. For reasons that are unclear, it appears that those who would retool the natural family in more progressive directions do not merely seek to be included in the institution's ranks. Very often, they seem to regard their social inclusion as a zero-sum game—i.e., as a prize that cannot be had without denigrating the more traditional forms of family life.[9] This kind of simmering antagonism toward the traditional family cannot help but chip away further at the confidence that individual men and women who *are* in traditional homes bring to the many sacrifices demanded of those who labor to build competent natural families. Any way one looks at it, this dynamic amounts to throwing more stones at an institution already pelted for decades by the sexual revolution—and much else.

And what, meanwhile, of Christianity itself? How will *that* institution fare in a world where the natural family recedes as a social model?

Anyone reading this far in these pages will already guess this book's answer. How—apart from the Holy Spirit—*could* Christianity thrive and prosper at such a time, given what appears to be its multilayered dependence on the selfsame battered family?

After all, and as we have seen, Christianity needs the family in more ways than one. It leans on the family to transmit the Word through generations. It needs the analogy of the family to tell its most fundamental story, the creation of the Son of God as man. It needs—or at least appears to benefit from—that elemental, powerful feeling of connection to the supernatural that is a commonplace of the experience of birth for many parents. And from the sheer point of view of institutional health and vitality, the churches have also been boosted by the similarly powerful desire of mothers and fathers to situate their children in a like-minded moral community—the phenomenon reviewed earlier in these pages of kids "driving parents to church." In all these ways that we have visited, and probably in others too, the "Family Factor" has contributed since the beginning to Christianity's very existence.

At a time when more and more Western men and women are choosing to live in nontraditional or antitraditional family settings—or for that matter, in no families at all—how could the churches be in any straits other than dire?

Let us drive the nails in deeper. In earlier chapters, we looked from different angles at the much discussed question of "American exceptionalism," or the seeming puzzle that Americans generally have been and remain more religious than similarly well-off Europeans. I have argued that what is called American exceptionalism is really not a puzzle at all, but rather just a hitherto misunderstood offshoot of the fact that Americans have more marriage and children than Europeans, and that marriage and children as this book argues are inextricably tethered to the Christian religion. All this remains sound logic, as far as it goes.

But now that we are contemplating the (admittedly rather large) question of Christianity's future, we must ask another question: Is America really so exceptional after all? Americans may yet exhibit higher levels of practice and belief than do Europeans; studies seem to say as much, and experts have been struck by the same disparity. But if we look instead at the family patterns across the West— patterns that, as I have argued, are bound to continue to have an enormous impact on Western Christianity—can we really sustain the thought that Americans are so inexplicably special in their clinging to religion? Do we not see instead that America in the longer run is heading toward the same de-Christianized future as large parts of the Continent—only at a somewhat more sedate pace?

Look again at the rapidly increasing share of children born out of wedlock. "Between 1970 and 2009," as a report from Child Trends summarized the numbers, "the percentage of all births that took place outside of marriage increased from 11 to 41 percent."[10] This means that illegitimacy in the general population is now far higher than it was when Senator Daniel Patrick Moynihan, then assistant secretary of labor, published his fabled Report in 1965 ("The Negro Family: The Case For National Action"). The focus of that report, which would go on to become one of the most contested government documents of the century, was what he regarded as the alarming rate of illegitimacy among American blacks. Yet this rate then, however unprecedented at the time, was a relatively mere 23.6 percent— "mere," that is, when measured against today's rate for all births in America, which is fully 17 points higher.[11]

Moreover, the out-of-wedlock birthrate in America today fairly begs to be compared not only to the rate in America in the past, but also to rates in *European* countries not so long ago—a comparison that once again raises the question of just how different and exceptional America is . . . or is not. The proportion of live births outside of marriage in the United States today is actually *higher* than the average for the European Union.[12] Finland—to take a particularly striking example—had a 2010 out-of-wedlock birth ratio *identical* to America's today.[13] In 1980, to offer one more example that may come as a surprise, less than 40 percent of Swedish babies were being born out of wedlock—a fact that is somewhat astonishing, given that Sweden was attracting international attention even back then as a petri dish for illegitimacy rates never before seen in the advanced

West.[14] Yet by our own day, the United States is further along than Sweden was then in its share of babies born to unmarried parents.

What are all these numbers, but statistical shorthand for the message that the United States is indeed home to the same patterns of family and marital decline now defining much of Western Europe? It is hard to make a case for American "exceptionalism" in family matters when a few decades of comparative family statistics like these are added to the mix—in other words, when America appears are only a few years or decades away from where, say, the Netherlands is right now.

Now let us consider some of the implications for Christianity of these enormous numbers of (typically) fatherless children, this new norm across the West. These rates of illegitimacy *alone* make any hypothetical Christian renaissance amount to an extraordinary uphill climb. That is because what used to be called "illegitimacy" puts people at odds with the traditional Christian moral code. Of course—to clarify the theological point—having a child out of wedlock is no more a permanent roadblock from the *church's* perspective, even in the strictest churches, than is homosexuality, adultery, abortion, or any of the other behaviors called sins by Christianity. The churches, as pastors like to remind, exist for sinners, not saints.

But all that, however laudable, is irrelevant. The point is that out-of-wedlock births institutionalized on today's scale work against the churches in a different way. Once again, at stake here are some fundamental issues of religious anthropology, or how people come to understand, believe, and practice religion in the first place—or not. And one thing that the experience of illegitimacy does is to pit a great many people's actual *experience* of the world—say, of growing up with an absent or delinquent father—against the very foundation of the Judeo-Christian tradition: to repeat, the notion that God can be understood as a benevolent, protecting male parent. How can that relationship between creature and Creator be understood when the very word "father" may be associated more with negative than with positive characteristics?

Similarly, how can the story of the Holy Family be understood in a world where a family is increasingly said to be whatever anyone in possession of voluntary associations wants it to be? It was one thing, say, for children to understand the figure of the adoptive father Joseph at a time when most came from traditional homes, and Joseph was easily grasped as someone "like" one's own father. But to ask children who do not have such protectors to understand what it is like to have one, and to encourage them to build their lives and souls around a concept that some will find elusive or even incredible is a very different conceptual challenge—and one that, to repeat, has not been faced by Christian leaders of the past, because it did not exist in the past on anything like today's scale. Once again, the realities of today's intentionally created and often fractured family life potentially impede grasping Christianity or finding it appealing, often in subtle and unexpected ways.[15] On balance, these relatively new social realities have to be a net minus for Christianity's future prospects.

Moreover, and leaving all those births aside, there also remain the many millions of Western men, women, and children affected by divorce, as well as the smaller but influential numbers of anti-traditional families featuring same-sex marriage, androgyny, polygamy, same-sex adoption, and other creative attempts to redefine the Western family. Some spokespeople for these efforts, as we have seen, are overtly hostile both to the traditional family as well as to traditional Christian teaching. And even without those influential hostile advocates, the mere proliferation of broken homes across the West poses one more problem of its own for receptivity to the Christian message.

That final problem is the defensiveness that those from nontraditional or antitraditional families feel toward the traditional family held up as the norm by the Christian church. This may seem abstract, but in reality it is anything but. "My family is just as good as yours" are surely the first fighting words any child ever learns, whether the family in question is the Medicis vs. the Sforzas, the Hatfields vs. the McCoys—or the child from a nontraditional home defending his domestic turf as he sees it against another child enjoying the benefits of biological parents.

The more nontraditional and antitraditional families become the norm, the more difficult it becomes to defend the traditional family, let alone to grant it any privileged position in policy or anywhere else. The question of who benefits and who loses in this arrangement will be argued over for a long time to come. But surely the biggest loser is plain already—and that is the church that has made defense of the family a cornerstone of its teaching, both benefiting from that unique sanctification and in turn reinforcing it.

Once again, it appears that one spiral in the helix can only be as strong as the other—and given all we now know about the diminution of the family in our time, the diminution of Christianity alongside it seems the educated forecast most in keeping with the social and demographic weather.

# ≈ 9

## The Future of Christianity and the Family: The Case for Optimism

As the preceding chapter goes to show, the case for pessimism about the future of Christianity in the West is a powerful one—to say nothing of intuitively obvious, even and perhaps especially to readers who wish matters were otherwise.

But is it the only plausible scenario? In a paradoxical twist, the case for optimism about the twin futures of Christianity and the family shares some of the same key facts as the case for pessimism. The case for optimism, one might say, is more or less the case for pessimism turned on its head and examined from a radically different angle.

Begin by meditating briefly on an insight from the late sociologist Pitirim Sorokin, founder of Harvard's Department of Sociology and one of the most seminal social thinkers of the mid-twentieth century. Sorokin wrote at a time when sociology was performed not with statistical fine work—the equivalent in painting of pointillism, say—but rather with the broadest possible brush and on wide historical canvases. As it happens, in one of his influential works, *Man and Society in Calamity* (1942), Sorokin dedicated his powers to a project with possible implications for our own. He sought to disentangle the ways in which historical catastrophes of various kinds—principally wars, famines, and pestilence—end up setting countervailing social forces into motion.

To borrow from his analysis and to apply it to these matters of faith and family raises an intriguing question—namely, whether the situation in which the Western world currently finds itself might now qualify as a decline that is just thoroughgoing enough, and just serious enough, to initiate its own reversal.

"Calamities," Sorokin observed, "generate two opposite movements in different sections of the population. One is a trend toward unreligiousness and demoralization; the other is a trend toward extreme religious, spiritual, and moral exaltation."[1] Reviewing large chunks of religious and other history, including some from beyond the West and Christianity alone, Sorokin believed that he spied a general rule: that "the principal steps in the progress of mankind toward a spiritual religion and a noble code of ethics have been taken *primarily* under the impact of great catastrophes [emphasis added]." Calamity, he concluded, is not only one possible inducement to religious revival; it may even be the *sine qua non* thereof.[2]

How does Sorokin's work on calamity and his vision of religion rising from the ashes of catastrophe fit the facts of today's time? At a minimum, the case could be made. Perhaps the first and most compelling pertinent fact suggesting the relevance of Sorokin's argument is this: the financial crisis that crashed upon the Western world in 2008. This is, as mentioned earlier, a multifaceted crisis that continues to shake the very political, social, and economic foundations of the advanced nations. This very crisis may ultimately contain the seeds of a turnaround for the institution of the family—and with it, for the institutions whose fortunes are inseparable from that of the family itself, i.e., the Christian churches.

Sorokin is not the only authority who can be brought to bear in defense of such a forecast. Over the years, some other people with sharp and educated eyes have also recognized the possibility of just such a dynamic. Their collective case reads something like this. The decline of the natural family has been taken more or less in stride depending upon how secure societies have been about the state's ability to do what the family once did—in other words, upon Western affluence. It is affluence that has effectively bankrolled today's rates of divorce, single motherhood, cohabitation, and the rest of the modern splintering of the family unit. To put the point another way, family breakup is a luxury item—in the sense that it is terrifically expensive not only for the individuals affected (just ask any single mother how much child care costs), but also for the societies constantly reinventing institutions to take up the slack.

So what happens if the affluence taken for granted during most of the postwar years isn't forever after all? That is the question stalking not only Europe, but the entire West. Writing thirty years before the economic collapse of 2008, sociologist David Popenoe eerily foresaw that one consequence of diminished affluence might be the most unexpected of all: namely, the possibility of reviving the institution of the family. After all, he observed, families perform a function little appreciated yet crucial to all societies: they do for free what would otherwise cost money to accomplish. And "the importance of this family care-giving function," as he wrote, "becomes clear when we consider what might happen if modern societies ever again fall into a serious economic depression."[3]

In the case of Sweden, for example, it appeared as of Popenoe's writing (1988) that the most advanced welfare state on earth had indeed managed the seemingly impossible—i.e., the substitution of what had been largely unpaid family services by the paid services of the welfare state. Yet imagine as he does that Sweden were to suffer a loss of the prosperity that made all same substitution possible—which is, to repeat, an exercise easier post-2008 than it was thirty years before. What would happen then? As Popenoe asked, "Will Swedish households and families, suddenly cut off from government services, be able to survive through voluntary mutual aid as well as will households and families in societies where families have maintained to a larger degree the practice of self-sufficiency?"[4]

In other words, will the post-welfare state do what the agricultural state did for many centuries—restore economic value to childbearing and marriage and family ties, in however inadvertent and default a way?

Again, Popenoe proposed this scenario well before the long-term consequences of Western welfare states crossed with Western fertility implosion became altogether apparent. During the past ten years or so, other thinkers have also started worrying over what that collision means for the future of the West.[5] As Theodore Dalrymple, a British psychiatrist and pundit, has put the point well, "The incontinent spending of many European governments, which awarded whole populations unearned benefits at the expense of generations to come, has . . . produced a crisis not merely economic but social, political, and even civilizational."[6]

Now let us look more closely at that crisis. It is also, perhaps above all, a family crisis: meaning that it has been brought about by the welfare state stepping in and doing what were historically the duties of the family. These include but are not limited to the most primal duties of all: care of the young, the sick, and the old.

These duties have been transferred in the modern West from families to the state for deep reasons. Perhaps the primary one is that in a time when family breakup has reached current levels, the family is too frail a reed to be counted upon for the levels of responsibility known to history hitherto. It is one thing to expect a single mother to be able to care for a school-age child; quite another to add an indigent parent or two and a chronic illness to the mix.

Second, as reiterated here and there already, families are smaller now. The many (mostly female) hands throughout history that have soothed the sick, tended the hearth, rocked the cradle, put on daily meals, and shouldered most of the rest of the domestic burden are now fewer, both literally and figuratively. Many women no longer live near extended family and hence do not enjoy such a network—and even those who do are pulled by the gravitational force of the paid marketplace.

Yet when the ultimately unsustainable welfare states of the West shrink, as they are just now beginning to do in a process that may go on for centuries, so it is the family—and only the family—that can be imagined stepping into the vacuum. The power of the state and the power of the family are at odds with one another. In fact most of the time, as we noted in chapter 8, they amount to a zero-sum game. As Milton Friedman once put it: "Consider Social Security. The young have always contributed to the support of the old. Earlier, the young helped their own parents out of a sense of love and duty. They now contribute to the support of someone else's parents out of compulsion and fear. The voluntary transfers strengthened the bonds of the family; the compulsory transfers weaken those bonds."[7]

Moreover, one need not imagine a full-scale crisis to see how the pressures of a shrinking and aging Western population might force a new consideration of the family. To quote social scientist Stanley Kurtz again, usefully staking out the particulars:

> It wouldn't take a full-scale economic meltdown, or even a relative disparity in births between fundamentalists and secularists, to change modernity's course. Chronic low-level economic stress in a rapidly aging world may be enough. There is good reason to worry about the fate of elderly boomers with fragile families, limited savings, and relatively few children to care for them. A younger generation of workers will soon feel the burden of paying for the care of this massive older generation. The nursing shortage,

already acute, will undoubtedly worsen, possibly foreshadowing shortages in many other categories of workers. Real estate values could be threatened by population decline. And all these demographically tinged issues, and more, will likely become the media's daily fare. In such an atmosphere, a new set of social values could emerge along with a fundamentally new calculation of personal interest. Modernity itself may come in for criticism even as a new appreciation for the benefits of marriage and parenting might emerge.[8]

Are we seeing before us in 2012 the beginnings of an instantiation of Sorokin's point about calamity? Are those who spy a family phoenix arising from the ashes of the welfare state correct? In fact, there is tantalizing, albeit preliminary, evidence that just such an unforeseen consequence of the West's economic morass may already have begun. Consider the matter of divorce. According to figures kept by the American Academy of Matrimonial Lawyers, for example, the divorce rate in the United States dropped 24 percent in 2008 and 57 percent in 2009—that is, immediately following the housing collapse.[9] The rates then began creeping back up in 2010: in other words, as the American economy improved a bit. The president of the AAML, like other insiders watching the trend, drew the obvious conclusion: the drop was a response to the financial hits many were taking. Less money equaled putting off breaking up some homes.

Or consider another unintended consequence of the economic crisis that might also amount to a boost for the natural family: the return of many adult children to the homes of their parents. According to the U.S. Census Bureau, "59 percent of men age 18 to 24 and 50 percent of women that age resided in their parents' home in 2011, up from 53 percent and 46 percent, respectively, in 2005."[10] So prevalent has the phenomenon become that pundits have even coined a term to describe it: "boomerang generation." Yet might not this movement back to the nest, though undertaken for reasons of empty young wallets, nevertheless have an unintentional consequence—the strengthening of the family unit via this inadvertent restoration of the extended family? And might it not in turn have another unseen outcome—leading some people back to church because they are *living* again in families, rather than by themselves?

It is interesting, as well, that both marriage rates and childbearing among relatively affluent educated American women now seem to be slightly on the uptick. Sociologists are debating why, and no one knows. Is it so unthinkable that at least in part, learning from the recent past—in particular from the manifold problems often seen in nontraditional family structures—might be part of the backstory to that change? Or that over time, the accumulated knowledge of those problems will continue to increase incentives toward the natural family? Single motherhood, for example, though cheered by feminists a generation ago in the name of "liberation," is now widely seen for what it really is: an inhumanly difficult task for almost any woman to execute, let alone the poorer and more vulnerable women among whom it has become common.[11]

Perhaps someday today's rates of fatherless homes will come to be seen as the equivalent of William Hogarth's depiction of the gin alleys in London in the mid-1700s—a regrettable fact to which all human beings may be prone, but that society, seeing the unfortunate consequences for some people, has nevertheless decided collectively to try to reduce.

Of course it is possible that the economic crisis of the modern welfare state will also have the opposite effect of weakening the family rather than enhancing it. After all, the same media that report the divorce rate to be in decline also report that other people have postponed their decisions about marrying or having children until the financial climate improves. Maybe less money also equals less family, at least for some people. Like any other great social phenomenon that changes lives, the crisis of the Western welfare state can be expected to have a multiplicity of effects.

In sum, though, it is not *impossible* to imagine a turnaround of some kind in family decline across the West—if only because the economics of subsidizing such decline have become untenable. And because of that, it is indeed possible to imagine a world that learns from its experience of those problems that the natural family has been an undervalued stock with strong fundamentals. Surely at least some people are already inferring that the ever-more expensive state can no longer be trusted to do what the family does better and cheaper. Bit by bit, given changing minds, the incentives toward maintaining a family network might come to trump some of the disincentives that the affluent society inadvertently puts in the way of such efforts.

In other words, a revival of the natural family may seem unlikely, but it is not out of the question. And if *that* revival is possible—*pace* the great thinkers of modernity—then neither is it impossible to imagine a revival of Christianity because of the dictum discussed earlier: *one spiral in the double helix is only as strong as the other*. Given the close relationship now established between the strength of the natural family and the strength of Christianity, Christian revival could accompany such a revival of the family.

One more point weighing hard against pessimism is intellectual humility. Claiming inevitability for *any* social trend is a risky business, as modernity itself goes to show—including the inevitability of family or religious decline.

After all, the historical road behind us is littered with discarded prognostications and overruled claims of inevitability; why should these be different? Is low fertility, for example, an unchangeable social fact of the future? History itself via its variations suggests otherwise. The aristocrats in the late Roman Empire, for example, very nearly stopped having children; so did much of Europe, a century before the Pill was even invented. These are examples of how the natural family has weakened in different places and times, in response to different events. There are also converse examples of its strengthening. To the surprise of almost all demographers, for example, and as we have seen, the middle of the twentieth century saw a "baby boom" across the Western world. Various governments are currently tinkering with tax codes to see if the birthrate will go up, to some limited but clear success in France, for example. Would more radical financial incentives have more radical effects? Only experiments of the future will tell. Meanwhile, agnosticism about the demography of the future would seem the most prudent stand.

And what about other proxies for the natural family, such as marriage? These too have fluctuated throughout history. Moreover, as the work of the great Harvard sociologist Carle Zimmerman in particular goes to show, the family throughout history has shown a pattern of strengthening following periods of decay which have brought on mounting social costs—work highly germane to our own situation, and one more reason for believing that family decline, in Western Europe or elsewhere, may not be inevitable after all.[12]

As for the decline of Christianity, it too appears no more inevitable under the lens of history than any other movements famous for claiming inevitability on their own behalf. After all, what might family revival mean for Christianity? If the argument presented here is correct, and people come to religious practice much of the time, or even just *some* of the time, because of their experience of the natural family rather than vice versa, then a very different verdict about the fate of religiosity might yet be written on the decades and centuries to come. If there is a family renaissance, there may be a religious renaissance too. And a religious renaissance in turn would make that family renaissance stronger for the same reasons already seen—because strengthening one spiral cannot help but reinforce the other.

Moreover, we can see that religion's obituary is no more assured than that of the family, for the same reason—it has thrived in too many places and times and diminished in too many others to suggest that any iron law of progressive deterioration is at work. Remember that the last boomlet of faith across the West—during the years, as we have seen, immediately following World War II—remains something that happened in the lifetime of at least some people reading these words.

That is to say: It is not only in the remote fog of the past that the churches managed to hold their own, but also in the not-very-distant Western past. Consider this evocative account of those years by Will Herberg, the foremost sociologist of religion in America during the mid-twentieth century. So religious had the United States become that in his classic work, *Protestant-Catholic-Jew*, this renowned authority of the scene could observe that:

> Through the nineteenth century and well into the twentieth America knew the militant secularist, the atheist or "freethinker," as a familiar figure in cultural life, along with considerably larger numbers of "agnostics" who would have nothing to do with churches and refused to identify themselves religiously. . . . The village atheist is a vanishing figure. . . . Indeed, their kind of anti-religion is virtually meaningless to most Americans today. . . . This was not always the case; that it is the case today there can be no reasonable doubt. *The pervasiveness of religious identification*

*may safely be put down as a significant feature of the America that has emerged in the past quarter of a century* [emphasis added].[13]

In the gap between his assessment of the religiosity of his day and our own assessment of its decline less than sixty years later, we see once more that religion ebbs and flows in the world, including even the modern world, in ways more mysterious than we first understood—and that point away from the conclusion that decline is inevitable.

One final and counterintuitive fact from which those on the side of religion and the family might take comfort in the future is what might be called Christianity's ultimate "secret weapon"—its manifest and singular and even somewhat perverse track record of resonating unexpectedly across disparate cultures and times.

Throughout its history, after all, the Christian church has found no shortage of converts, martyrs, and other witnesses who embrace it for exactly the reason that so many today despise that institution: exactly *because* it is believed to be the unchanging repository of truth and as such, immune from the importunings of its surroundings. In his classic work *A History of Christianity*, first published in 1953, the great Yale historian Kenneth Scott Latourette ponders a genuine conundrum concerning the origins of Western civilization:

> How shall we account for the fact that, beginning as what to the casual observer must have appeared a small and obscure sect of Judaism, before its first five centuries were out had become the faith of the Roman state and of the vast majority of the population of that realm and had spread eastward as far as Central Asia and probably India and Ceylon and westward into far away Ireland?[14]

Of course there is no single answer to his question. Nonetheless, the master historian himself cites Christianity's surprisingly strong combination of flexibility and inclusivity on the one hand and "uncompromising adherence to its basic convictions" on the other. "In striking contrast with the easy-going syncretism" of the time, he emphasizes, "Christianity was adamant on what it regarded as basic principles.[15] Similarly, in a well-known essay defending the church's continuing ban on artificial contraception, twentieth-century phi-losopher Elizabeth Anscombe reviewed the early Christian bans on infanticide, abortion, and nonmarital sex, arguing "the known fact that Christianity drew people out of the pagan world, always saying no to these things."[16]

Ironically, therefore, at least from the point of view of today, what many modern people take to be the signal weakness of the Christian creed proved early on to be perhaps its greatest strength. In yet another example of the double helix at work, sociologist Rodney Stark has put these same pieces together in his own explanation of how Christianity grew from a small sect to a world religion—because, he argues, Christianity's prizing of marriage and its ban-ning of infanticide and abortion all contributed to a demographic advantage for believers.[17] Once again, the faith appears to have bol-stered families; and families in turn appear to have been bolstered by faith.

What was true as Christianity took the Greco-Roman world by storm remains true today. The more an age forthrightly rejects the Christian code, the more does the forceful insistence that there is a right and wrong exert a gravitational pull all its own, with or without the demographic advantages of living according to the law. The failure to recognize that power—one experienced by converts from St. Paul, to St. Augustine, to some of the Anglicans studying the catechism today—may be one final and underappreciated way in which the attempt to jettison the traditional code weakened both the natural family on which traditional Christianity depended, and the institutions themselves. But it is one among several other under-rated factors pointing the way toward a possible optimism for those who sense that the end of the story of Christianity in Europe and other parts of the West remains to be written, and that brighter days than these remain to come. Therein—and only therein—lies the case for optimism about the future of family and the faith.

# Conclusion

## Why Does Any of This Matter?

WHAT IS THE "take-home" of these relatively rarified discussions for general readers—the practical implication of all this armchair sociology?

For those interested in that more pragmatic subject, this conclusion will switch gears once more—away from the advancement of a new theory of secularization, which for better or worse is now out of the closet, and toward this sensible and more earthbound question: *Why even bother with all this?*

Why would it matter if the double helix of faith and family were real—if, contrary to current understanding, the health of Christianity somehow depended at least in part on the health of the family? It matters because both believers and unbelievers have a stake in having believers do what they do—and the data that affirm this point comes not from theologians and family-firsters, but rather from secular social science. It makes sense, then, that in these closing pages we visit briefly but in a concentrated way just some of the empirical evidence indicating that <u>both believers *and* secularists benefit in public ways from Christian faith and the natural family</u>—whether they mean to do so or not, and regardless of whether they consider religion itself a toxic issue. Let us make the case in two parts, beginning with religion.

*Does the health of Christianity in the West matter?*
*How and to whom?*

To religious believers, of course, the answers to both of these questions are self-evident. The point of being a Christian is to save one's own soul and to get to heaven. Many tests and requirements might be involved along one's earthly path to that ultimate goal—good works, attendance in church, the practicing of virtues and the resisting of vices, and so on. Yet again from the point of view of the believer, these demands, however strenuous, are actually mere stepping stones to what being a Christian is really all about—which is the pursuit of an eternal space in the kingdom of God.

And so, for example, Christian Samantha volunteers in soup kitchens, serves as a foster parent to a troubled teenager, fundraises by phone for the local unwed mothers' shelter, and otherwise does what she feels compelled to do because of her creed. At the same time, however, these activities are not things she does in and of themselves; they are instead activities that serve a higher purpose—to Samantha's way of thinking, the highest purpose of all.

This is exactly where what might be called the "take-home" of the situation to secularists comes in. What is fascinating about the unintended consequences of Samantha's Christianity is this fact, which cutting-edge social science now illustrates beautifully: what Samantha does in pursuit of the kingdom of Heaven, *even though she does not do these things as ends in themselves,* nevertheless has a great many practical consequences on this earth.

And so the first nonreligious answer to the questions of why these things matter becomes:

*The fate of Christianity matters even to nonbelievers, because Christianity on balance is a force for good in modern society.*

Some people would ferociously dispute that assertion, of course. They would point—as the new atheists point—to the long list of crimes and misdeeds committed in the name of Christianity or by self-professed Christians, including centuries of religious wars, corruption at the highest levels of both church and church-influenced state, seemingly limitless sex scandals, and the rest of the shameful and familiar list of historical iniquities committed by people marching under a crucifix. Church critics and Church-bashers would also point, as we saw in chapter 7, to the much-lamented Christian rule book that restricts human liberty in ways that modern, secularized individuals increasingly find intolerable.

Who can blame them for making the case? There is a reason why the new atheists have had such rhetorical success in invoking Old Testament massacres, the Inquisition, religious wars, corrupt popes, sexual hypocrisy, and other historical examples of churches and especially the Church failing miserably to live up to their creed. Probably nothing has hurt Christianity more in living memory than the priest-boy sex scandals that were finally exhumed and held to light across the West in the 2000s. The fact of Christian leaders exploiting the youngest and most vulnerable with the protection of some of the very people posing as guardians of the young continues to exact a global toll.[1] The enemies of Christianity—for that matter, any readers of the news here and there—can find no shortage of evidence for their anti-Christian manifestoes.

Even so, and without minimizing the dark historical deeds committed by sinners and criminals acting in Christianity's name, the empirical truth—*pace* those dangling handcuffs at the Pope—is that people of this faith are *on balance* a net plus for modern society. All one needs to verify that claim is a quick tour through reliable, intriguing, and perfectly secular social science about the relationship between private religious belief and public action.

This is not to say that people of other faiths have different profiles in generosity, public service, and other forms of altruism summarized below; remember, we are limiting our inquiry here to Christians (though for the record, the evidence does look similar for observant Muslims and Jews).[2] But neither is the evidence of their contributions to society small enough to sweep under any conceptual rug. It is no disservice to Secular Sydney, say, to point out that statistically speaking, Christian Samantha is more likely to be contributing certain benefits to society. Let us count some of the ways.

*Believers give more to charity.*

Recent scholarship has documented a perhaps unexpected and fascinating difference between Western churchgoers and Western seculars: the distinct "charity gap."

In the United States, for example, 91 percent of people who identify themselves as religious conservatives are likely to give to charity, as opposed to 67 percent of those who do not so identify themselves.[3] They also volunteer at a rate 10 points higher than the general population.[4] Or consider a different measure of religiosity than self-description: prayer. People who pray every day are 30 percentage points more likely to give to charity than people who never pray.[5]

These and other arresting numbers testifying to the charity gap can be found in the work of social scientist Arthur Brooks, who is perhaps the best-known numbers expert in the United States on this subject of the relationship between religious believing and charitable giving. But, critics might ask, aren't the religious "only" giving to their own—i.e., to houses of worship? No, they are not, according to Brooks—and when the meaning of "giving" is broadened to include other acts of donation in addition to check-writing, an even starker picture emerges of the contrast between believers and nonbelievers. Religious people, reports Brooks, are also "far more likely to donate blood than secularists, to give food or money to a homeless person, to return change mistakenly given them by a cashier, and to express empathy for less fortunate people."[6]

These are not just American results; they span the West. A European churchgoer, Brooks estimates from the charity numbers, is 30 percentage points more likely than the secularist to volunteer and 15 points more likely to volunteer for even nonreligious charities.[7] In a particularly excellent example comparing secular French people with religious Americans, and holding constant for education, income, age, sex, and marital status, Brooks summarizes that 27 percent of the secular French could be expected to volunteer in a given year—as opposed to 83 percent of the religious Americans.[8]

"Religious people," Brooks summarizes, "are, inarguably, more charitable in *every measurable way* [emphasis in the original]."[9] Of course this does not necessarily make Christian Samantha a better person than Secular Sydney. But what the charity gap does go to show is that what Christianity makes, the world takes.

*Believers live longer and are healthier.*

Following in the tradition of Émile Durkheim, who believed that the atomized nature of modern society was linked to higher rates of modern suicide, secular researchers have also thought to investigate the connections between religious beliefs and other social goods—including mental and physical health.

One particularly comprehensive recent volume, for example, the 2001 *Handbook on Religion and Health*, analyzed over 1,200 studies and other material to find that religion was consistently associated with better mental and physical well-being.[10] "In the vast majority of the cross-sectional studies and prospective cohort studies we identified," the authors summarize, "religious beliefs and practices rooted within established religious traditions were found to be consistently associated with better health and predicted better health over time."

Of particular interest, especially for the West's increasing numbers of graybeards, are two findings. One is the apparent connection between attendance at religious services and mortality itself. In a particularly compelling study published in *Demography* in 1999, for example, researchers used a nationally representative sample of U.S. adults combined with mortality data on those same subjects from a nine-year follow-up period. The results were stark: "Religious involvement," they summarize, "is strongly associated with adult mortality in a graded fashion. Those who never attend services exhibit the highest risk of death, and those who attend more than once a week exhibit the lowest risk."[11]

Just how does the social science language here apply to the realm of everyday life? The researchers do the math: "*This translates into a seven-year difference in life expectancy at age 20 between those who never attend and those who attend more than once a week* [emphasis added]."[12]

As a related matter, people who practice religious beliefs not only live longer, generally speaking, but also appear to be happier in old age. One study in 2007 on "religion and depression in older medical inpatients" found that less religiously observant people were more likely to be depressed, *and* that less religious people were more likely to have depression that was severe.[13] Another study of 850 elderly ill men found similarly that "depressive symptoms were inversely related to religious coping," and that "religious coping was the only baseline variable that predicted lower depression scores at follow-up."[14] Yet another found that when people diagnosed with HIV became more religious, they had slower disease progression four years later than did their less religious counterparts.[15]

*Believers are more likely to be happy.*

Of all the correlations that secular social science has lately drawn between religiosity and its apparent benefits to the believer, this particular connection may be the most heavily and ubiquitously documented.

The Gallup Organization, the National Opinion Research Center, and other institutions dedicated to studying public opinion have repeatedly turned up the finding that religious people are happier than secularists.[16] "In survey after survey," as researcher David G. Myers summarizes of North America and Western Europe in another book that seriously examines the existing research on happiness, "actively religious people have reportedly markedly greater happiness and somewhat greater life satisfaction than their irreligious counterparts."[17] People of faith, he adds, tend to cope with crises somewhat better than people without. They also recover more quickly from ominous life events—including bereavement, divorce, unemployment, and serious illness.[18]

So more God seems to equal more grins. Conversely, studies have also found that religion seems to have a protective effect against negative behaviors. Religious people are less likely to get depressed, less likely to become addicted to alcohol or drugs, and less likely to commit suicide.[19] Apparently, having God as one's copilot reduces the likelihood of too many drinks and other dangerous or self-destructive activities in the cockpit.

*Believers are less likely to commit crime.*

Especially compelling evidence for this claim appears in a landmark book published in 2010 by criminologist Byron Johnson called *More God, Less Crime: Why Faith Matters and How It Could Matter More.* Johnson's ambition was to examine all the studies of the effect of religiosity on crime conducted between 1944 and 2010—a total of 273 different works. His conclusion is that 90 percent of the time, more religion is associated with less crime—and that the sheer number of studies confirming that finding in different ways more than offsets methodological quarrels about what exactly is causing what.[20]

Johnson's work has also been endorsed by the late James Q. Wilson, one of the country's most distinguished social scientists. Reviewing Johnson's book for the *Wall Street Journal*, Wilson singled out as exemplary one particular study by Harvard social economist Richard Freeman. Interviewing over two thousand young black men in inner-city neighborhoods, Freeman found that "going to church," in Wilson's summary, "is associated with substantial differences in how young men behave. More churchgoing, less crime, less alcohol and fewer drugs."[21]

Commenting from outside the academic world, the late evangelical Christian Chuck Colson—whose Prison Fellowship pioneered the effort to use religion as a gravitational force against that of criminality—also affirmed the same link based on his extensive work with actual prisoners. Citing the comparison of prisoners who graduated from the Fellowship's "InnerChange Freedom Initiative" in Texas with others who did not, Colson pointed to the fact that "after two years the post-release re-incarceration rate is 8 percent for our graduates against 20.3 percent for the matched comparison group."[22] "We've been right all along," Colson concluded.

"The Gospel changes lives, and it's the best hope for keeping men and women out of prison."

The notion that more Christianity means less crime has also been argued outside American borders. In a 2004 book called *The Strange Death of Moral Britain*, sociologist Christie Davies of Reading maintains at length that the collapse of Christianity in Britain had been accompanied by a striking rise in deviant behaviors, including drug and alcohol abuse and violent crime, which he attributed to the fact that traditional religious constraints against these behaviors had imploded.[23] In 2009, James Arthur, dean of the education college at the University of Birmingham, reached a similar conclusion. Arthur led a team of researchers to investigate the origins of teenage violence. The resulting report—which was presented at 10 Downing Street—included the perhaps unexpected finding that Muslim teenagers were more law abiding than their non-Muslim counterparts.[24] The difference, Arthur and the team concluded, had to do with religion and intact families. "No government or other secular tradition has been able so far to replace the Judeo-Christian moral tradition," he summarized.[25]

*Believers contribute to "social capital."*

In his *Bowling Alone*, mentioned earlier, Robert D. Putnam repeatedly counts the ways in which religious believers contribute to society.[26] Of course he is talking about all religious believers, and not merely Christians. Still, the United States despite its pluralism remains a majority Christian country; and therefore we can safely substitute the word "Christian" for "worshippers" in the following passage:

> Religious worshippers . . . are much more likely than other persons to visit friends, to entertain at home, to attend club

meetings, and to belong to sports groups; professional and academic societies; school service groups; youth groups; service clubs; hobby or garden clubs; literary, art, discussion, and study groups; school fraternities and sororities; farm organizations; political clubs; nationality groups; and other miscellaneous groups.[27]

In another major book mentioned earlier, *American Grace*, Robert D. Putnam and David E. Campbell add more details to our understanding of how individual religious belief influences social behavior. "Deeply religious people," they summarize, "are, in fact, more generous in terms of their own giving and volunteering for social service, so in this sense religious people seem to walk the walk."[28] Religious believers also have greater marital stability and report higher levels of marital satisfaction.[29]

It bears repeating, especially to balance such a compelling litany: Christianity is no monolith built of saints. To paraphrase St. Paul, where there is grace, sin has also been known to abound. But for the purpose of settling the personal and civic track record here, so what? If the evidence is in, anyone can read it. Christians today are just more likely to do the sorts of things that most people would say are a net plus for society—including people who never go to church.

Hence all people, including secular people, benefit from the social and other capital created by religious people. More God means better health and more well-being—meaning less dependence on the services of the overburdened welfare state. Whether society is for Christianity or against it, society profits from allowing religious people to do their thing.

So is it in society's interest to encourage Christian practice? The answer is: only insofar as it is in society's interest to encourage quality of life, enhanced health, happiness, coping, less crime, less depression, and other such benefits associated with religious involvement.

Having called on secular social science to help answer that question, let us now look at social science again in considering this related question: *Is it similarly in society's interests to encourage the natural family?*

Is society built upon the family—or is the family the enemy of society itself? That question has been an object of dispute among Western thinkers stretching back at least to Plato. Ever since that Greek philosopher argued famously in his *Republic* that the best society would dispense with the family and turn children over to the rational child-rearing of the state, other people have taken up the challenge of figuring out how family and state ought to coexist—or not. Roughly speaking, their answers have fallen into two opposed groups.

*The family is the enemy of society, progress, or the state— or all of the above.*

One camp is that established by Plato, in which other revolutionaries and other discontents over the millennia have also planted their flags. According to this shared view, the natural family with its inherent limitations and inequities is a threat—in particular, a threat to plans for a new and more rational and more egalitarian ordering of society.

Preceded by the Utopian Socialists in the early nineteenth century, Marx and Engels argued famously that the family was intrinsically exploitative, and predicted that it would pass away along with the stage of capitalism it was tied to—strongly implying good riddance to it.[30] Though not all Communists and socialists could justifiably be called as antifamily as Marx and Engels were—Pierre-Joseph Proudhon was a particular exception—in the main, most other socialist thinkers sided with these two masters, seeing the family as either a microcosm or outgrowth of a failed political and economic system. Perhaps best known among these attacks on the institution of family is Engel's 1884 treatise, *The Origin of the Family, Private Property, and the State*, published after Marx's death. An early classic in what would become the intellectual history of feminism, it famously described conventional marriage as "the subjugation of the one sex by the other."[31]

The grain of truth in this enmity between collectivist visionaries on the one side and the family on the other is this: the collectivists have been quite right in understanding that the primal connections of family bind most people more tightly than do abstractions like revolution and utopia—which fact renders the family a natural enemy of collectivism.

"The family," as British writer Ferdinand Mount observed in an interesting book about this very phenomenon, "is a subversive organization. . . . Only the family has continued throughout history and still continues to undermine the state."[32] Alexis De Toqueville, Mount argues, was among the few to understand this fundamental antagonism between family and state—as witness the great Frenchman's observation that "as long as family feeling is kept alive, the opponent of oppression is never alone."[33] Hence, collectivists throughout history have brought coercive power to bear in the hopes of diminishing the elemental power of family—from the Bohemian Bolsheviks to the Communist Chinese government's long-running attempt to break family power by enforcing the "one-child only" policy.

This is not to say that political opposition has been the only source of attack on the family—far from it.

The reputation of the family took another serious beating later on in the nineteenth century, on the couch of psychoanalysis. Freudians and like-minded critics painted the family as a hotbed from which sprang necessary but still excruciating weeds of neurosis, repression, and other problematic eruptions. Gone was the Victorian image of the happy hearth surrounded by proud parents and beaming children. Instead, Freudians believed, the family unit seethed with toxicity, including where none had been detected before—such as putative sexual longings by infants, murderous feelings toward parents perceived as sexual competitors, and lust for the parent of the opposite sex.

Though both Marxism and Freudianism would fall precipitously from grace by the end of the twenty-first century, it seems safe to say that their antifamily legacies linger on in Western culture. The 1960s, in particular, witnessed an explosion of calls for new and improved family forms given what were often said to be the unbearable oppressions of the family unit. The notion that there is unique misery associated with hearth and home has also been a theme of modern literature sounded by more writers than one can list here, among them Virginia Woolf, George Bernard Shaw, Tennessee Williams, Arthur Miller, Philip Roth, J. D. Salinger, and more.

More recently, the family has also been the whipping boy of choice for generations of Western feminists missing no opportunity to blame the family first for the problems of modern women. Most of these attacks have amounted to one or another translation of Engels' fundamental point: the institution of the family is inimical to the individual interests of human beings—most especially women.

"The women . . . who grow up wanting to be 'just a housewife' are in as much danger as the millions who walked to their own deaths in the concentration camps," as Betty Friedan rather infamously put it in *The Feminine Mystique*.[34] "Friedan would later fear that some of her fellow feminists had taken the attack on the family too far—and certainly farther than most other American women would choose to go. Some openly celebrated the replacement of the traditional two-person married family with homes headed only by single mothers.[35] Others delivered their verdicts in book titles like *The Baby Trap* and *Marriage Is Hell*.[36] As other examples could go to show, the die was plainly cast; the family was coming up snake eyes.

Though it is easy to caricature some of these efforts, critiques of the family do make certain points worth weighing carefully. Compared to any egalitarian ideal, the family is indeed an intrinsically unfair institution, with authority and responsibility and labor all unevenly distributed among generations. The family is also, at least for parents, the hardest work many humans will ever undertake, with relentless decision making and seemingly nonstop obligations just two of the inescapable companions of the mothers and fathers of the world.

There is also no doubt that the sacrifices entailed by family life have real live consequences of the kind that feminists have so persistently identified (and resented). A mother who takes her work seriously might indeed find her career derailed by the demands of family, at any level of education or achievement and at any stage of a minor child's life. So might a father. As the first and original collective, the family does not put individualism first.

Moreover, critics like sociologist Judith Stacey who argue in favor of nontraditional family forms make a significant point too: those types have proliferated in the West following the sexual revolution, and they show every sign of gaining more ground in the future. Single motherhood, unwed motherhood, no-fault divorce, the piecemeal legalization of gay marriage: just as "secularization" has translated in part into believers having to cohabit the world with a growing number of unbelievers, so have the forces contributing to postmodern family formation meant that traditional households now coexist alongside what appears to be a growing number of nontraditional households. As Stacey observes, the rise of single-mother households and the concomitant demise of the two-parent, sole-breadwinner family means at least that "we cannot rewind the historical wheel in the quest to escape postmodern family life, however much some might wish to do so."[37]

But what does contemporary *empirical* evidence for its (often overlooked) part tell us about the role of family in society? This brings us to the opposing camp in these family matters—the one that believes functioning natural families to be essential to society and even good government itself.

*The family is the partner of society, progress,*
*or the state—or all of the above.*

Just as we saw earlier that common wisdom about the supposed toxicity of religion is trumped by the empirical evidence of what religious believers contribute to society, so too, in exactly parallel fashion, does other evidence back the proposition that society itself depends on the health of the family—and by "family" I do not mean just any arrangement that people might call a family, but rather the two-parent, biologically connected, intact natural family. This is the family form that has been studied in the research summarized ahead—and *pace* critics who might wish otherwise, it is that form of the family that has been associated most often with the best results not only for children, but for adults too.

So let us bring an open mind to the following survey. A great deal of evidence now goes to show the unwitting contributions made by the intact nuclear family to society at large—so much evidence, on so many fronts, that as the late James Q. Wilson once quipped, "Even some sociologists now believe it."[38]

That quote is taken from a remarkable lecture given by Wilson in 1997, outlining just how much difference the family makes. A hundred years earlier, Wilson observed, the great British Prime Minister Benjamin Disraeli had distinguished between "two nations" in that country—the rich and the poor, "between whom there is no intercourse and no sympathy; who are as ignorant of each other's habits, thoughts, and feelings, as if they were dwellers in different zones, or inhabitants of different planets,"[39] in Disraeli's words. Much the same formulation, Wilson argued, could apply to the United States today—only the dividing line is no longer one of money, but rather of family situation.

Wilson's argument has particular force because of his extraordinary career as a social scientist, including as former head of the prestigious American Political Science Association. Consider just some of the evidence he summarized from the available studies and surveys and other empirical instruments:

- Children in one-parent families, compared to those in two-parent ones, are twice as likely to drop out of school.

- Boys in one-parent families are much more likely than those in two-parent ones to be both out of school and out of work.

- Girls in one-parent families are twice as likely as those in two-parent ones to have an out-of-wedlock birth.[40]

Truancy, unemployment, and fatherless homes all rise in proportion to the rise in broken homes. Emphasizes Wilson: "These differences are not explained by income. Children in one-parent families are much worse off than those in two-parent families *even when both families have the same earnings* [emphasis added]."[41]

It is common for cynics to say that statistics mean whatever anyone with an agenda wants them too; and any reasonable person will grant that data can be misused. But so overwhelming is the contrary evidence cited by Wilson and other scholars that it simply trumps any such objections. The benefits to society and to individuals of the intact family are not wild suppositions pulled from one or two controversial studies. They are instead verifiable evidence of what the family delivers to society—evidence built out of a library of secular social science, as Wilson observed, in the course of many decades.

Thus, for example—quoting Wilson's summary—"When the Department of Health and Human Services studied some thirty thousand American households, it found that for whites, blacks, and Hispanics and for every income level save the very highest, children raised in single-parent homes were more likely to be suspended from school, to have emotional problems, and to behave badly." Private schools and all the other benefits that come with money apparently cannot equalize the effects of a broken home. "Another study," Wilson reports, "showed that white children of an unmarried woman were much more likely than those in a two-parent family to become a delinquent, *even after controlling for income* [emphasis added].[42] Once again, we are accustomed to thinking of the dividing line in society being between rich and poor. But it is the difference in family structure, not the difference in family income, that best explains why children from intact homes are the statistical winners.

So social science has also established that children do best when they grow up with married, biological parents in the home, and that children who do not enjoy that advantage are at higher risk for a large number of problems. We now "know" things like this empirically whereas previous generations knew them through anecdote or experience. Adolescent delinquency, adult criminality, illness and injury in childhood, sexual abuse, school problems, emotional troubles, early sexual behavior—all rise with the fatherless home (or for that matter, generally speaking, the home with the stepfather rather than the biological father). To quote Charles Murray once more, "I know of no other set of important findings that are as broadly accepted by social scientists who follow the technical literature, liberal as well as conservative, and yet are so resolutely ignored by network news programs, editorial writers for the major newspapers, and politicians of both major political parties."[43]

There is no point in dwelling upon the reasons why some scholars speak with such frustration about the unwillingness of others to acknowledge these truths. Fear of offending people and a concomitant reluctance to believe in these results because of where else they might lead—such as social and professional ostracism—are powerful barriers to candor. Nonetheless and for what it is worth, James Q. Wilson's side of the debate wins handily—not Plato's, not Marx's, and not that of other adversaries of the traditional home. There is not much data yet on the effects on children of growing up in the experimental family forms being tried today. But we already have the data we need to render a verdict about the question before us, which is whether sound families make for a sound society. Just as Christianity is a net plus for modern societies, as measured by the data in the last chapter, so too is the functioning family unit. First, the family—if it is competent—reduces the need for state intervention, state subsidy, state substitutes, and the rest of the fiscal burden that poorly functioning families place on everyone else. Second, the family—again if it is competent—acts as the original safety net, lowering the risks to its members of adverse outcomes and raising the likelihood that its members will contribute to society in turn.

# EPILOGUE

A Reflection on What Nietzsche
and His Intellectual Heirs Missed,
and Why They Might Have Missed It

HAVING MADE the case that all of us, secularists as well as believers, have a stake in the twin fates of Christianity and the family, whatever our personal beliefs, I would like to close with a few final thoughts about the thesis put forward in this book.

Which account better fits the facts about the decline of faith and family in the West—Nietzsche's and that of modern sociology, or one that takes the Family Factor into account? Which image best describes how Western people have *actually* come to believe and not believe in their historical churches—a two-dimensional, unidirectional timeline, according to which religion would ultimately get pushed off the track of humanity altogether; or the more intricate and elegant double helix, which depends for its very movement and replication on mutually reinforcing dynamics?[1]

The answer seems to depend on *which* people of the West we are talking about. On Nietzsche's model, a few *übermenschen* in possession of truths that would be unbearable to others spread the word slowly—in this case of the death of God, which will take centuries—thus beginning a process that will someday trickle down to the unknowing mass of men. The mechanism of such a transfer appears mysterious; after all, not many people avoid church these days because of the Copernican revolution, say, or because of

Galileo's vindication, or because of other specific events that caused some in the history of philosophy to lose their faith.

But let us leave this issue of trickle-down secularism aside and give Nietzsche's madman the benefit of the doubt for now. There are surely people who do indeed learn and decide, believe and disbelieve, in the rational and atomistic way he describes; or at least, this is the story they tell themselves.

Even so, the majority of people, to continue this complementary religious anthropology, do not reinvent the theological wheel this way. They learn religion in communities—beginning with the community of the family. They learn it as the philosopher Ludwig Wittgenstein once brilliantly observed that language is learned: not by individuals independently making up their own tongues, but in a *community* of users sharing the same linguistic rules.

Wittgenstein countered philosopher René Descartes's dualism by observing that the philosophical question Descartes was most famous for—*how do I know that I am?*—contained the seeds of its destruction in the very phrasing: only by *presupposing* a community of language believers, Wittgenstein argued, could this question about radical oneness make sense.[2] In other words, what Wittgenstein dubbed "private language," as he argued, was impossible, for it was something that only could be done in groups. It is a fascinating exercise to extend this profound philosophical insight to the case of religion.

What if Christianity (like other religions) is like language—something that can really only be practiced in groups? What if, just as people enhance their language skills by exposure to other people, those who are most connected to other people are more likely to develop "religious skills" too?

This is a different way of looking at Christianity and secularization, but it does seem to describe ordinary experience—not for the *übermenschen* of Nietzsche's imaginings, perhaps, but for at least some of the other human beings who have lived their lives in natural families and worshipped a deity and have obviously found it natural to connect major family events like birth, death, and marriage with religious ritual. With daily experience of the family community now greatly weakened in formerly Christian Europe and other parts of the West, many people—to continue the speculation—now tack toward secularism instead. Like the fabled wolf boy of Germany whose time growing up alone in the forest left him disadvantaged in speech for the rest of his life, so might the relative solitude and disconnection from family of many Westerners today render them severely disadvantaged when it comes to understanding another language: religion.

But that current state of affairs, *pace* the secularists and the new atheists, has not proved once and for all that Christianity is over. It has proved rather that the *kind* of human community on which religious apprehension depends—i.e., one in which the family enjoys some kind of critical social mass—is in serious trouble. Trying to believe without a community of believers is like trying to work out a language for oneself—something that a few *übermenschen* might be up for attempting, but that most of us ordinary mortals are not.

As the chapters of this book have also gone to show, there is another deep reason why Nietzsche and his heirs may have overlooked the Family Factor, or the notion that there is something critical about the natural family in the transmission of Christianity. It is that *secular modern thinkers have never had an adequate explanation for why people believe in God in the first place.*

As we saw back in the beginning and at some length, the going speculations about theotropism fail to satisfy. For one thing, it is not only the unwashed masses who are religious; in fact, as we have seen, historical evidence supports the perhaps counterintuitive claim that they are often the *least* religious. As Hugh McLeod documented in his classic *Class and Religion in the Late Victorian City*, among Anglicans in London during that period, "The number of . . . worshippers rises at first gradually and then steeply with each step up the social ladder."[3] In the United States today, as we also reviewed, Protestant evangelicals and members of the Church of Jesus Christ of Latter-day Saints are among the most highly educated groups—and also the most religious.

Also as we have seen, the related explanation by many secularists—that religious belief disappears as people become more knowledgeable and less superstitious—is similarly vulnerable to criticism. As John Micklethwait and Adrian Wooldridge show ably in *God Is Back*, the spread of Pentecostalism today, like the persistent success of evangelicalism, by itself confutes the idea that more education means less religion.[4]

In sum, because it treats belief as an atomistic decision taken piecemeal by individuals rather than a holistic response to what is evidently a profound desire to tether family life to something transcendent, Nietzsche's madman and his academic offspring present an incomplete version of how some considerable portion of human beings actually come to think and behave about things religious—not one by one and all on their own, but rather mediated through the elemental connections of husband, wife, child, aunt, great-grandfather, and the rest.

As a related matter, it is historically striking—and also unremarked-upon—how many of the great atheists and secularists pronouncing over the grave of Christianity have been childless. These include the great Friedrich Nietzsche himself, who died without recorded children and never knew a spouse. His atomized life appears to be a forerunner of the mass of Europeans to follow, increasing numbers of whom live alone or otherwise insulated against the ancient rhythms of birth, death, and rebirth of generations. Could the philosopher's relative familial inexperience have left him less than well equipped to understand the symbiotic relationship between Christianity and the family? For that matter, could the relative familial inexperience of many modern Western people today similarly render them tone-deaf to religious words—even the Word?

Jean-Jacques Rousseau, another towering founder of modern thought and antagonist of Christianity, did have children, at least technically speaking—five of them. But *père* Rousseau sent them all to an orphanage as infants where they are presumed to have died; and he did not marry any of his series of mistresses either.[5] Might not someone who abandoned his own children one by one be at something of a conceptual disadvantage when it comes to understanding religion that revolves around a Father and a Son and a holy mother—a religion that begins with a baby?

Or to put the speculation another way—to conjecture about what might be called *secularist* anthropology—which came first for Rousseau and some of Christianity's other ferocious critics: the public hatred of religion, or the profound and elemental desire to act in defiance of some of its deepest tenets?

Of course we will never know the full answers to those deliberately provocative questions. But given the evidence, our understanding of secularization would appear to benefit from grasping the Family Factor, or the inextricable way in which Christianity and the family depend for their support on one another. Perhaps, as conventional theorists claim, some people do just sit in a corner and decide what they do and don't believe about the profoundest things. Perhaps for some people, such as the childless philosopher Nietzsche, Christianity does indeed go in or out the door as he described it: in a top-down process hammered out by a tortured soul sitting in a study and then left for intellectual heirs to disseminate.

But for most other men and women, it seems safe to wager by now, this conventional religious anthropology fails to describe why things are the way they are. The history of the modern West, in which declines in fertility and marriage and other measures of the strength of family life ran right alongside declines in religious practice, must be grasped in full—not just in isolated measures of church attendance or unmarried births or other relevant measures, but as a whole in which all these measures lock the helix together.[6] In a way that we are only just beginning to understand, it appears that the natural family as a whole has been the human symphony through which God has historically been heard by many people—not the prophets, not the philosophers, but a great many of the rest; and the gradual but by now recognizable muffling of that symphony is surely an important and overlooked part of the story of how certain Western men and women came not to hear the sacred music any more.

# Acknowledgments

THE ESSAY that ended up being the prolegomenon to this book first appeared in *Policy Review* in 2007; thanks to editor and longtime friend Tod Lindberg for his confidence in its argument. Susan Arellano, head of Templeton Press, asked me to follow the logic of that essay into book form. She's been agent, editor, and publisher rolled into one, and her persistence and enthusiasm are much appreciated. Thanks also to managing editor Natalie Silver and everyone else at the Press for putting up with the manuscript (and its author) throughout many drafts and revisions.

Three scholars read the first draft and provided detailed comments and criticism: political scientist Eric Kaufmann; anthropologist Stanley Kurtz; and sociologist W. Bradford Wilcox. I'm grateful to each for their sharp insights, their tactful corrections, and their patience with a nonspecialist lumbering through their turf.

Thanks of an indirect sort go out to George Weigel, whose 2005 meditation about the fate of Christianity in Europe, *The Cube and the Cathedral*, first interested me in the puzzle of secularization; and similarly to Joseph Bottum for his 2008 essay, "The Death of Protestant America."

I'm deeply indebted to Sean Fieler, Greg Pfundstein, and Ed Whelan, president of the Ethics and Public Policy Center. Thanks to them I'm now a Senior Fellow at EPPC, than which there's no finer place to hone ideas and enjoy colleagues. The Hoover Institution at Stanford University supported some of my work during the years that went into this book, including two highly informative research trips in 2011; Sharon Ragland and Stephen Langlois are thanked for those. I am grateful to the Earhart Foundation, which stepped in with critical grant support during the writing of the middle chapters of this work; and to the Lynde and Harry Bradley Foundation and the William E. Simon Foundation, both of which provided assistance during the final year of writing. Their support has been the *sine qua non* of this undertaking.

Friends and colleagues helped by listening, correcting, and opining. They include Andrew and Denise Ferguson, Kathryn Jean Lopez, Charles Murray, Mary Anne Novak, Michael Novak, P. J. and Tina O'Rourke, Fr. Arne Panula, Austin and Cathy Ruse, Fr. William A. Ryan of Togo, Apoorva Shah, Mary Rose Somarriba, Gayle Trotter, and Andreas Widmer. Fr. Justin Huber deserves special mention for the helpful database he put together. Thanks are also due to my father-in-law, Frederick Eberstadt.

In London, thanks for interesting discussions and interviews to Fernanda Eberstadt and Alastair Bruton, Cornelia Grassi and Tommaso Corvi-Mora, Tarka Kings, Dominic Lawson, John Micklethwait, Constantine Normanby, Fr. Alexander Sherbrooke, Nicola Shulman, and Adrian Wooldridge. In Rome, *grazie* to Monsignor Ettore Balestrero, the Vatican's undersecretary for relations with states; Monsignor Anthony Frontiero of the Pontifical Council for Justice and Peace; Fr. Victor Ghio, Pontifical Council for the Family; Luisa Arrezo of the paper *Liberal*; Fr. Roberto Odorico; Fr. John Wauck; and Alberto Mingardi of the Bruno Leoni Institute.

Finally, I acknowledge (though without implicating him in any way) the contributions of demographer/economist Nicholas Eberstadt, my husband. Here as elsewhere, his erudition and expertise have been exploited as fully as I'm capable of understanding them. Any mistakes are, as usual, all mine.

Anything useful in these pages is to the credit of Frederick, Catherine, Isabel, and Alexandra, to whom this work is dedicated.

# Notes

INTRODUCTION

1. The definition of "the West" for purposes of these pages runs more or less along the lines of one offered recently by George Weigel: "What we call 'the West'—and the distinctive forms of political and economic life it has generated—did not just happen. Those distinctive forms of politics and economics—democracy and the market—are not solely the product of the continental European Enlightenment. No, the deeper taproots of our civilization lie in cultural soil nurtured by the fruitful interaction of Jerusalem, Athens, and Rome: biblical religion, from which the West learned the idea of history as a purposeful journey into the future, not just one damn thing after another; Greek rationality, which taught the West that there are truths embedded in the world and in us, and that we have access to those truths through the arts of reason; and Roman jurisprudence, which taught the West the superiority of the rule of law over the rule of brute force and sheer coercion." George Weigel, the Eleventh William E. Simon lecture, reprinted in *National Affairs* as "The Handwriting on the Wall," no. 11 (Spring 2012): available online at http://www.nationalaffairs.com/publications/detail/the-handwriting-on-the-wall.

2. The best-known verse of "Dover Beach" (1867) reads: *"The Sea of Faith / Was once, too, at the full, and round earth's shore / Lay like the folds of a bright girdle furled. / But now I only hear / Its melancholy, long, withdrawing roar / Retreating to the breath / Of the night-wind, down the vast edges drear / And naked shingles of the world."*

3. Measurements of decline are open to debate, but here is one relatively straightforward example: the European Values Study (EVS), which includes data from four "waves" (1981, 1990, 1999, and 2008). These waves make it possible to compare, say, religious attendance today with attendance eighteen years ago. In nine out of eleven countries, for example, belief in God dropped between 1981 and 1999. All but one country (Italy) also showed a decline in church attendance during these same years. The number of nonaffiliated individuals concomitantly rose in every country. A falling percentage of people believe in hell and other particulars of the Christian creed; and so on. For more data, see http://www.europeanvaluesstudy.eu/evs/data-and-downloads. As for the United States, according to the Pew Forum on Religion & Public Life, the percentage of American adults claiming no religious affiliation grew from 15 to 20 in the five years between 2007 and 2012. Cary Funk and Greg Smith, Senior Researchers, "Nones on the Rise: One-in-Five Adults Have No Religious Affiliation," published by Pew Research Center, Washington, DC, October

9, 2012, available online at http://www.pewforum.org/uploadedFiles/Topics/Religious_Affiliation/Unaffiliated/NonesOnTheRise-full.pdf.

4. To repeat, the phrase "natural family" is not intended here as a pejorative, or as an indication that other kinds of families are thereby "unnatural." It refers instead to what ought to be an uncontroversial definition: the natural family is the one form of family that other forms might imitate, but never replicate—i.e., it is the form of family based on biological ties. Only one woman may be a biological mother, for example, to a given child, though other women may be stepmothers, adoptive mothers, or otherwise "like" a natural mother. To put the matter another way, one's actual biological ties to relatives are intrinsically limited and unchangeable, whereas one's figurative, family-like associations are not.

5. The term "Christophobia" is commonly attributed to legal scholar Joseph Weiler. George Weigel, *The Cube and the Cathedral: Europe, America, and Politics without God* (New York: Basic Books, 2006), 19.

6. In Great Britain in 2011, to give one emblematic example, a Pentecostal couple was barred from giving foster care by a judge who cited their Christian beliefs on homosexuality as "inimical" to children's well-being. See "Christian Foster Couple Lose 'Homosexuality Views' Case," BBC News, February 28, 2011, available online at http://www.bbc.co.uk/news/uk-england-derbyshire-12598896. Other and similar collisions between traditional Christian teaching and changing views of Christianity have occurred within the last few years, and organizations have accordingly sprung up to track such incidents. According to Dr. Gudrun Kugler, for example, lead author of a 2011 *Report on Intolerance and Discrimination against Christians in Europe* published by the Austrian nonprofit group Observatory Intolerance against Christians (Europe), "Studies suggest that 85% of all hate crimes with an anti-religion background in Europe are directed against Christians. . . . We also notice professional restrictions for Christians: a restrictive application of freedom of conscience leads to professions such as magistrates, doctors, nurses and midwives as well as pharmacists slowly closing for Christians. Teachers and parents get into trouble when they disagree with state-defined sexual ethics." The report is available online at http://www.intoleranceagainstchristians.eu/fileadmin/user_upload/Press_Release_Report_2011_English_01.pdf.

7. For an engaging account of Christianity's vibrancy elsewhere, see, for example, John Micklethwait and Adrian Wooldridge, *God Is Back: How the Global Revival of Faith Is Changing the World* (New York: Penguin Press, 2009).

8. For more information, see the group's website: http://uk-england.alpha.org/.

9. See, for example, Rob Williams, "Modern-Day Pilgrims Beat a Path to the Camino," *The Guardian*, May 2, 2011. Also in 2011, this pilgrimage became the premise of a movie called *The Way*, produced by Emilio Estevez and starring Martin Sheen.

10. Philip Jenkins, *God's Continent: Christianity, Islam, and Europe's Religious Crisis* (New York: Oxford University Press, 2011), 36.

11. On the rise of Islam in Europe, see, for example, Bruce Bawer, *While Europe Slept: How Radical Islam Is Destroying the West from Within* (New York: Doubleday, 2006); Claire Berlinksi, *Menace in Europe: Why the Continent's Crisis Is America's Too* (New York: Crown Forum, 2006); Ian Buruma, *Murder in Amsterdam* (New York: Penguin Press, 2006); Christopher Caldwell, *Reflections on the Revolution in Europe: Immigration, Islam, and the West* (New York: Doubleday, 2009); Walter Laqueur, *The Last Days of Europe: Epitaph for an Old Continent* (New York: Thomas Dunne Books, 2007); and Melanie Phillips, *Londonistan* (New York: Encounter Books, 2006). See also Jenkins, *God's Continent*.

12. See, for example, Sam Harris, *The End of Faith: Religion, Terror, and the Future of Reason*, reprint ed. (New York: W. W. Norton, 2005) and *Letter to a Christian Nation* (New York: Knopf, 2006); Daniel C. Dennett, *Breaking the Spell: Religion as a Natural Phenomenon*, reprint ed. (New York: Penguin, 2007); Richard Dawkins, *The God Delusion* (Boston, MA: Houghton Mifflin, 2006); Christopher Hitchens, *God Is Not Great: How Religion Poisons Everything* (Boston, MA: Twelve Books, 2007); Michel Onfray, *Atheist Manifesto: The Case against Christianity, Judaism, and Islam*, English language ed. (New York: Arcade Publishing, 2005); Victor J. Stenger, *God: The Failed Hypothesis: How Science Shows That God Does Not Exist* (Amherst, NY: Prometheus Books, 2007).

13. "Papal Visit Scuppered by Scholars," BBC News, January 15, 2008, available at bbc.co.uk.

14. In fact, as George Weigel observed of the controversy provoked by Pope Benedict XVI's historic trip to the UK in 2010, some of the protesters had become "people so perfervid, so over-the-top, in their antipathies as to be dismissed as fundamentally unserious." Weigel, "Richard Dawkins & Co.=Paisley 2.0?" September 29, 2010, available online at http://www.firstthings.com/onthesquare/2010/09/richard-dawkins—co—paisley-20/george-weigel.

15. Historically, some version of this "natural family" has been near-ubiquitous—from illiterate tribes in the Amazon rainforest to the civilizations of Mesopotamia on up to poor much-maligned (but very clearly in the human majority) *Ozzie and Harriet* of television yore.

16. Eurostat, *Demography Report 2010*, http://epp.eurostat.ec.europa.eu/portal/page/portal/population/documents/Tab/report.pdf.

17. It is true, as experts like to emphasize, that there are variations on the theme of Western birth decline. Birthrates are lowest in Southern Europe, for example, and highest in Scandinavia, France, and the Anglo Saxon countries. (Thanks to Eric Kaufmann for this nuanced observation. E-mail correspondence, March 2012.) It is also true that the relationship between fertility and marriage appears to be a complicated one. Perhaps counterintuitively, births are highest in countries with higher out-of-wedlock births, and appear lowest of all in

countries with relatively strong marriage patterns; Eric Kaufmann, ibid. For a wide-ranging discussion of these and other fine points, see also Eric Kaufmann and W. Bradford Wilcox, eds., *Whither the Child?: Causes and Consequences of Low Fertility* (Boulder, CO: Paradigm Publishers, 2012). Fascinating though the variations may be, however, these too amount to leaves in the forest for now. Surveying the trees instead, as it were, we can easily see the dramatic trend: down, down, down.

18. Data derived from Eurostat, http://appsso.eurostat.ec.europa.eu/nui/show .do?dataset=demo_find&lang=en

19 For example, in a classic work written almost a quarter century ago called *Disturbing the Nest: Family Change and Decline in Modern Society* (Piscataway, NJ: Aldine Transaction, 1988), sociologist David Popenoe offered a ten-point list of particulars about the change in what he called the "ecology of childrearing." He argued on the basis of his list that the family as an institution was, and is, in decline across the West (spearheaded by Sweden, the particular object of his study). He included among others the empirical facts that families have become smaller; have fewer joint activities; that contact time between parents and children has been reduced; that families have less time for family-centered routines and traditions; that children have less regular contact with relatives and neighbors than before; that children have less association with the work of their parents than before; that children are also more likely to find that their parents do not remain together; and a number of other findings bolstering his case for declinism. And this is just one checklist of the systemic weakening of family ties across the West, for better or worse; there are many others one could name.

20. See, for example, David Blankenhorn, *Fatherless America: Confronting Our Most Urgent Social Problem* (New York: Basic Books, 1995); James Q. Wilson, *The Marriage Problem: How Our Culture Has Weakened Families*, reprint ed. (New York: Harper paperbacks, 2003); Kay S. Hymowitz, *Marriage and Caste in America: Separate and Unequal Families in a Post-Marital Age* (Chicago, IL: Ivan R. Dee, 2006).

21. Nicholas Eberstadt, quoted in Chrystia Freeland, "The Problems of a Graying Population," *New York Times*, global ed., July 28, 2011, available online at http://www.nytimes.com/2011/07/29/world/americas/29iht-letter29.html.

22. Nicholas Eberstadt and Hans Groth, "Demography and Public Debt," discussion paper for the World Demography Association forum, no. 2010/1, p. 4, available online at http://www.aei.org/files/2010/08/06/EberstadtTime DemographicStressTest.pdf.

23. Ali Alichi, quoted in Freeland, "The Problems of a Graying Population."

24. As Rich Lowry, editor of *National Review*, noted at the time: "Julia begins her interaction with the welfare state as a little tot through the pre-kindergarten program Head Start. She then proceeds through all of life's important phases, not Shakespeare's progression from 'mewling and puking' infant to 'second

childishness and mere oblivion,' but the Health and Human Services and Education Departments version: a Pell grant (age 18), surgery on insurance coverage guaranteed by Obamacare (22), a job where she can sue her employers for more pay thanks to the Lilly Ledbetter Fair Pay Act (23), free contraception (27), a Small Business Administration loan (42) and, finally, Medicare (65) and Social Security (67)." See "A Nation of Julias," National Review Online, May 4, 2012, available online at http://www.nationalreview.com/articles/298936/nation-julias-rich-lowry.

25. For a discussion of the impact of these changes on contemporary childhood in addition to Popenoe's, see Mary Eberstadt, *Home-Alone America: The Hidden Toll of Day Care, Behavioral Drugs, and Other Parent Substitutes* (New York: Sentinel, 2004).

26. Peter Laslett, *The World We Have Lost: England before the Industrial Age*, 3rd ed. (New York: Charles Scribner's Sons, 1984), 21.

27. See Elizabeth Marquardt, Norval D. Glenn, and Karen Clark, *My Daddy's Name Is Donor: A New Study of Young Adults Conceived Through Sperm Donation* (New York: Institute for American Values, 2010), 8, available online at http://www.familyscholars.org/assets/Donor_FINAL.pdf.

28. See, for example, David McNeill, "How Japan Succumbed to a Massive Attack of Puppy Love," *The Independent*, June 11, 2004. "Manufacturers," he observes, "have stepped in to fill the human void [of Japan's low fertility and marriage rates] with electronic substitutes. Sega Toys has sold millions of toy dogs and nearly half a million of its Yumeneko cats in Japan. Takura has enjoyed runaway success with a device called Bow-lingual and its follow-up Meow-lingual, by boasting that they translate dog barks and cat meows into human speech. Bandai . . . has enjoyed another huge hit with a cuddly toy called PrimoPuel, a talking robot marketed as a 'comfort product' to lonely women. 'It has an internal clock so it knows when it's Christmas and will demand a Christmas present,' says Bandai President Takeo Takasu. 'And it also has a built-in sensor so it knows when it's too hot or too cold. We've sold 900,000 of these at 6,900 yen each, mostly to middle-aged and older women.'"

29. Christopher White, "Surrogates and Their Discontents," *The Public Discourse*, August 16, 2012, http://www.thepublicdiscourse.com/2012/08/6137. India is a popular destination for "surrogacy tourism," or shopping for wombs that can be used temporarily by paying customers who cannot bear their own children or choose not to.

30. See James D. Watson, *The Double Helix: A Personal Account of the Discovery of the Structure of DNA* (New York: Atheneum Publishers, 1968). In dragooning the helix into service as metaphor, I am not pretending to understand anything other than its image and the fact that each side requires the other to reproduce—in other words, it is intended as a literary device, not a scientific one.

31. See, for example, Phillip Jenkins, *The Next Christendom: The Coming of Global Christianity* (New York: Oxford University Press, 2002).

32. It happens that I am a Roman Catholic Christian, an affiliation stated here up front in the interests of transparency. It is worth noting that many people who write about secularization do not identify their own beliefs (or lack thereof)—though it might be helpful to readers if they did.

33. As historian Eamon Duffy—whose compelling revisionist work on the Reformation will be mentioned in the pages ahead—once summarized his own interest in these matters, "There is, of course, no such thing as a presupposition-less observer." Bearing in mind the deep truth of that observation, I have tried to look with heightened scrupulosity at the roads down which my own preconceptions might lead. Eamon Duffy, *The Stripping of the Altars: Traditional Religion in England 1400–1580* (New Haven, CT: Yale University Press, 1992). The quote continues: "All historians who aspire to be more than chroniclers derive their imaginative insight and energy from somewhere, and if reading and research provide the core materials, our own experience provides us with the sensitivities—and no doubt the blind-spots—which make what we do with that material distinctive." These are the best words I have found that capture the observer interference we all carry with us in matters of religion (and for that matter, in everything else in life that is interesting), and they've been a touchstone of sorts in researching this work. Thus, for example, in assessing the evidence of Christianity's decline and arguing for a new theory of what has happened, I have tried to resist the daring but perhaps overreaching optimism that some scholarly religious believers have brought to the discussion. Where there is historical and contemporary evidence of religious decline, I do not try and wish it away; conversely, where there is evidence of religious vitality, that phenomenon too is given appropriate credit.

34. Charles Taylor, *A Secular Age* (Cambridge, Massachusetts, and London, England: The Belknap Press of Harvard University Press, 2007), 25.

## Chapter 1

1. The *Time* magazine reference is to the cover story "Is God Dead?" one of the most famous in the institution's history, published on April 8, 1966.

2. Pippa Norris and Ronald Inglehart, *Sacred and Secular: Religion and Politics Worldwide* (New York: Cambridge University Press, 2004), 3.

3. Peter L. Berger, ed. *The Desecularization of the World: Resurgent Religion and World Politics* (published jointly by the Ethics and Public Policy Center in Washington, DC, and Wm. B. Eerdmans, Grand Rapids, MI, 1999), 2.

4. Whittaker Chambers, *Witness* (Mattituck, NY: Amereon Ltd., 2011), 25. First published in 1952.

5. On the role of John Paul II in the demise of Communism, see especially George Weigel, *The End and the Beginning: Pope John Paul II—The Victory of Freedom, the Last Years, the Legacy* (New York: Doubleday, 2010). See also John

O'Sullivan, *The President, the Pope, and the Prime Minister: Three Who Changed the World* (Washington, DC: Regnery History, 2006).

6. Robert Royal, *The God That Did Not Fail: How Religion Built and Sustains the West* (New York: Encounter Books, 2006), xxiii; for other counterattacks on various aspects of secularization theory, see Weigel, *The Cube and the Cathedral*, and Michael Novak, "The End of the Secular Age," Conference on Religion and the American Future, American Enterprise Institute (October 26–27, 2006). See also Eric Kaufmann, "God Returns to Europe: The Slow Death of Secularism," *Prospect* (November 2006); and Berger's preface to *The Desecularization of the World*.

7. See, for example, David Berlinski, *The Devil's Delusion: Atheism and Its Scientific Pretensions* (New York: Crown Forum, 2008); Dinesh D'Souza, *What's So Great About Christianity* (Washington, DC: Regnery Publishing, 2007); Antony Flew and Roy Abraham Varghese, *There Is a God: How The World's Most Notorious Atheist Changed His Mind* (New York: HarperOne, 2007); Peter Hitchens, *The Rage Against God: How Atheism Led Me to Faith* (Grand Rapids, MI: Zondervan, 2010); Michael Novak, *No One Sees God: The Dark Night of Atheists and Believers* (New York: Doubleday, 2008). For a satire of the new atheism, see Mary Eberstadt, *The Loser Letters: A Comic Tale of Life, Death, and Atheism* (San Francisco: Ignatius Press, 2010).

8. Berger, ibid., 2.

9. Peter Berger, "Religion in a Globalizing World," event transcript, Pew Forum biannual Faith Angle Conference on religion, politics, and public life, moderated by Michael Cromartie, December 4, 2006, available online at http://www.pewforum.org/Politics-and-Elections/Religion-in-a-Globalizing-World(2).aspx.

10. José Casanova, *Public Religions in the Modern World* (Chicago: University of Chicago Press, 1994), 5.

11. Micklethwait and Wooldridge, *God Is Back*, 16, 17, and 4, respectively.

12. Owen Chadwick, *The Secularization of the European Mind in the Nineteenth Century* (Cambridge: Cambridge University Press, 1975), 4.

13. Chadwick, ibid., 3.

14. Rodney Stark, "Secularization, R.I.P.," *Sociology of Religion* 60, no. 3 (1999): 249–73; see especially 255–60.

15. Ibid., 255.

16. Ibid., 259.

17. Michael Snape, "War, Religion and Revival: The United States, British and Canadian Armies during the Second World War," in *Secularisation in the Christian World: Essays in Honour of Hugh MacLeod*, ed. Callum G. Brown and Michael Snape (Surrey, England: Ashgate Publishing, 2010), 135–58. He concludes, "The soldiers of the United States, British and Canadian armies were exposed to an institutional process of rechristianisation during the Second

World War, a process that was widely reinforced by a deepening of religious faith at a personal level" (151).

18. Rodney Stark, "Secularization, R.I.P.," 259.

19. Rodney Stark and Roger Finke, *Acts of Faith: Explaining the Human Side of Religion* (Berkeley: University of California Press, 200), 40.

20. See Rodney Stark and Laurence R. Iannaccone, "A Supply-Side Reinterpretation of the 'Secularization' of Europe," *Journal for the Scientific Study of Religion* 33, no. 3 (Sept. 1994): 230–52.

21. Steve Bruce, *God Is Dead: Secularization in the West* (Oxford: Blackwell Publishing, 2002), 45.

22. Ibid., 56.

23. Eamon Duffy, *The Stripping of the Altars: Traditional Religion in England 1400–1580*, 2nd ed. (New Haven, CT: Yale University Press, 2005).

24. Ibid., 4.

25. Ibid., "Preface to the Second Edition," xviii.

26. Raphaël Franck and Laurence R. Iannaccone, "Why Did Religiosity Decrease in the Western World during the Twentieth Century?" preliminary draft, Nov. 9, 2009, available online at http://econ.hevra.haifa.ac.il/~todd/seminars/papers09-10/franck_iannaccone_religiosity.pdf.

27. Robert D. Putnam and David E. Campbell, *American Grace: How Religion Divides and Unites Us* (New York: Simon and Schuster, 2010), 79–80.

28. Callum G. Brown, *The Death of Christian Britain: Understanding Secularization 1800–2000* (London: Routledge, 2001), 7.

29. Ibid., 8.

30. Ibid., 188.

31. Émile Durkheim, *The Elementary Forms of the Religious Life* (Oxford: Oxford University Press, 2001; first published in 1912). On the other hand, to say that Durkheim thought religion to be "real" is not to say that he believed it to correspond to supernatural reality. Particular thanks to Stanley Kurtz for discussions clarifying Durkheim's and Freud's thoughts on religion.

32. Andrew M. Greeley, *Unsecular Man: The Persistence of Religion*, 2nd ed. (New York: Shocken Books, 1985), 1.

33. Charles Darwin, *The Descent of Man, and Selection in Relation to Sex* (Charleston, SC: Forgotten Books, 2007), 513. First published in 1871.

34. Ibid. The full passage reads:

"On the other hand a belief in all-pervading spiritual agencies seems to be universal, and apparently follows from a considerable advance in man's reason, and from a still greater advance in his faculties of imagination, curiosity and wonder. I am aware that the assumed instinctive belief in God has been used by many persons as an argument for His existence. But this is a rash argument, as we should thus be compelled to believe in the existence of many cruel and malignant spirits, only a little more powerful than man; for the belief in them is far more general than in a beneficent Deity. The idea of a universal and beneficent Creator does not seem to arise in the mind of man, until he has been elevated by long-continued culture." (394–95)

Note the interesting if questionable syllogism embedded in Darwin's rejection of the idea that belief in God could arise from an underlying religious reality. Belief in spirits, he says, is more universal than belief in a beneficent God; and since we cannot possibly be asked to believe in spirits (hidden premise), we cannot be asked either to believe in God. The reason for rejecting belief in other supernatural forces than God is merely asserted, not explained.

35. Steven Pinker, "The Evolutionary Psychology of Religion" (paper presented at the annual meeting of the Freedom from Religion Foundation, Madison, WI, October 29, 2004), available online at http://pinker.wjh.harvard.edu/articles /media/2004_10_29_religion.htm.

36. For an overview for the general reader, see Robin Marantz Henig, "Darwin's God," *New York Times Magazine*, March 4, 2007.

37. See, for example, Nicholas Wade, "The Evolution of the God Gene," *New York Times*, November 14, 2009, available online at http://www.nytimes.com/2009 /11/15/weekinreview/12wade.html.

38. See, for example, Jonathan Wynne-Jones, "Rowan Williams Hits Out at Atheist Dawkins," *The Telegraph*, October 14, 2007.

39. Stark, "Secularization, R.I.P.," 249.

40. Jenkins, *God's Continent*, 31, 33, and 37, respectively.

41. Phil Zuckerman, *Society without God: What the Least Religious Nations Can Tell Us about Contentment* (New York: New York University Press, 2008).

42. Ibid., 6–11.

43. Jonathan Wynne-Jones, "Clergy Told to Take On the 'New Atheists,'" *The Telegraph*, February 6, 2011.

44. See Jürgen Habermas and Joseph Ratzinger, *The Dialectics of Secularization: On Reason and Religion* (San Francisco: Ignatius Press, 2005).

45. See, for example, Joseph Cardinal Ratzinger, Address to Catechists and Religion Teachers, Jubilee of Catechists, December 12, 2000, http://www.ewtn .com/new_evangelization/Ratzinger.htm

46. "Pope Creates New Office to Fight 'Eclipse of God' in the West," Catholic News Agency, October 12, 2010, available online at http://www.catholicnewsagen cy.com/news/pope-creates-new-office-to-fight-eclipse-of-god-in-the-west/.

47. Jeffrey Cox, "Master Narratives of Religious Change," in *The Decline of Christendom in Western Europe, 1750–2000*, ed. Hugh McLeod and Werner Ustorf (Cambridge: Cambridge University Press, 2003), 203.

48. David Voas, "The Rise and Fall of Fuzzy Fidelity in Europe," *European Sociological Review* 25, no. 2 (2009): 155.

49. Particular thanks to Msgr. Ettore Balestrero, undersecretary for relations of state at the Vatican, for a lengthy conversation clarifying some of the themes in this section.

50. For an excellent summary of the demographic and financial straits of mainline churches, see, for example, Joseph Bottum, "The Death of Protestant America," *First Things*, Aug./Sept. 2008, available online at http://www.firstthings.com /article/2008/08/001-the-death-of-protestant-america-a-political-theory-of-the-protestant-mainline-19.

51. Dean M. Kelly, *Why Conservative Churches Are Growing: A Study in Sociology of Religion with a New Preface* (Macon, GA: Mercer University Press, 1996); and Laurence R. Iannaccone, "Why Strict Churches Are Strong," *The American Journal of Sociology* 99, no. 5 (March 1994): 1180–211.

52. Bottum, "The Death of Protestant America."

53. Hilary White, "Italy's Last Catholic Generation? Mass Attendance in 'Collapse' among Under-30s," lifesitenews.com, August 9, 2010, available online at http://www.lifesitenews.com/news/archive/ldn/2010/aug/10080901.

54. Sandro Magister, "Who Goes to Mass and Who Doesn't: The Uncertain Tomorrow of Catholic Italy," available online at http://chiesa.espresso.repub blica.it/articolo/1344389?eng=y.

55. Jenkins, *God's Continent*, 32.

56. Ibid., 28.

57. Pope John Paul II at a Mass before 350,000 during his first trip to France, 1980. Quoted in George Weigel, *Witness to Hope: The Biography of Pope John Paul II* (New York: HarperCollins, 1999), 377.

58. Brad Miner, "Data Mining and Stock Grading," *thecatholicthing.org*, October 24, 2010.

59. Ibid.

60. Ulrich Beck, quoted in Jenkins, *God's Continent*, 30.

61. Jenkins, ibid, 29.

62. Charles Taylor, *A Secular Age* (Cambridge, Massachusetts, and London, England: The Belknap Press of Harvard University Press, 2007), 522.

63. Stanley Kurtz, "Culture and Values in the 1960s," in *Never a Matter of Indifference: Sustaining Virtue in a Free Republic*, ed. Peter Berkowitz (Palo Alto, CA: Hoover Institution Press, 2003), 50.

64. Ibid., 31.

65. Grace Davie, *Religion in Britain Since 1945: Believing without Belonging* (Hoboken, NJ: Wiley-Blackwell, 1994). The author's main theme is "the increasingly evident mismatch between statistics relating to religious practice and those which indicate levels of religious belief" (4).

66. Grace Davie, "Believing without Belonging: Just How Secular Is Europe?" event transcript, Pew Forum biannual Faith Angle Conference on religion, politics and public life, moderated by Michael Cromartie, December 5, 2005, available online at http://www.pewforum.org/Politics-and-Elections /Believing-Without-Belonging-Just-How-Secular-Is-Europe.aspx.

67. Eric Kaufmann, *Shall the Religious Inherit the Earth? Demography and Politics in the Twenty-First Century* (London: Profile Books, 2011), 17.

68. Bruce, *God Is Dead*, 75–105. Particularly interesting is Bruce's emphasis on the consumerism inherent in New Age practice. "The New Age," he comments, "is eclectic to an unprecedented degree and it is so dominated by the principle that the sovereign consumer will decide what to believe that, even if it were the case that we have some innate propensity to spirituality, we will not get from where we are now to any sort of religious revival" (105).
69. Kaufmann, *Shall the Religious Inherit the Earth?* 17.
70. Chadwick, *The Secularization of the European Mind*, 266.

## Chapter 2

1. About "Sex Weeks," see, for example, Douglas Quenqua, "On Campus, Opening Up Conversations about Sex," *New York Times*, April 16, 2012, available online at http://www.nytimes.com/2012/04/17/science/college-students-opening-up-conversations-about-sex.html?pagewanted=all. It is now over sixty years since a young William F. Buckley lamented the ubiquity of atheism and secularism on America's elite campuses in *God and Man at Yale*, the book that catapulted him to national fame. William F. Buckley, *God and Man at Yale: The Superstitions of "Academic Freedom,"* 50th ed. (Washington, DC: Regnery Publishing, 1986).
2. Sociologist Philip S. Gorski discriminates among the fates assigned to religion by the secularization paradigm as follows: transformation, privatization, disappearance, and decline. "Historicizing the Secularization Debate," *American Sociological Review*, 2000, Vol. 65, 142, figure 1.
3. Karl Marx, *Critique of Hegel's Philosophy of Right*, ed. Joseph O'Malley (Cambridge, UK: Press Syndicate of the University of Cambridge, 1970), 131. The full quote reads: "The wretchedness of religion is at once an expression of and a protest against real wretchedness. Religion is the sigh of the oppressed creature, the heart of a heartless world and the soul of soulless conditions. It is the opium of the people."
4. Sigmund Freud, "A Philosophy of Life," *New Introductory Lectures on Psychoanalysis*, Lecture 35 (London: Hogarth Press, 1933). http://www.marxists.org/reference/subject/philosophy/works/at/freud.htm.
5. Michel Onfray, *Atheist Manifesto: The Case against Christianity, Judaism, and Islam* (New York: Arcade Publishing, 2007), 1.
6. Harris, *End of Faith*, 14.
7. Dawkins, *God Delusion*, 163–207. Dawkins has also advanced a theory of his own about the origins of religion, which he calls "the gullible child theory." A similar thought is offered by the late Christopher Hitchens, *God Is Not Great*, 161: "Credulity may be a form of innocence, and even innocuous in itself, but it provides a standing invitation for the wicked and the clever to exploit their brothers and sisters, and is thus one of humanity's great vulnerabilities. No honest account of the growth and persistence of religion, or the reception

of miracles and revelations, is possible without reference to this stubborn fact."

8. Quoted in George Weigel, "Christian Number Crunching," *First Things*, February 9, 2011, available online at http://www.firstthings.com/onthesquare /2011/02/christian-number-crunching.

9. To grasp something of John Paul II's effect on world history, see the definitive biographies of Karol Woytila by George Weigel, *Witness to Hope* and *The End and the Beginning: Pope John Paul II—The Victory of Freedom, the Last Years, the Legacy* (New York: Image, 2011).

10. "Voltaire" was the pen name of François-Marie Arouet, born in 1694.

11. Hitchens, *God Is Not Great*, 277–83; quotation on p. 283.

12. Alan Charles Kors, "The Enlightenment, Naturalism, and the Secularization of Values," *Free Inquiry*, April/May 2012, available online at http://www.secu larhumanism.org/index.php?section=fi&page=kors_32_3.

13. McLeod and Ustorf, *Decline of Christendom in Western Europe*, 16.

14. Michael Weisskopf, "'Gospel Grapevine' Displays Strength in Controversy over Military Gay Ban," *Washington Post*, February 1, 1993, A1.

15. Hugh McLeod, *Class and Religion in the Late Victorian City* (Hamden, CT: Archon Books, 1974), 28–29.

16. Ibid., 29.

17. Brown, *Death of Christian Britain*, 149.

18. Putnam and Campbell, *American Grace*, 252.

19. Ibid., 253.

20. Charles Murray, *Coming Apart: The State of White America* (New York: Crown Forum, 2012), 12.

21. Ibid., 200.

22. W. Bradford Wilcox, ed., *When Marriage Disappears: The Retreat from Marriage in Middle America* (Institute for American Values, New York, and the National Marriage Project of the University of Virginia, Charlottesville, VA, 2011).

23. Andrew Cherlin, Matthew Messel, Jeremy E. Ueker, and W. Bradford Wilcox, "No Money, No Honey, No Church: The Deinstitutionalization of Religious Life Among the White Working Class," in *Religion, Work and Inequality, Research in the Sociology of Work*, ed. Lisa A. Keister, John McCarthy, Roger Finke (Bingley UK: Emerald Group Publishing Limited), 23:227–50.

24. Brian Alexander, "Who Is Going to Church? Not Who You Think, Study Finds," msnbc.com, August 21, 2011, available online at http://www.msnbc .msn.com/id/44192469/ns/health-behavior/t/who-going-church-not-who- you-think-study-finds/#.UBstx6BOzng.

25. See Murray, *Coming Apart*, 206.

26. The Pew Forum on Religion & Public Life, "Mormons in America: Certain in Their Beliefs, Uncertain of Their Place in Society," January 12, 2012, available online at http://www.pewforum.org/Christian/Mormon/mormons-in -america-beliefs-and-practices.aspx.

27. Ibid.

28. The Holocaust is the major reason why the question of secularization among Jews in the postwar era is largely cordoned off from this book—because the Holocaust can be presumed to have had a uniquely catastrophic impact on Jewish faith. Even if that presumption is incorrect, it would take at least a book-length treatment to determine as much. Hence, though "Judeo-Christianity" is considered in these pages where the theological influence of Judaism on Christianity is clear, this book is nevertheless limited to Christianity and not inclusive of other faiths as the test of secularization theory—though once more, the application of its argument to other faiths remains an open question.

29. Snape, "War, Religion and Revival," 135–58.

30. Brown, *Death of Christian Britain*, 5.

31. Wolfhart Pannenberg, "Letter from Germany," *First Things*, March 2003, available online at http://www.firstthings.com/article/2007/01/letter-from-germany-21.

32. Hans-Peter Schwarz, *Konrad Adenauer: A German Politician and Statesman in a Period of War, Revolution and Reconstruction: From the German Empire to the Federal Republic, 1876–1952* (Oxford, NY: Berghahn Books, 1995), 1:357. Adenauer also said in that speech that "Germany is one of the most irreligious and un-Christian peoples of Europe. It was so even before 1914. Though the Berliners have many valuable characteristics, even at that stage I always felt that in Berlin I was in a heathen city."

33. Arthur Simon, *How Much Is Enough? Hungering for God in an Affluent Culture* (Grand Rapids, MI: Baker Book House, 2003).

34. Ibid., 16.

35. See, for example, *Rerum Novarum* (1891) and *Quadragesimo Anno* (1931), both of which warn of untrammelled capitalism. See also the encyclical letters of Pope John Paul II, particularly in *Sollicitudo Rei Socialis* (1987) and *Centesimus Annus* (1991), which address among other subjects the pitfalls of consumerism.

36. Bonnie Malkin, "Pope Benedict XVI Urges Pilgrims to Reject 'False Idols' of Consumerism," *The Telegraph*, July 17, 2008, available online at http://www.telegraph.co.uk/news/worldnews/australiaandthepacific/australia/2419531/Pope-Benedict-XVI-urges-pilgrims-to-reject-false-idols-of-consumerism.html.

37. One exception to this tendency is what is known as "prosperity theology," or the "health and wealth gospel." It holds that financial blessings are the logical fallout to believing Christians. Obviously, according to this model, prosperity and Christianity are not in conflict at all. That said, the "health and wealth" gospel remains a minority view in light of the larger Christian tradition, in which warnings about the tension between God and Mammon suggest that the two forces exist in a relationship more competitive than symbiotic.

38. Norris and Inglehart, *Sacred and Secular*, 14: "We regard the absence of human security as critical for religiosity."

39. Michel Onfray, *Atheist Manifesto: The Case Against Christianity, Judaism, and Islam*, trans. Jeremy Leggatt (New York: Arcade Publishing, 2005), 33.

40. Harris, *Letter to a Christian Nation*, 91.

41. Émile Durkheim, "The Dualism of Human Nature," in Émile Durkheim and Mustafa Emirbayer, *Émile Durkheim: Sociologist of Modernity* (Malden, MA: Blackwell Publishing, 2003), 274.

42. Thanks to Stanley Kurtz, former Harvard anthropologist, for helping to clarify these points. E-mail discussion, April 2012.

43. Or as Durkheim puts it in the aforementioned essay, "There is no moral act that does not imply a sacrifice, for, as Kant has shown, the law of duty cannot be obeyed without humiliating our individual, or, as he calls it, our 'empirical' sensitivity." Durkheim, "The Dualism of Human Nature," 273.

44. Sigmund Freud, *Civilization and Its Discontents*, tr. James Strachey (New York: W.W. Norton and Company, reprint edition, 2010). Originally published in 1930.

45. Max Weber, *The Protestant Ethic and the Spirit of Capitalism: and Other Writings* (New York: Penguin Classics, 2002). Originally published in 1905.

46. Ronald A. Lindsay, "An Unprecedented Time in Human History," *Free Inquiry*, April/May 2012, available online at http://www.secularhumanism.org/index .php?section=fi&page=lindsay_32_3.

## CHAPTER 3

1. David Martin, *On Secularization: Toward a Revised General Theory* (Burlington, VT: Ashgate Publishing Company, 2005), 3.

2. Bruce, *God Is Dead*, 36. His summary of the theory: "It is not an accident that most modern societies are largely secular. Industrialization brought with it a series of social changes—the fragmentation of the lifeworld, the decline of community, the rise of bureaucracy, technological consciousness—that together made religion less arresting and less plausible than it had been in pre-modern societies. That is the conclusion of most social scientists, historians, and Church leaders in the modern world." Note how family and kin are missing from the list.

3. Norris and Inglehart, *Sacred and Secular*, 6. Note the clear causal vector here, which is standard in the wider literature as well.

4. W. Bradford Wilcox, "As the Family Goes," *First Things* 173 (May 2007), available online at http://www.firstthings.com/article/2007/04/as-the-family -goes-14.

5. Steven L. Nock, *Marriage in Men's Lives* (New York: Oxford University Press, 1998), 100.

6. Ross M. Stolzenberg, M. Blair-Loy, and Linda J. Waite, "Religious Participation in Early Adulthood: Age and Family Life Cycle Effects on Church Membership," *American Sociological Review* 60 (1995): 94.

7. Wilcox, "As the Family Goes."

8. Murray, *Coming Apart*, 202.

9. Wilcox, "As the Family Goes."

10. Eric Kaufmann, "Faith's Comeback," *Newsweek*, 148, no. 20, November 13, 2006, 34–35.

11. See, for example, Eli Berman, "Sect, Subsidy and Sacrifice: An Economist's View of Ultra-Orthodox Jews," *The Quarterly Journal of Economics* 115, no. 3 (August 2000): 936, table VI.

12. Eric Kaufmann, "Islamism, Religiosity, and Fertility in the Modern World" (paper prepared for 2009 ISA conference, New York, unpublished; sent by the author).

13. Kaufmann, "Islamism, Religiosity, and Fertility in the Modern World," 21, figure 7.

14. This remains true even though there is another, lesser-known side of the story: Muslim fertility across the world is also dropping fast. See Nicholas Eberstadt and Apoorva Shah, "Fertility Decline in the Muslim World: A Veritable Sea-Change, Still Curiously Unnoticed," The American Enterprise Institute Working Paper Series on Development Policy, Number 7, December 2011, available online at http://www.insideronline.org/summary.cfm?id=16526.

15. See, for example, Tim B. Heaton and Kristen L. Goodman, "Religion and Family Formation," *Review of Religious Research* 26 (1985): 343–59.

16. Conrad Hackett, "Why Is Congregational Participation Associated with Higher Fertility?" paper presented at the annual 2009 Population Association of America conference in Detroit, MI, April 30–May 2, available online at http://paa2009.princeton.edu/download.aspx?submissionId=91839.

17. Tomas Frejka and Charles A. Westoff, "Religion, Religiousness, and Fertility in the U.S. and Europe" (working paper [WP 2006-013], Max Planck Institute, Rostock, Germany, May 2006), available online at http://www.demogr.mpg.de/papers/working/wp-2006-013.pdf.

18. Ibid., 12.

19. This is the verse that inspired the name of Quiverfull, the evangelical organization (largely but not entirely American) that rejects birth control and celebrates procreation as an essential part of the divine plan.

20. Moreover, even Catholics are not enjoined to have all the children that they can, but rather to use their reason and weigh responsibilities in the matter of family size.

21. David Kinnaman, with Aly Hawkins, *You Lost Me: Why Young Christians Are Leaving Church . . . and Rethinking Faith* (Grand Rapids, MI: Baker Books, 2011). The reasons given were:
    - Reason #1—Churches seem overprotective.
    - Reason #2—Teens' and twentysomethings' experience of Christianity is shallow.

- Reason #3—Churches come across as antagonistic to science.
- Reason #4—Young Christians' church experiences related to sexuality are often simplistic, judgmental.
- Reason #5—They wrestle with the exclusive nature of Christianity.
- Reason #6—The church feels unfriendly to those who doubt.

22. Mark Regnerus, "The Case for Early Marriage," *Christianity Today*, August 2009, available online at http://www.christianitytoday.com/ct/2009/august/16.22 .html.

23. Putnam and Campbell, *American Grace*, 448.

24. Tom W. Smith, "Beliefs about God across Time and Countries," report of the National Opinion Research Center at the University of Chicago, April 18, 2012, available online at http://www.norc.org/_layouts/NORC.Website /Pages/SearchResults.aspx?k=religion.

25. Ibid., 4.

26. Putnam and Campbell, *American Grace*, 448.


CHAPTER 4

1. Ansley J. Coale and Susan Cotts Watkins, eds., *The Decline of Fertility in Europe: The Revised Proceedings of a Conference on the Princeton European Fertility Project* (Princeton, NJ: Princeton University Press, 1986).

2. "Cohabitation rate and prevalence of other forms of partnership," OECD Family Database, last updated 01/07/2010. Available online at http://www .oecd.org/els/socialpoliciesanddata/41920080.pdf.

3. For an overview, see, for example, John Caldwell, "Paths to Lower Fertility— Education and Debate—Statistical Data Included," *British Medical Journal* (October 9, 1999), http://www.accessmylibrary.com/article-1G1-57041723 /paths-lower-fertility-education.html. See also Jean-Claude Chesnais, "Below-Replacement Fertility in the European Union (eu-15): Facts and Policies, 1960–1997," *Review of Population and Social Policy* 7 (1998). http://www.ipss .go.jp/publication/e/R_s_p/No.7_P83.pdf. See especially table 7.

4. David Garrioch, *The Making of Revolutionary Paris* (Berkeley: University of California Press, 2002), 189.

5. Ibid. These facts appear in his chapter "Secularization," 184–206.

6. Ibid., 189.

7. Ibid.

8. See, for example, the chart on p. 78 of *The European Culture Area: A Systematic Geography* by Alexander B. Murphy, Terry G. Jordan-Bychkov, Bella Bychkova Jordan (Lanham, MD: Rowman and Littlefield Publishers, 2008). It shows how fertility decline began first in France and spread eventually throughout the rest of Western Europe.

9. Graham Tibbetts, "Most Children of British Mothers Born Out of Wedlock," *The Telegraph*, July 11, 2008, available online at http://www.telegraph.co.uk

/news/uknews/2285670/Most-children-of-British-mothers-born-out-of-wedlock.html.

10. Jacinta Ashworth and Ian Farthing, *Churchgoing in the UK: A Research Report from Tearfund*, April 2007, available online at http://news.bbc.co.uk/2/shared /bsp/hi/pdfs/03_04_07_tearfundchurch.pdf.

11. Russell Shorto, "Keeping the Faith," *New York Times*, April 8, 2007, available online at http://www.nytimes.com/2007/04/08/magazine/08pope.t.html?pa gewanted=all.

12. See, for example, Andrew M. Greeley, "What Ever Happened to Ireland?" *America*, July 16, 2007. Greeley argues that what is commonly called "secularization" is in fact shorthand for popular objection to a church hierarchy that resists change. He believes that "people do not lose their faith or their religion in this kind of secularization. Rather, they lose their willingness to accept the apodictic rules of church authority." But does not "religiosity" in any commonly used sense of the word depend exactly upon accepting the rules of *some* acknowledged authority—including the church?

13. Tom Hundley, "How Catholicism Fell from Grace in Ireland," *Chicago Tribune*, July 9, 2006, available online at http://www.chicagotribune.com/news/nation-world/chi-0607090342jul09,0,3397459.story.

14. Press release, Catholic Communications Office, Irish Bishops Conference (October 28, 2006).

15. See, for example, "Decline of the Irish Catholic Church," *Religion & Ethics Newsweekly*, July 15, 2011, http://www.pbs.org/wnet/religionandethics/episo des/july-15-2011/decline-of-the-irish-catholic-church/9146/.

16. Robert D. Putnam, *Bowling Alone: The Collapse and Revival of American Community* (New York: Simon and Schuster, 2000).

17. Ibid., 228.

18. Kaufmann, *Shall the Religious Inherit the Earth?* 14.

19. Historian David Garrioch, mentioned earlier, advances one other way in which urbanization hit Christianity hard: because "the mobility of much of the population made the job of the parish clergy next to impossible. . . . Journeymen and servants moved from employer to employer. Poor families were forced to move if they could not pay their rent. . . . Enforcement of religious observance was thus extremely difficult." Garrioch, *Making of Revolutionary Paris*, 200. Again, I am not saying the "Family Factor" is the *only* explanation for secularization—merely that it is the most important historically overlooked one.

20. Chadwick, *Secularization of the European Mind*, 94.

21. Jon Butler, *Awash in a Sea of Faith: Christianizing the American People* (Cambridge, MA: Harvard University Press, 1990), 31.

22. *Population, Urbanization, and Quality of Life* (United Nations Center for Human Settlements [HABITAT], Nairobi, 1994), http://collections.infocollections .org/ukedu/uk/d/Jha15pe/.

23. "Gender Brief," prepared by the OECD Social Policy Division, March 2010 version, http://www.oecd.org/dataoecd/23/31/44720649.pdf.

24. See, for example, Richard F. Tomasson, "Modern Sweden: The Declining Importance of Marriage," *Scandinavian Review*, Autumn 1998, http://houstonhs.scsk12.org/~mrobinson/Mr._Robinsons_Web_Site_at_Houston_High_School/Contemporary_Issues_Resource_Page_files/The%20declining%20importance%20of%20marriage.pdf.

25. Ibid., 2.

26. Eric Klinenberg, *Going Solo: The Extraordinary Rise and Surprising Appeal of Living Alone* (New York: Penguin Press, 2012), introduction.

27. Again, we will investigate these and other questions of religious anthropology in chapter 7.

28. Phillip Longman, *The Empty Cradle: How Falling Birthrates Threaten World Prosperity and What to Do About It* (New York: Basic Books, 2004).

29. Mark Steyn, *America Alone: The End of the World as We Know It* (Washington, DC: Regnery Publishing, 2006).

30. Eric Kaufmann, *Shall the Religious Inherit the Earth?*

31. Phillip Longman, "Survival of the Godliest: Does Strong Religious Belief Provide an Evolutionary Advantage?" bigquestionsonline.com, November 11, 2010.

32. Tony Judt, *Postwar: A History of Europe since 1945* (New York: Penguin Press, 2005), 331.

33. Murray, *Coming Apart*, 202.

## Chapter 5

1. For a discussion see Nicholas Eberstadt, "'Demographic Exceptionalism' in the United States: Tendencies and Implications," *Agir 29* (January 2007).

2. Dawkins, *God Delusion*, 61.

3. As Peter Berger has observed, for example, "Strongly felt religion has always been around; what needs explanation is its absence rather than its presence." See also Grace Davie, "Europe: The Exception That Proves the Rule?" in Berger, *Desecularization of the World*, 65–83.

4. Murray, *Coming Apart*, 136.

5. Ibid., 137.

6. This religious gender gap is also a subject of vigorous debate. See, for example, Leon J. Podles, *The Church Impotent: The Feminization of Christianity* (Dallas: Spence Publishing, 1999), and David Murrow, *Why Men Hate Going to Church* (Nashville: Thomas Nelson, 2004).

7. Putnam and Campbell, *American Grace*, 233.

8. Loek Halman and Veerle Draulans, "How Secular Is Europe? *The British Journal of Sociology* 57 no. 2 (2006): 269.

9. Ibid.

10. Tony Walter, "Why Are Most Churchgoers Women? A Literature Review," *Vox Evangelica* 20 (1990): 73–90, available online at http://biblicalstudies.org.uk /pdf/vox/vol20/women_walter.pdf.

11. Ibid., 74.

12. The stipulation is that males are slightly more likely to be represented on either end of the curve; i.e., slightly more likely to be geniuses on one end, or severely retarded on the other. See Charles Murray and Richard Herrnstein, *The Bell Curve* (New York: Free Press, 1996), 275.

13. Norris and Inglehart, *Sacred and Secular*, 14: "We regard the absence of human security as critical for religiosity."

14. Franck and Iannaccone, "Why Did Religiosity Decrease in the Western World during the Twentieth Century?" preliminary draft, Nov. 9, 2009, available online at http://econ.hevra.haifa.ac.il/~todd/seminars/papers09-10/franck _iannaccone_religiosity.pdf, 1.

15. Brown, *Death of Christian Britain*, 188.

16. Hugh McLeod, *The Religious Crisis of the 1960s* (Oxford, UK: Oxford University Press, 2007), 264.

17. Brown, *Death of Christian Britain*, 179.

18. McLeod, *Religious Crisis of the 1960s*, 259.

19. Ibid.

20. Faramerz Dabhoiwala, *The Origins of Sex: A History of the First Sexual Revolution* (London: Allen Lane, 2012).

21. Ibid., 201.

22. George Gilder, *Sexual Suicide* (New York: Quadrangle Books, 1973).

23. Lionel Tiger, *The Decline of Males* (Darby, PA: Diane Publishing Company, 1999).

24. Ibid., 231.

25. Midge Decter, *The New Chastity and Other Arguments Against Women's Liberation* (New York: Perigee Books, 1974).

26. See, for example, Danielle Crittenden, *What Our Mothers Didn't Tell Us: Why Happiness Eludes the Modern Woman* (New York: Simon and Schuster, 1999); Carolyn Graglia, *Domestic Tranquility: A Brief against Feminism* (Dallas, TX: Spence Publishing Company, 1998); Mary Eberstadt, *Home-Alone America*; and Mary Eberstadt, *Adam and Eve after the Pill: Paradoxes of the Sexual Revolution* (San Francisco: Ignatius Press, 2012).

27. For a contrarian view of the sexual revolution's fallout, see Eberstadt, *Adam and Eve after the Pill*.

28. Robert Wuthnow, *After Heaven: Spirituality in America since the 1950s* (Berkeley: University of California Press, 1998).

29. Ibid., 67.

30. Conversation with Father Victor Pablo Ghio, March 2011.

CHAPTER 6

1. Taylor, *A Secular Age*, 424.
2. Roderick Phillips, *Untying the Knot: A Short History of Divorce* (Cambridge, UK: Cambridge University Press, 1991), 12.
3. Ibid., 33.
4. Mary Eberstadt, "Christianity Lite," *First Things*, February 2010, http://www .firstthings.com/article/2010/01/christianity-lite.
5. "Religion: The Birth-Control Debate," *Time*, Dec. 21, 1959, http://www.time .com/time/magazine/article/0,9171,865161,00.html.
6. By 1959, for example, the World Council of Churches, representing 171 Protestant, Anglican, and Orthodox denominations, would make an announcement that was judged tantamount to removing any stricture whatever from the use of contraception. See "Concerning Birth Control," *Time*, October 19, 1959, http://www.time.com/time/magazine/article/0,9171,869310,00.html.
7. George Dugan, "Graham Sees Hope in Birth Control," *New York Times*, December 13, 1959, 49.
8. William Murchison, *Mortal Follies: Episcopalians and the Crisis of Mainline Christianity* (New York: Encounter Books, 2009), 152.
9. Andrew Brown, "Runcie: I Ordained Gay Priests," *The Independent*, May 16, 1996.
10. Rowan Williams in Eugene F. Rogers, Jr., ed., *Theology and Sexuality: Classic and Contemporary Readings*, Blackwell Readings in Modern Theology (Malden, MA: Wiley-Blackwell, 2002), 320.
11. Minutes of the Evangelical Lutheran Church on Marriage and Family, archives, 1954, https://www.elca.org/Who-We-Are/History/ELCA-Archives/Archival -Documents/Predecessor-Body-Statements/Augustana-Lutheran-Church /Marriage-and-Family.aspx.
12. "Welcoming Gay and Lesbian People," ELCA Churchwide Assembly Action, CA95.06.50, 1995, available online at http://www.elca.org/What-We-Believe /Social-Issues/Resolutions/1995/CA95,-p-,06,-p-,50-Welcoming-Gay-and-Lesbian-People.aspx.
13. Report Examines the State of Mainline Protestant Churches," Barna Group, Dec. 7, 2009, http://www.barna.org/barna-update/article/17-leadership/323 -report-examines-the-state-of-mainline-protestant-churches.
14. McLeod, *Religious Crisis of the 1960s*. See the chapter "Aggiornamento," 83–101.
15. Ibid., 84.
16. Ibid.
17. John Robinson, *Honest to God*, 40th anniv. ed. (Louisville, KY: Westminster John Knox Press, 2003), 118.
18. Here is one more fascinating question that cannot be followed up adequately here: Does the relaxing of dogma drive people from church, or does the decline in attendance push leaders to relax dogma? Certainly these two forces, too,

are joined at the causal hip somehow. As fabled Catholic convert Monsignor Ronald Knox observed in an essay some eighty years ago, "The Decline of Dogma and the Decline of Church Membership": "The evacuation of the pew and the jettisoning of cargo from the pulpit" have been going on side by side. Ronald Arbuthnott Knox, *The Belief of Catholics* (San Francisco: Ignatius Press, 2000), 8.

19. Andrew Greeley, Michael Hout, and Melissa Wilde, "Demographics of Mainline Decline," *Christian Century*, October 4, 2005. https://sociology.sas.upenn .edu/sites/sociology.sas.upenn.edu/files/Birth_Dearth_Christian_Century .pdf.

20. Ibid., 26.

21. Adrian Hamilton, "Will the Last Person to Leave the Church of England Please Turn Out the Lights," *The Independent*, April 18, 2011.

22. John Allen, "What Comunione e Liberazione Is," *National Catholic Reporter*, August 26, 2005, available online at http://www.nationalcatholicreporter.org /word/word082605.htm.


## Chapter 7

1. Whittaker Chambers, *Witness*, reissue edition (Washington DC: Regnery Publishing, 1987), 16.

2. Elizabeth Marquardt, *Between Two Worlds: The Inner Lives of Children of Divorce* (New York: Crown Books, 2005).

3. Elizabeth Marquardt, *Between Two Worlds*, 158.

4. Nicholas Kulish, "A Papal Homecoming to a Combative Germany: Benedict Faces Calls for Change," *New York Times*, September 22, 2011, A6.

5. Ibid.

6. Raphael Minder, "Protests Greet Visiting Pope as Austerity Grips Spain," *New York Times*, August 18, 2001.

7. See "Papal Visit: Thousands Protest against Pope in London," BBC News, bbc .co.uk, December 18, 2010.


## Chapter 8

1. Murray, *Coming Apart*, 149.

2. Wilcox, *When Marriage Disappears: The Retreat from Marriage in Middle America* (Institute for American Values, New York, and the National Marriage Project of the University of Virginia, Charlottesville, VA, 2011), http://state ofourunions.org/2010/when-marriage-disappears.php.

3. Barbara McMahon, "Mamma's Boys Fuel Italy's Soaring Divorce Rate," *The Observer*, November 12, 2006.

4. Marta Dominguez, Teresa Castro Martin, and Letizia Mencarini, "European Latecomers: Cohabitation in Italy and Spain" (paper prepared for the annual

meeting of the Population Association of America, New York, March 29–30, 2007), 3.

5. Ibid., 6.

6. "Spain Has Highest Divorce Rate in Europe: Study," expatica.com, May 24, 2007, available online at http://www.expatica.com/es/news/local_news/spain-has-highest-divorce-rate-in-europe-study-40129_36503.html.

7. Phillip Longman et al., "The Empty Cradle," in *The Sustainable Demographic Dividend: What Do Marriage & Fertility Have to Do with the Economy?* an international report from the Social Trends Institute, October 3, 2011, available online at http://sustaindemographicdividend.org/articles/the-empty-cradle.

8. Rich Lowry, "Just Not the Marrying Kind," *Time*, March 5, 2012, available online at http://www.time.com/time/magazine/article/0,9171,2107496,00 .html; and Rachel Kramer Bussel, "Knocked Up and Proud: Louise Sloan, Single Mother by Choice," HuffPost, March 26, 2008, available online at http://www.huffingtonpost.com/rachel-kramer-bussel/knocked-up-and -proud-loui_b_93559.html.

9. Some work by sociologist Judith Stacey, for example—who is a leading representative of the notion that family is constructed rather than natural—illustrates this prevailing attitude on the part of those who champion nontraditional homes. In her book advocating gay adoption, for example, she argues that all known studies show that lesbian parents are indistinguishable from mixed-sex parents—except when they are being better. Judith Stacey, *Unhitched: Love, Marriage, and Family Values from West Hollywood to Western China* (New York: NYU Press, 2011), 84: "Apart from matters related to social stigma and discrimination, the studies find very few measurable differences between children raised by lesbian or straight couples, and the rare differences that show up in this research more often favor the children with two lesbian moms." Similar triumphalism can be found in the social-scientific literature on same-sex adoption. See, for example, Nanette Gartrell and Henny Bos, "US National Longitudinal Lesbian Family Study: Psychological Adjustment of 17-Year-Old Adolescents," *Pediatrics*, June 7, 2010, published online and available at http://pediatrics.aappublications.org/content/early/2010/06/07 /peds.2009-3153.abstract. Its conclusion: "According to their mothers' reports, the 17-year-old daughters and sons of lesbian mothers were rated significantly higher in social, school/academic, and total competence and significantly lower in social problems, rule-breaking, aggressive, and external-izing problem behavior than their age-matched counterparts in Achenbach's normative sample of American youth." Once again, the clear implication is that nontraditional parenting (in this case, lesbian) is not only *comparable* to traditional parenting, but *better*.

10. Elizabeth Wildsmith, Nicole R. Steward-Streng, and Jennifer Manlove, *Childbearing Outside of Marriage: Estimates and Trends in the United States* (Washington, DC: Child Trends Research Brief, November 2011), available

online at http://www.childtrends.org/Files/Child_Trends-2011_11_01_RB_NonmaritalCB.pdf.

11. For further discussion of the American pattern, see Nicholas Eberstadt, "White Families Are in Trouble Too," *Dallas News*, August 21, 2005, available online at http://www.aei.org/article/society-and-culture/citizenship/white-families-are-in-trouble-too/.

12. Eurostat, *European Illegitimacy Ratios 1960–2010*, last updated Dec. 19, 2011. According to the source, the number for 27 EU countries was 37.3 in the year 2009.

13. Ibid.

14. Ibid.

15. To be sure—and to temper the pessimism somewhat—this sort of conceptual problem may not be insurmountable for Christianity. In effect, it amounts to replacing "God the Father" with "God the Father you did not have"—which nevertheless surely remains one more uphill struggle for the next generations of theologians to take on.

## CHAPTER 9

1. Pitirim Sorokin, *Man and Society in Calamity* (New Brunswick, NJ: Transaction Publishers, 2010), 161. Originally published in 1942 by E. P. Dutton & Co.

2. Ibid., 226. He added, conversely, that "the periods of comparative stability, order, and material well-being, and hence of complacency, have scarcely ever given birth to a truly great religion or a truly lofty moral ideal. Here lies, perhaps, the justification for the signal tragedies of human history."

3. Popenoe, *Disturbing the Nest*, 339.

4. Ibid.

5. Longman, *Empty Cradle*; Ben Wattenberg, *Fewer: How the New Demography of Depopulation Will Shape Our Future* (Lanham, MD: Ivan R. Dee, 2004); Laurence J. Kotlikoff and Scott Burns, *The Coming Generational Storm: What You Need to Know about America's Economic Future* (Cambridge, MA: MIT Press, 2004); and Peter G. Peterson, *Running On Empty: How the Democratic and Republican Parties Are Bankrupting Our Future and What Americans Can Do About It* (New York: Farrar Straus and Giroux, 2004). For an excellent discussion of these and related works, see Stanley Kurtz, "Demographics and the Culture War," *Policy Review* no. 129, February/March 2005, http://www.hoover.org/publications/policy-review/article/7123.

6. Theodore Dalrymple, "The European Crack-up," *City Journal* 22, no. 1 (Winter 2012), available online at http://www.city-journal.org/2012/22_1_otbie-european-debt-crisis.html.

7. Milton Friedman, *Bright Promises, Dismal Performance: An Economist's Protest* (New York: Harcourt Brace Jovanovich, 1983), 98.

8. Stanley Kurtz, "Demographics and the Culture War."

9. Virginia Montet, "Rising U.S. Divorce Rates Signal U.S. Recovery," AFP, April 28, 2001, available online at http://www.google.com/hostednews/afp /article/ALeqM5ibKyCkXrV67Q_M4h6zC-rgc1YXnQ?docId=CNG .b3179216f55b905d4c8f5516b86569b9.261.

10. U.S. Census Bureau, "More Young Adults Are Living in Their Parents' Homes, Census Bureau Reports," press release, November 3, 2011, available online at http://www.census.gov/newsroom/releases/archives/families_households /cb11-183.html.

11. See, for example, Sara McLanahan and Gary Sandefur's landmark book, *Growing Up With a Single Parent: What Hurts, What Helps* (Cambridge, MA: Harvard University Press, 1994), in which McLanahan, who was herself then a single mother, surveyed a variety of data expecting to find no meaningful differences between intact and single-parent homes, only to be convinced otherwise that having a single parent raised the risks to a child of drug use, financial setbacks, and other negative outcomes. See also Barbara Defoe Whitehead's highly influential "Dan Quayle Was Right," *The Atlantic*, April 1993, which summarizes: "According to a growing body of social-scientific evidence, children in families disrupted by divorce and out-of-wedlock birth do worse than children in intact families on several measures of well-being. Children in single-parent families are six times as likely to be poor. They are also likely to stay poor longer. Twenty-two percent of children in one-parent families will experience poverty during childhood for seven years or more, as compared with only two percent of children in two-parent families. A 1988 survey by the National Center for Health Statistics found that children in single-parent families are two to three times as likely as children in two-parent families to have emotional and behavioral problems. They are also more likely to drop out of high school, to get pregnant as teenagers, to abuse drugs, and to be in trouble with the law. Compared with children in intact families, children from disrupted families are at a much higher risk for physical or sexual abuse."

Just a few of the works testifying to the material and other advantages of the intact, two-parent home include, for example, James Q. Wilson, *Marriage Problem*; Kay S. Hymowitz, *Marriage and Caste in America*; David Blankenhorn, *The Future of Marriage* (New York: Encounter Books, 2007); Mary Eberstadt, *Home-Alone America* (New York NY: Sentinel, 2004), which includes several chapters discussing the fallout of weakened families. For discussion of the negative effects of broken families on adulthood, see again Elizabeth Marquardt's *Between Two Worlds*, whose data are drawn from the first nationally representative sample of children of divorce, 1,500 randomly selected such subjects.

12. Carle Zimmerman, *Family and Civilization*, ed. James Kurth, (Wilmington, DE: Intercollegiate Studies Institute, 2nd abridged edition, 2008). Originally published in 1947.

13. Will Herberg, *Protestant-Catholic-Jew: An Essay in American Religious Sociology* (Chicago: University of Chicago Press, 1983), 46–47.

14. Kenneth Scott Latourette, *A History of Christianity, vol. 1: Beginnings to 1500* (New York: Harper & Row, 1975), 104–5.

15. Ibid., 106.

16. Elizabeth Anscombe, "Contraception and Chastity," in *Why Humanae Vitae Was Right: A Reader*, ed. Janet E. Smith (San Francisco: Ignatius Press, 1993), 119–46. This essay was first published in 1972.

17. Rodney Stark, *The Rise of Christianity: How the Obscure, Marginal Jesus Movement Became the Dominant Religious Force in the Western World in a Few Centuries* (New York: HarperOne, 1997), 119.

## CONCLUSION

1. As George Weigel has written, "The shock of seemingly widespread clerical misconduct, reported on an almost daily basis in the first months of 2002, was immeasurably intensified by what even sympathetic Catholics had to regard as some bishops' inept and irresponsible response to grave sins and crimes. In this instance, one plus one yielded something more than two: one plus one equaled an unprecedented crisis." Weigel, *The Courage To Be Catholic: Crisis, Reform, and the Future of the Church* (New York: Basic Books, 2002), 2.

2. Arthur Brooks, *Who Really Cares: The Surprising Truth about Compassionate Conservatism* (New York: Basic Books, 2006).

3. Ibid., 47.

4. Ibid.

5. Ibid., 36.

6. Ibid., 39.

7. Ibid., 126.

8. Ibid.

9. Ibid., 40.

10. Harold G. Koenig, Michael E. McCullough, and David B. Larsen, *Handbook of Religion and Health* (New York: Oxford University Press, 2001).

11. Robert A. Hummer, Richard G. Rogers, Charles B. Nam, and Christopher G. Ellison, "Religious Involvement and U.S. Adult Mortality," *Demography* 36, no. 2 (May 1999): 283.

12. Ibid.

13. H. G. Koenig, "Religion and Depression in Older Medical Inpatients," *American Journal of Geriatric Psychiatry* 15, no. 4 (2007): 282–91. Quote is from the abstract.

14. H. G. Koenig, H. J. Cohen, D. G. Blazer, C. Pieper, K. G. Meador, R. Shelp, V. Golit, and R. DiPasquale, "Religious Coping and Depression in Elderly Hospitalized Medically Ill Men," *American Journal of Psychiatry* 149 (1992): 1693.

15. G. Ironson, R. Stuetzie, and M. A. Fletcher, "An Increase in Religiousness/Spirituality Occurs after HIV Diagnosis and Predicts Slower Disease

Progression over 4 Years in People with HIV," *Journal of General Internal Medicine* 21 (December 2006): S62–68.

16. For a good summary, see, for example, David G. Myers, "Religion and Human Flourishing," in *The Science of Subjective Well-Being*, ed. Michael Eid and Randy J. Larsen (New York: The Guilford Press, 2008), 323–46.

17. Ibid., 324.

18. Ibid., 326.

19. See, for example, Timothy Smith, Michael McCullough, and Justin Poll, "Religiousness and Depression: Evidence for a Main Effect and Moderating Influence of Stressful Life Events," *Psychological Bulletin* 129, no. 4 (2003): 614–36, doi:10.1037/0033-2909.129.4.614. PMID 12848223.

20. Byron Johnson, *More God, Less Crime: Why Faith Matters and How It Could Matter More* (West Conshohocken, PA: Templeton Press, 2011).

21. James Q. Wilson, "In the Pew Instead of Prison: A Review of *More God, Less Crime*," *Wall Street Journal*, May 9, 2011, available online at http://online.wsj .com/article/SB10001424052748703778104576287043835803026.html.

22. Chuck Colson, "More God, Less Crime: The Evidence Is There," *Breakpoint* commentary, http://www.breakpoint.org/bpcommentaries/entry/13/17051.

23. Christie Davies, *The Strange Death of Moral Britain* (New Brunswick, NJ: Transaction Publishers, 2004), 45.

24. "Growing Up in Today's Britain," *Templeton Report*, December 2, 2009, http:// www.templeton.org/templeton_report/20091202/.

25. The quote appears in "The Roots of Britain's Riotous Rage," *Templeton Report*, September 7, 2011, http://www.templeton.org/templeton_report/20110907 /index.html.

26. Putnam, *Bowling Alone*.

27. Ibid., 67.

28. Putnam and Campbell, *American Grace*, 257.

29. See, for example, Andrew J. Weaver, Judith A. Samford, Virginia J. Morgan, David B. Larson, Harold G. Koenig, and Kevin J. Flannelly, "A Systematic Review of Research on Religion in Six Primary Marriage and Family Journals: 1995–1999," *American Journal of Family Therapy* 30, no. 4 (July 2002): 293–309.

30. See, for example, Richard Weikart, "Marx, Engels, and the Abolition of the Family," *History of European Ideas* 18, no. 5 (1994): 657–72, available online at http://www.csustan.edu/history/faculty/weikart/Marx-Engels-and-the -Abolition-of-the-Family.pdf.

31. Friedrich Engels, *The Origins of the Family, Private Property, and the State*, ed. Eleanor Burke Leacock (Long Island City, NY: International Publishers, 2001), 128. Originally published in 1884.

32. Ferdinand Mount, *The Subversive Family* (New York: Free Press, 1992), 1. A true contrarian, Mount also regards organized religion as one more institution engaged in an enduring power struggle with the nuclear family.

33. De Tocqueville, quoted in Mount, *Subversive Family*, 2.
34. Betty Friedan, *The Feminine Mystique* (New York: W.W. Norton & Co., 1963).
35. See for example Judith Stacey, *In the Name of the Family: Rethinking Family Values in the Postmodern Age* (Boston MA: Beacon Press, 1996). "The [nuclear married] family is dead. Long live our families!" (51).
36. Kathrin Perutz's *Marriage Is Hell* (New York: William Morrow, 1972); and Ellen Peck's *The Baby Trap* (New York: Bernard Geis Associates, 1971).
37. Stacey, *In the Name of the Family*, 11.
38. James Q. Wilson, "Two Nations," 1997 Francis Boyer Lecture to the American Enterprise Institute, December 4, 1997, available online at http://www.aei .org/speech/society-and-culture/two-nations-speech/.
39. Ibid.
40. Ibid.
41. Ibid.
42. Ibid.
43. Murray, *Coming Apart*, 158.

## Epilogue

1. Watson once remarked of his double helix that it was "too pretty not to be true." Watson, *Double Helix*, 134.
2. Ludwig Wittgenstein, *Philosophical Investigation*, tr. G.E.M. Anscombe, P.M.S. Hacer, and Joachim Shulte, 4th revised edition (Malden, MA: Wiley-Blackwell, 2009). See also the entry about Wittgenstein and private language in the Stanford Encyclopedia of Philosophy (last revised May 2012), http://plato .stanford.edu/entries/private-language/
3. McLeod, *Class and Religion in the Late Victorian City*, 26.
4. Micklethwait and Wooldridge, *God Is Back*, 169. They also summarize pithily some of the social functions of religion that secularists and atheists have failed to understand, though Durkheim and Weber certainly did: "Religion," they observe, "serves lots of social functions, functions that are becoming no less relevant as a result of 'modernization.' It helps suburbanites to form communities in the atomized world of the Sunbelt. It helps ordinary people all over America to deal with the problems of alcoholism and divorce, wayward children and hopelessness. And it helps the hard-pressed inhabitants of the inner city to deal with the chaos that surrounds them . . . inspiring all sorts of desperate people to turn their lives around."
5. Paul Johnson, *Intellectuals: From Marx and Tolstoy to Sartre and Chomsky* (New York: HarperCollins, 1989), 21–23.
6. For what it is worth, there is a coda of possible interest at the end of all this. The Family Factor just may shed light on an aspect of the Judeo-Christian tradition that has appeared mysterious to just about anyone ever pondering it. That is

the command from God himself, in Genesis, to "be fruitful and multiply." The enjoinder to do things that contribute to the strength and size of the natural family—from the multiplication command in Genesis to Jesus' and Paul's strict rules protecting marriage—is a constant, indeed one of *the* constants, of Judeo-Christianity itself. But why? Why is it said to be "not good for the man to be alone"? Why is more always made to seem merrier?

Maybe that connection, too, has been a two-way street all along. Maybe God's people have been constantly called upon to protect the family because the family was not only valuable to *them*, but also to Judeo-Christianity itself—as the primary means through which ordinary men and women, whether literally or figuratively, would hear God's voice and believe. It's one more speculation among many, admittedly. But whether you believe in God, or believe instead that other people made him up, you can still conclude either way that the biblical calls to fruitful multiplication mean that someone somewhere figured out the centrality of the family to Christianity early on and put it in the sacred books to work in religion's favor—as it has.

# Index

HB7